Thatcher and Thatcherism

The Making of the Contemporary World
Edited by Eric Evans and Ruth Henig
University of Lancaster

The Making of the Contemporary World series provides challenging interpretations of contemporary issues and debates within strongly defined historical frameworks. The range of the series is global, with each volume drawing together material from a range of disciplines – including economics, politics and sociology. The books in this series present compact, indispensable introductions for students studying the modern world.

Forthcoming titles include:

The Soviet Union in World Politics, 1945–1991
Geoffrey Roberts

The Uniting of Europe
From Discord to Concord
Stanley Henig

International Economy since 1945
Sidney Pollard

United Nations in the Contemporary World
David Whittaker

Latin America
John Ward

China Under Communism
Alan Lawrance

The Cold War
An interdisciplinary history
David Painter

The Green Movement
Dick Richardson

The Irish Question
Patrick Maume

Decolonization
Raymond Betts

Right Wing Extremism
Paul Hainsworth

Thatcher and Thatcherism

Eric J. Evans

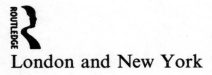

London and New York

First published 1997
by Routledge
11 New Fetter Lane, London EC4P 4EE

Simultaneously published in the USA and Canada
by Routledge
29 West 35th Street, New York, NY 10001

Typeset in Times by BC Typesetting, Bristol

Printed and bound in Great Britain by Mackays of Chatham PLC,
Chatham, Kent

British Library Cataloguing in Publication Data
A catalogue record for this book is available from the British Library

Library of Congress Cataloguing in Publication Data
Evans, Eric J., 1945–
    Thatcher and Thatcherism/by Eric J. Evans.
        p.   cm. – (Making of the contemporary world)
    Includes bibliographical references and index.
    ISBN 0–415–13694–6
    1. Thatcher, Margaret.   2. Conservatism–Great Britain-
History–20th century.   3. Great Britain–Politics and
government–1979-   4. Conservative Party (Great Britain)   5. World
politics–1945-   I. Title.   II. Series.
DA591.T47E94   1997
941.085′8′092–dc21   97-4317
                                                                                CIP

ISBN 0–415–13694–6

Contents

Acknowledgements		vi
1	The 1970s: explanations and origins	1
2	Election and depression, 1979–81	12
3	Thatcher triumphant, 1982–8	24
4	Thatcherism and the Conservative Party	40
5	The attack on the government ethic	53
6	The attack on the professional ethic	65
7	Thatcher abroad I: Europe	79
8	Thatcher abroad II: defence and The Americas	90
9	Thatcherism abroad: influence and prejudice	101
10	The fall	108
11	The legacy	115
Notes		125
Guide to further reading		136
Index		142

Acknowledgements

The production of this book has been greatly facilitated by the help of many who have shared their insights with me both in private conversation and by more formal comment. I would particularly like to acknowledge the contributions of three. My co-editor, Ruth Henig, has generously shared with me her much more hands-on knowledge of the contemporary political world. Mike Goldsmith, of Salford University, gave up a considerable amount of time to making detailed suggestions for improvingg the manuscript, not least by sharing with me his immense knowledge of local government scholarship. Heather McCallum's enthusiasm for the new *Making of the Contemporary World* Series, of which *Thatcher and Thatcherism* is an inaugural volume, has been vital. She has combined unfailing cheerfulness with the shrewdest appraisals of what is possible within the context of the series. Her astute judgement has had a considerable influence on the structure and shape, if not the argument, of this book and I am most grateful to her.

All of the above, and many others have saved me from much error. For that which remains I am entirely responsible.

Eric Evans
Lancaster, April 1997

1 The 1970s: explanations and origins

INTRODUCTION

Margaret Thatcher is an extraordinary phenomenon. She is the only woman prime minister in British history. She was prime minister from May 1979 to November 1990 and eleven and a half years is a comfortably longer stint than anyone else has achieved in the twentieth century. She also held the office for a longer continuous period than anyone for more than a century and a half – in fact since Lord Liverpool's fifteen-year tenure was prematurely halted by a stroke in 1827. She won three successive general elections, two of them by landslide majorities. No other party leader this century has won more than two, and then with smaller majorities overall. Thatcher claims to have changed the course of British history. Change as moral crusade is the *leitmotif* of her career. As early as 1977, when asked by the right-wing journalist Patrick Cosgrave, who was then acting as one of her special advisers, what she had changed, she replied, simply, 'Everything'.[1] When she was preparing her first Queen's Speech in 1979, a speech which many of her detractors say she would like to have given in person, it was uppermost in her thinking: 'If the opportunity to set a radical new course is not taken', she wrote in her Memoirs, 'it will almost certainly never recur. . . . I was determined to send out a clear signal of change'.[2]

Certainly, she shook the country up. Certainly, too, she has exercised the most profound effect on the structure and social composition of the Conservative Party which she led for nearly sixteen years, from February 1975 to November 1990. Her influence directly affected the nature and orientation of the governmental machine. She also required a fundamental reappraisal of the role and loyalties of a civil service, which, like most professional structures, she was determined to turn upside down.

Once she had found her feet, she addressed both the nation and international political leaders in hectoring tones. Straightforward, simplified, and frequently moralistic messages were conveyed with insistent, repetitive clarity. Thatcher transformed, by ignoring, the nuanced subtleties of international diplomacy. She is more readily recognized worldwide than any figure in British public life, except perhaps the most prominent, or notorious, members of the royal family. Her leadership, policies and personality alike have excited stronger passions – for and against – than have those of any other twentieth-century prime minister, with the possible exception of Lloyd George.

IDEAS?

Thatcher is also the only prime minister to have become eponymous. The use of the term 'Thatcherism' might be taken to imply a more or less coherent body of thought or ideology, much as well-established terms such as 'Liberalism', 'Marxism' or, indeed, 'Conservatism' do. Thatcherism is markedly different from any of these. It offers no new insights and, although profoundly ideological on one level, it is better seen as a series of non-negotiable precepts than as a consistent body of thought.

Most modern commentators share the present writer's view that Thatcherism does not represent a coherent ideology. Jim Bulpitt sees Thatcherism continuing a traditional Conservative preoccupation with 'statecraft' – by which is meant winning elections and retaining control of high politics. The editor of *The Daily Telegraph*, in a sympathetic valedictory piece written the day after she announced her resignation in November 1990, asserted that 'Thatcherism . . . is not really an economic doctrine at all. It is a powerful collection of beliefs about the capacities of human beings in political society'. Sheila Letwin, another Thatcher sympathiser, sees individualism as the key attribute. Her view is that, since people naturally follow what they perceive as their own interests, Thatcher was merely drawing upon basic human motivation, rendering it as political programme relevant to the circumstances of the late 1970s and 1980s.[3]

Those who see Thatcherism as an ideology tend to fall into two categories. Tory 'wets', like Gilmour and Prior (see below, p. 14), accused her of slavish adherence to monetarism when traditional Conservatism was rooted in pragmatism, flexibility, compromise and common sense.[4] Marxists (see pp. 28, 120), who rarely think other than ideologically anyway, tend to see Thatcherism as an ideological campaign, in the interests of the capitalist rich and powerful, to create new forms of political and cultural domination over the under-privileged.[5]

Debates about ideology, often politically motivated and intellectually sterile, should not be allowed to deny Thatcherism its visceral power. Thatcherites have no difficulty identifying what they are *against*: state interference with individual freedom; state initiatives which encourage an ethos of 'dependency'; woolly consensuality; high levels of taxation; the propensity of both organized labour and entrenched professional interests to distort market forces; and a reluctance to be 'pushed around', either personally or as a nation state. In one sense, being 'against' all of these implies that their obvious antitheses will guide policy: individual rights; private enterprise within a free market; firm, perhaps authoritarian, leadership; low levels of personal taxation; union- and vested-interest-bashing; simple patriotism.

Thatcherism embodies a series of interconnected political attitudes rather than a coherent body of thought. Few of these attitudes are new. Free-trade ideology developed out of Adam Smith's distinctive contribution to the eighteenth-century European Enlightenment and reached its apogee in the Liberalism of William Gladstone, who fought – and lost – a general election in 1874 on the policy of abolishing income tax. Disraeli and Salisbury in the last third of the nineteenth century both exploited patriotism, through the burgeoning British empire, as an effective vote winner for the Conservatives in the first age of mass politics. Attacks on the grasping, exploiting professions were the small change of eighteenth-century satire, while trade unions were widely tolerated in Victorian society only when their members – usually a highly skilled minority of the labouring population – used collective activity in the furtherance of capitalist objectives rather than as a challenge to the dominant ideology of the age.

The importance of Thatcherism, therefore, lies not in the novelty of its ideas but in the context of their operation in the late 1970s and 1980s. The key to understanding Thatcher herself lies in two facts. First, she actually believed in, and drew strength from, a set of precepts which most sophisticated politicians in the 1970s – not least in her own party – found almost unbelievably crude and shallow. Second, she retained throughout her career the unshakeable conviction that the domestic virtues she had absorbed from a dominating father in a lower-middle-class, non-conformist home – hard work, taking personal responsibility, prudence, thrift, plain-dealing and an overriding concern to see that the books balanced – could be transferred into the public sphere as guiding principles for government. In a television interview broadcast in January 1983, she asserted that her views were 'born of the conviction which I learned in a small town from a father who had the conviction approach'.[6]

The reasons for Margaret Thatcher's political success are complex and will be examined in some detail later in the book. However, it should be mentioned here that Thatcher's political skills were of a very high order. She extracted maximum benefit from the fact that she was not an orthodox political 'insider' at a time when 'insider politics' were coming under increasingly hostile scrutiny. She could engage with the aspirations of the lower middle classes because she had been one of them, and she developed a genius for presenting her attitudes, values and beliefs as if they were beacons of common sense. At least from the early 1970s, she viewed established politics – mired and ensnared by misbegotten notions of consensus and the enfeebling apparatus of state provision – much as early nineteenth-century radicals viewed the system before 1832: as 'Old Corruption'. She offered a battered and disillusioned electorate a new beginning based on old truths. She presented herself as a 'conviction politician' who would roll back the frontiers of the state. As she told the House of Commons in 1983, her vision was of 'long-term economic growth' based on the creation of an 'enterprise culture'.[7]

EARLY CAREER

The 'newness' of Thatcherism was personal and political, not ideo-logical. Thatcher was not an original thinker. Furthermore, little in her career before the early 1970s suggested that she was in any way an exceptional, still less a mould-breaking, politician. She served her constituents in the north London suburb of Finchley capably but unremarkably from her first election at the Conservative landslide of 1959. She rose steadily, and loyally, in the Party hierarchy during the leadership of Edward Heath from 1965 to 1970. By the time of his rather unexpected victory at the election of 1970, she was suffi-ciently senior to be promoted to the middle-ranking post of Secretary of State for Education. Here, although she reversed Labour policy by halting the drive towards compulsory comprehensive schooling, she nevertheless assented to the creation of more comprehensive schools than any Education Secretary before or since. Although she already enjoyed a good argument, she revealed little of her later fierce reputa-tion for shaking received departmental orthodoxies and humiliating civil servants and junior ministers who disagreed with her. She was a rather conventional Secretary of State by the standards of the time, though, ironically in view of her later reputation, she did succeed in preserving her ministry from the severe expenditure cuts which were a feature of the first two years of Heath's government. She attracted widespread publicity only for withdrawing free school milk from children over the age of seven. Though the easy slogan 'Margaret Thatcher, milk snatcher' was regularly heard, the policy was not an example of robust radicalism. Rather it reflected the dominant perception that the health value of free school milk was a declining asset when most families were enjoying rising living standards and a much more varied diet.

Before the end of the Heath government, therefore, Thatcher was no dynamic new force in British political life. But politics is a volatile and uncertain business in which luck plays a quite outrageous part. It is likely that, had the Conservatives won fewer popular votes but four more seats than Labour in the February 1974 general election, rather than the other way round, then the Thatcher phenomenon would not have been unleashed upon the world. Criticism of Heath's government had become forceful within the Conservative Party after the collapse of the economic boom engineered by his Chancellor of the Exchequer, Anthony Barber. This was followed by the imposition of wage controls, industrial unrest and the imposition of a power-saving three-day week. Heath gambled that he could break a damaging strike by the mine workers by appealing to the country on the cry of 'Who governs Britain?'. The gamble almost paid off; the election could have gone either way. As we have seen, in terms of votes cast and seats won, it did. For a few days afterwards, an electoral pact with the Liberals, which would have kept Heath in Downing Street, seemed possible. However, he lost office in March 1974 and failed to win it back in October when the Labour prime minister, Harold Wilson, called another election to secure an overall majority, which he only just achieved. Nevertheless, in both elections the Conservative share of the popular vote dropped below 40 per cent – the only occasions it has done so since 1945. Indeed, the Party's share in October 1974 was the lowest in the century until the unprecedented debacle of 1997.

THE CONSERVATIVE LEADERSHIP

Heath had therefore lost two desperately close elections within eight months. Had he won either, he would have retained, or regained, the premiership. Margaret Thatcher would, in all probability, have remained a tolerably loyal and efficient, if unimaginative, cabinet minister. By the time Heath would have retired, or resigned, five or more years later, other challengers would most likely have made their mark. The Conservative Party is, however, notoriously intolerant of electoral defeat, and Heath's departure after the second election of 1974 was inevitable. What was *not* inevitable, however, was Thatcher's succession. During the last months of the Heath administration, it is true, she had become increasingly disenchanted with the way in which yet another post-war government elected with high promise seemed unable to break out of the cycle of economic boom followed by slump, unable to control the power of the unions, unable to halt Britain's apparently inexorable economic decline. The rapid, and largely unforeseen, rise in oil prices in 1973–4 served to heighten the sense of crisis. It was now much easier to argue that only a radical new approach would do.

Thatcher allied herself with the radicals on the right of the Tory Party. She was not, however, their intellectual leader. Sir Keith Joseph fulfilled that role, and even he had inherited it from the now hopelessly marginalized Enoch Powell, probably the twentieth-century politician with the largest brain and the smallest amount of common sense. Joseph articulated a coherent critique of what was known as 'consensus politics', and advocated most of the economic policies which later became known as distinctively Thatcherite. He called for reduced functions by the state, sharp reductions in taxation and greater incentives for businessmen to chase markets. As they won profits, they would create new jobs in industry and help to reverse the years of economic decline. Successful competition within a free market was a much more effective means of securing full employment than the essentially defensive, spoiling tactics of an over-powerful and arrogant trade union movement. At a speech in Preston in September 1974, Joseph argued that *a priori* government commitment to full employment was cruelly mistaken. The state could not guarantee jobs. It could only pay for them on borrowed, or printed, money. In the longer term, such a policy would destroy the very objective it sought.[8]

This frontal assault on the central tenet of Keynesianism – that governments could 'manage' demand in order to secure full employment – was immensely influential. Above all, following the theories of the so-called Chicago school of anti-Keynesian economists, F. A. Hayek and Milton Friedman, he called for strict control of the money supply.[9] Put crudely, Joseph and the right-wing economists who had influenced him believed that successive governments had paid for welfare provision by printing money. The consequence was inflation, the rate of which had been increasing. As it did so, inflation ate away at the value of people's savings, demoralized and literally devalued a lifetime of effort. It was also likely to lead to political instability and social conflict, even in mature democracies. For monetarists, therefore, inflation was the prime target.

Although Keith Joseph was the most senior, and probably intellectually the best equipped, advocate of policies which were becoming increasingly influential within the Conservative Party, he had considerable weaknesses as a potential leader. Like many who are excited by ideas, he tended to spend much more time on reflection than on action. He did not always distinguish well between small print and large. The civil servants with whom he worked, most of whom admired him enormously, could nevertheless be driven to distraction both by the delays taken in reaching even straightforward decisions and by the retrospective hand-wringing which followed complex ones. Perhaps fatally for his leadership prospects, he did not always distinguish effectively between the logical conclusion of a closely reasoned argument and the need to make such conclusions politically attractive or expedient. He suffered enormous political damage during a speech about social policy in Edgbaston a week after the October election by suggesting that those feckless and disorganized folk in the lowest social classes whose high birth rates were a disproportionate charge on the social services budget should be directed to practise contraception. Partly because of this gaffe, but mostly because he was clear-headed enough to realize his own political limitations, he stood aside when the challenge to Edward Heath's leadership was launched in November 1974.

Into the breach stepped Margaret Thatcher. She would not have stood against Joseph but was now the only cabinet minister prepared to oppose the Conservative leader. Her performance in the first leadership ballot by Tory MPs vindicated her decision. She won 130 votes to Heath's 119 – a more than respectable performance for a candidate who was relatively untried; it was, however, short of the 15 per cent lead required for a knock-out victory. However, a combination of Heath's stubbornness and the misplaced loyalty shown to him by William Whitelaw, the standard-bearer of the left-centre, played into Thatcher's hand. Much of her support came from MPs who wanted Heath out far more than they wanted her in. Wits at the time called it the 'Peasants' Revolt', knowing that most of those who voted for her had been backbenchers vexed by Heath's high-handed ways and bemused by the shock of losing two elections in a year. In no sense did their votes represent a commitment to monetarist policies or, come to that, to the views of the ordinary delegates to Conservative

Party conferences. Had Whitelaw, a classic example of the principled Tory gent, pressed his own claims earlier, there is little doubt that the centre of the Party would have rallied to him. As it was, his moment passed. Margaret Thatcher won almost twice as many votes as Whitelaw in the second ballot, gaining an eighteen-vote majority over both him and the three other contenders. For the first time – but certainly not the last – Thatcher benefited from taking a clear stand against the established elite of her own party. The Tory Party faithful had gained a leader who understood their motivation and prejudices.

CONTEXT

The immediate context of Thatcher's great experiment in government needs more exposition. Three closely linked factors can usefully be identified. The first revolves around Britain's growing economic troubles during the period of the so-called Keynesian consensus, roughly from 1945–73. This period saw both unprecedented social advance – characterized by effective welfare provision, better housing, sharply rising living standards, and successive consumer booms – and accelerating relative economic decline. For right-wing thinkers, the social successes were, if not illusory, then certainly unsustainable. In the period 1950 to 1970 they had been funded by economic output which had increased by approximately two-thirds. The problem was that other nations' output had been increasing much faster. Britain had, therefore been slipping down a succession of league tables. During the decade 1962–72, for example, France sustained an annual growth rate of 4.7 per cent, while Britain could manage only 2.2 per cent. In the period 1969–73 the annual rate of gross domestic product per employee for EEC countries was 4.63 per cent, while in Britain it was 2.79 per cent. This represented a substantial improvement on the position in the late 1950s although still a relative decline. Whereas Britain had been ninth in the international league table of GDP per head, it had fallen to fifteenth in 1971 and would fall further – to eighteenth – by 1976.[10] Right-wing theorists tend to look particularly hard at a culture which permits restrictive practices in labour to flourish. They were, therefore, fiercely critical of the powerful role exercised by British trade unions, particularly during periods of Labour government. Statistics showing that labour productivity in the United States ran approximately 50 per cent higher than that in Britain, while West Germany was more than a quarter higher,[11] suggested to economists and right-wing politicians alike that trade unions should receive particular attention in the developing critique. The circumstances surrounding the fall of Heath's government – the only Tory administration during what was to prove a fifteen-year period dominated by Labour – gave extra force to the argument.

The second relevant factor is the crisis of confidence caused by the end of the long post-war boom in the late 1960s. By the early 1970s, international agreements on fixed exchange rates were breaking down, creating a volatile economic climate which was substantially worsened by the oil crisis of 1973–4. Britain, like many countries following Keynesian prescriptions, attempted to sustain domestic demand in order to keep unemployment levels low. Even so, by 1971, the number of people out of work reached almost a million – roughly three times the average levels of the 1950s and 1960s. Keynesian anti-unemployment policies could only be pursued at the risk of building up inflationary pressures. These were exacerbated during periods of economic growth when British consumers developed an understandable, but economically distressing, preference for over-seas manufactures – particularly Japanese cars and electronics. Adverse balance of payments figures mounted alarmingly. A trade deficit of £110 million in 1965 had reached £1,673 million by 1975.[12] The quadrupling of oil prices at the end of 1973, which brought a short period of growth to a shuddering halt, threatened to put inflation into orbit. In Britain, it reached a peak of 26.9 per cent in August 1975.[13] The value of the pound continued to plummet on international markets. Formally devalued in 1967, it lost a further 30 per cent of its value between 1971 and 1975.

The symbolic nadir of Britain's decline was the revelation in 1971 that Rolls Royce, for so long the talisman of the nation's manu-facturing excellence, was bankrupt. It was saved from going under, but only at the cost of creating a government-owned company which ate up huge amounts of tax-payers' money. By the middle of the 1970s, the tide seemed to have turned decisively in favour of monetarism. Keynesianism seemed to be a busted flush: a one-way street to hyper-inflation and political instability. Restrictions on money supply and tight restrictions on government expenditure appeared to be the only roads back to economic virtue and governability.

The third contextual factor requires a brief look at the economic policies of the Wilson–Callaghan Labour governments which stag-gered on, first with a tiny parliamentary majority and later by virtue of a pact with the Liberal Party, from 1974 to 1979. The electorate had invested limited confidence in Labour in 1974, probably on the basis that only a party which had close links with the trade unions could save the country from ungovernability at a time of profound economic strain. Labour attempted to respond. A 'Social Contract' was cobbled together whereby the governing party agreed to discuss with union leaders, almost on a basis of equality, the major questions of the day. In return for this the unions agreed to recognize an obligation wider – more patriotic even – than their members' pay packets. For a time, the Contract seemed to deliver. Both inflation and pay demands became more moderate in the years 1976–8. From the mid-1970s, significant amounts of North Sea oil and gas were beginning to become available. In 1978, North Sea oil produced more than half the country's energy needs. The prospects both of energy self-sufficiency, and perhaps even of permanent economic recovery, began to brighten.

Labour's experiment with consensus, however, went hand in hand with policies for meeting continuing short-term crises. One such appeared during 1976 and it had profound consequences. Labour's Chancellor of the Exchequer, Denis Healey, proposed to deal with yet another run on the pound by a strict set of economic measures: stringent reductions in expenditure, wage restraint and moves towards a balanced budget. These, of course, were the key tenets of monetarist economic policy and it is worth stressing that the first post-war moves towards deflation and sound money came not from Thatcher or her new-right gurus, but from a Labour government. Callaghan told the Labour Party conference directly in 1976: 'You cannot spend your way out of recession'[14] – but neither he nor Healey was a free agent. The Bank of England's reserves were so depleted, and the currency so depreciated that the government felt an international loan necessary to stave off the prospect of currency collapse or even bankruptcy. The International Monetary Fund's loan of $3.9 million naturally came with further deflationary strings attached in the form of additional expenditure cuts. Although in part externally imposed, and therefore internally divisive, monetarist economic policies were alive and well within the Labour Party in the years 1976–8. The advent of a Thatcher government did not bring them about.

Naturally, the Tories exploited Labour discomfiture and disunity. Much was made of a Labour government needing to go cap in hand to international bankers. A key feature of opposition speeches in the years 1976–9 was loss of sovereignty and a weakening of the authority of government. Thatcher was also keen to stress the importance of Britain's full commitment to the North Atlantic Treaty Organisation and, particularly, to the alliance with the United States. To this extent, she was stressing traditional Tory commitment to a strong

Britain linked to its powerful 'natural' ally. She seems not to have considered the extent to which Americans any longer saw Britain as at all 'special'. In economic terms, Thatcher naturally stressed her commitment to new-right, deflationary policies. However, since Denis Healey was busy putting many of these into place anyway, the general theme was that Labour was acting under duress. Only the Tories could be trusted to continue with policies of prudence and sound money.[15]

Two factors brought the Callaghan government down. The first is the one most usually stressed. The internal contradictions of maintaining a deflationary policy in a party whose pay-master was the trade unions proved too much during the winter of 1978/79 – the so-called 'winter of discontent', which followed the unions' rejection of yet another pay restraint – this time a 5 per cent limit. The Social Contract, which the Conservatives had always claimed to be an illusion, finally fell apart. The rash of strikes brought back to the centre of debate claims about 'ungovernability' and the need for firm action. Popular hostility to unions 'holding the nation to ransom' was gleefully stoked by a generally anti-Labour press. The second factor in Labour's demise has received less attention, at least in England. However, it was the Party's failure to carry through its proposals for devolution in Scotland and Wales which alienated the minority parties and which left Callaghan vulnerable to a vote of no-confidence, which he eventually lost by a single vote on 28 March 1979.[16] 'We shall take our case to the country', Callaghan defiantly told the Commons when the result was announced. Privately, he was far from confident that the coming general election was winnable.

2 Election and depression, 1979–81

THE SIGNIFICANCE OF 1979

Good fortune contributed at least as much to Margaret Thatcher's becoming prime minister in 1979 as it had to her winning of the Conservative leadership four years earlier. Not surprisingly, this crucial element was given little emphasis by Thatcher herself. Her clear, but simplified and determinist explanation of the victory allowed for luck only in terms of how sensibly the public would react to a demonstrably superior Tory message:

> The Government's defeat in the confidence debate symbolized a larger defeat for the Left. It had lost the public's confidence as well as Parliament's. The 'winter of discontent', the ideological divisions in the Government, its inability to control its allies in the trade union movement, an impalpable sense that socialists everywhere had run out of steam. . . . The Tory Party, by contrast, had used its period in Opposition to elaborate a new approach to reviving the British economy and nation. Not only had we worked out a full programme for government; we had also taken apprenticeships in advertising and learnt how to put a complex and sophisticated case in direct and simple language. We had, finally, been arguing that case for the best part of four years, so our agenda would, with luck, strike people as familiar common sense rather than as a wild radical project.[1]

That Thatcher's explanation contains considerable truth is not to be doubted, but how 'new' was the Tory approach, and how consistently, and insistently, had it been put across since Thatcher became leader? Thatcher, quite rightly, laid great stress on the electoral consequences of the Winter of Discontent. She might have had to put her 'complex and sophisticated case' across in less favourable circumstances. With the International Monetary Fund's 1976 stringencies fading from the memory and an election to win, the Chancellor of the Exchequer's spring budget of 1978 had been reflationary. One author has called it 'Healey's last Keynesian fling'.[2] Healey was providing the prime minister with the normal platform for electoral recovery, while the Party attempted to re-establish some semblance of unity behind a realistic pay policy.

While Healey's budget can be seen in retrospect as storing up trouble by encouraging expectations which the government could not meet, in the short term his financial manipulations opened up a window of electoral opportunity. Despite the traumas of the past three years and unemployment at 1.2 million – in post-war terms, damagingly high – signs were appearing by the summer that the government was beginning to regain popularity. Callaghan, who had made something of a speciality of common-sensical television 'fireside chats', booked himself an appearance in early September. The general expectation was that, in the course of one of his standard-issue avuncularities, the prime minister would announce a general election for the following month. Unsure how robust Labour's partial political recovery would prove to be during the rough and tumble of an election campaign however, he confided that there would be no immediate election. Perhaps a leader who had held a longer lease on power (Callaghan had been prime minister only since the spring of 1976 and loved the job, particularly his weekly audience with the Queen) would have taken the risk. As it was, during the winter which followed, the fates, the Scottish nationalists and – above all – the unions combined to bring crashing down that rickety edifice which was Labour's election chances. The loss of a confidence motion in the Commons (see Chapter 1) also deprived Callaghan of the most valuable perk available to a prime minister: the ability to choose an election date to maximize his party's chances of victory. Thatcher *might* have won in October 1978; she could hardly have lost in May 1979.

How united were the Tories? Thatcher and her advisers, notably Keith Joseph and the economist Alfred Sherman, had indeed long planned her 'new approach' for reviving the economy. A new right-wing 'Centre for Policy Studies' had been set up in 1974 to challenge financial and other orthodoxies. It was, however, far from clear that her party was willing to swallow their bitter medicine of savage deflation and free-market determination of wages which the right advocated with increasing stridency during the years of opposition. The shadow employment secretary, James Prior, certainly was not. *The Right Approach to the Economy*, published in October 1977 as the basis of the Party's programme for the next election, demonstrated clearly enough the battle which was being waged for the soul of the Party. Crucially, the question of whether it believed in incomes policy was fudged in generalities about consultation with both employers and unions.

Thatcher had beaten Heath for the leadership in 1975, but this did not mean that she could do as she wished. Nearly all of her initial shadow cabinet had voted for Heath. Even after she had dismissed six Heathites, replacing them with more congenial right-wingers like John Biffen and Angus Maude, most of the shadow cabinet remained in the centre, or centre-left, of the Party. Some – like Prior, Maudling and Hailsham – were too senior to sack. Many had inherited wealth and had been brought up to old-style traditions of service. They distrusted ideology – believing it to be inimical both to the proper practice and the electoral prospects of Conservatism. Their most elegant writer, Ian Gilmour, had been delivering a waspish and snobbish, if coded, warning about the dangers of leadership by the defensive lower middle classes as early as 1975:

> We cannot really believe that this is the moment for the party of Baldwin and Churchill, of Macmillan and Butler, of the Industrial Charter and the social advances of the 1950s to retreat behind the privet hedge into a world of narrow class interests and selfish concerns.[3]

In 1977, Gilmour published *Inside Right*, a developed statement of his centre-leftist philosophy of Conservatism. Replete with historical and theological allusions, it savaged Thatcherite economics, denouncing 'the *sans culottes* of the monetarist revolution'. Gilmour also cheekily attempted to distance the Conservative Party from any contamination with ideology.[4] The leader had, indeed, marked him down for the tumbril but could not afford to sharpen the guillotine just yet. After all she still had to pass her own acid test: winning a general election. She knew perfectly well, as she told the television interviewer and ex-Labour MP, Brian Walden, that the still-entrenched party elite would allow her only one chance at that.[5] As the election approached, Edward Heath made a speech to the Party conference of 1978 in which he advocated the continuance of pay policy under an incoming Conservative government. In her reply, Thatcher made clear her own strong preference for free collective bargaining. As so often, she spoke directly to the minds of the Party faithful, who cheered her to the rafters. She knew, however, that many shadow cabinet colleagues remained unconvinced and was unsure whether she could sell her message to the electorate. The Winter of Discontent changed the political landscape dramatically, making it much easier for Thatcher to argue that her view must prevail. Conciliation, accommodation and consensus had all been tried, yet the winter's rash of damaging strikes, particularly in the public sector, demonstrated their futility.

The Conservative Manifesto, which had been planned almost a year earlier, underwent minor revisions largely to capitalize on the public's anti-union mood. It promised to tackle the problem of secondary picketing, whereby those not directly involved in a strike turned up, often in threateningly large numbers to 'offer support' to their fellow workers. The Manifesto also contained a pledge to help more people own their own homes. Overall, however, it looked little different from the 1970 Manifesto on which Edward Heath had won. Pledges to improve education and health services found a prominent place, as did support for the police and a commitment to strengthen Britain's defence systems. The Tory Manifesto of 1979 offered some evidence of Margaret Thatcher's distinctive sense of mission. It promised to rebuild the economy and offer fresh hope to 'a divided and disillusioned people'.[6] Specific statements about economic policy, however, were rare. For example, no mention was made of privatization, which was to be the central plank of Thatcherite economic policy during the 1980s.

During the campaign, also, Thatcher reined in her natural combativeness. She took lessons in speech delivery and presentation from the Tory Director of Publicity, Gordon Reece; she lowered her voice, learned to speak more slowly and generally softened her image. The effect was certainly less strident, but also eerily synthetic. Party managers nevertheless claimed to detect increased voter appeal and Reece would gain a knighthood for his skills in image manipulation. As the campaign proceeded, Thatcher deployed a fine range of political skills. She presented herself as someone passionate for change in order to rebuild Britain's morale yet not as someone likely to veer off in wild or uncharted directions. In April and early May 1979 she frequently relied upon that caution and canniness which is an important, but under-stressed, part of her political make-up. Knowing that the Labour Party and its union supporters had all but lost the election before it started, she avoided risk.

Callaghan attempted to exploit one of the very few advantages which Labour possessed in 1979: his greater personal popularity than Thatcher. He dropped into his practised, indeed threadbare, routine as the experienced uncle who had seen it all, was solid, unflappable and secure. He could be trusted both to see it through and

Britain right. Old voters must have been reminded of Stanley Baldwin, the long-serving, pipe-smoking Conservative prime minister of the 1920s and 1930s. One newspaper cartoon summed up Callaghan's image brilliantly: 'If you want a Conservative prime minister, I'm your man'. Baldwin, however, never had to face a Winter of Discontent and when faced with a challenge from the unions – in the General Strike of 1926 – he defeated it. The Callaghan image was anyway duplicitous. The outgoing prime minister was never as nice as he seemed; he could be testy, overbearing and manipulative. Thatcher anyway had a nice riposte for Callaghan's promotion of consensus as the way forward. In one of the few examples in which that notoriously humourless lady used irony wittingly and with success, she told an interviewer who charged her with divisiveness:

> The Old Testament prophets did not say 'Brothers I want a consensus'. They said: 'This is my faith, this is what I passionately believe. If you believe it too, then come with me.'[7]

The Tories' election advertising was also superior to that of Labour. Saatchi and Saatchi, in charge of this aspect of the campaign, produced one spectacularly effective poster. It depicted a dole queue snaking into the distance and it carried the caption: 'Labour isn't working'. It was perfectly true that deflationary policies had driven unemployment comfortably over the million mark. Naturally, the Tories concealed the fact that they planned to see it rise much higher still.

Thatcher's victory was decisive, but not overwhelming. The Conservatives won 339 seats to Labour's 269 and had an overall majority of 43 seats. They won just short of 43.9 per cent of the popular vote, the lowest proportion in modern times for a party winning a clear overall majority. The swing away from the government, however, was larger than had been achieved at any election since 1945. Who had voted for Thatcher, and for what, in practice, had they voted?

Firstly, considerably more had voted against Labour than had voted positively for the Conservatives. Nevertheless, negative votes produce positive outcomes, and some striking new patterns emerged in May 1979. Labour's long-term position had been jeopardized by a decline in the number of manual workers in the electorate. Twice as many manual workers normally voted Labour than Conservative, but they now formed only 56 per cent of the electorate. When Wilson won narrowly in 1964, they had formed 63 per cent. Worse, as the political scientist Ivor Crewe's detailed study showed, they were beginning to turn against the trade unions – alienated, no doubt, by the shen-

nanigins of the winter of 1978–9.[8] By contrast, Tory policies stressing
wider home-ownership proved very popular, particularly among the
upper working classes of southern England.

Electoral geography, it can now be seen, was of much greater significance than short-term swings or the precise numbers of seats won.
Historically, the Conservative Party has always been stronger in
England than in the other countries of Britain. It has also performed
better in the rural areas and small towns of England than in its industrial heartlands.[9] Within England, however, it has usually been able to
show a reasonable spread of support. The 1979 election showed a significant change. Swings to the Conservatives were much less pronounced in the north of England than in the south. Compared with
1955, when the Tory lead over Labour in terms of seats was very similar to 1979, Thatcher's Conservative Party won thirty-four more seats
in the south and midlands, twenty fewer in the north of England and
fourteen fewer in Scotland. Thatcher was winning where the economy
was relatively strong and losing where it was contracting. Clearly her
message of effort, thrift and individual self-reliance struck a chord
where economic opportunity was likely to reward these virtues and
not, indeed spectacularly not, where jobs were in much shorter
supply. As Peter Jenkins put it: 'Labour was becoming the party of
decline, the Conservative Party the party of growth. Slowly the political culture of the south was moving northwards . . . colonising the
Midlands, ghettoising Labour's strength in the inner cities and the
urban centres of manufacturing decline'.[10]

This chasm would widen over the next decade and is one of the main
reasons why Thatcher's period in office proved to be one of such
bitterness. Whereas in the 1870s, Benjamin Disraeli worked with considerable success to make the Conservatives permanently electable
by stressing its 'one-nation' appeal, almost exactly a century later
Margaret Thatcher's first electoral success showed that the Conservatives could win power by appealing to the better off. Regulation soothing, mendacious platitudes on the steps of No. 10 Downing Street the
day after an election apart – and Thatcher was brazen enough to quote
St Francis of Assisi there on the afternoon of 4 May 1979: 'Where
there is discord, may we bring harmony' – the message appeared to
be that the British people had elected a government which believed
in the virtues of competition but which now needed only to appeal
to that competition's winners in order to hold power. Nothing symbolized the end of the cross-party consensus more starkly.

THE COURAGE OF HER CONVICTIONS?

Winning general elections is one thing, using the power they bestow to effect change quite another. In Thatcher's view, Harold Wilson and Edward Heath had achieved the former while spectacularly failing in the latter. Thatcher was determined not to repeat their mistakes. It was her rooted conviction that the biggest mistake they had made was in trying to preserve a played-out consensus. She was also aware that the profound economic destabilization of the 1970s had affected most western democracies. Everywhere, so it seemed, high-taxing, big-government administrations were in trouble. Thatcher had some justification for believing that the great experiment she now intended to launch could become part of a change which would affect the whole of the developed world.

Great thoughts are, however, often belittled by practicalities. Thatcher the free-market visionary yielded place in important respects to Thatcher the hard-headed politician. Large pay rises were immediately granted to the police and armed forces. After all, a visionary government might need to defend itself and Thatcher anyway knew well enough how well the redemption of this election pledge would play with her natural constituents. A second pledge, however, was much more tactical and much more costly. The Conservatives had agreed during the election campaign to honour any recommendations which might be made by Hugh Clegg to rectify pay anomalies which had opened up in recent years between workers in the public and private sectors. The general tendency during the 1970s had been for workers with muscle to bludgeon and threaten their way to large pay awards and for those without to lag behind. Callaghan had appointed Clegg, an academic but an old Labour man and sympathetic to the unions, to reintroduce elements of fairness into the process. Instinct told Thatcher that this type of redistributive activity conflicted with her vision of Conservatism; political reality, however, told her that it would lose the support of too many floating voters who were not members of powerful unions to renege on Uncle Jim's promise of largesse. Through 1979 and 1980 the bills for public-sector pay awards kept piling up and, with them, inflation. After a year in office, inflation stood at 22 per cent, more than double what it had been in the last days of Labour. A government pledged to rebirth and renewal by squeezing inflation out of the system had not got off to a good start.

It was because the government knew of inflationary pressures building up that the first budget of the new Chancellor, Geoffrey Howe, actually raised taxes. This was done, however, in ways of which most Conservatives approved since Howe initiated a radical shift from direct to indirect taxation. The top rate of income tax was reduced from 83 per cent to 60 per cent, therefore, to give wealth creators what was deemed the necessary incentive to chase markets and engender elusive economic growth; at the same time, the standard rate went down from 33 per cent to 30 per cent. The key indirect tax, Value Added Tax (VAT) was almost doubled – from 8 per cent to 15 per cent. Although VAT did not apply to food and some other necessities, taxes on consumption nearly always hit the poor hardest since they must spend a larger proportion of their income on the basics. Thatcher knew well enough how controversial the measure would be. She later explained that a government could only get away with it 'at the beginning of a parliament, when our mandate was fresh'.[11] Her overriding concern, however, was to use this structural shift 'to boost incentives'. Interest rates were also raised to 14 per cent and would reach 17 per cent by the end of the year. Most who reflected on its implications concluded that the budget helped the rich at the expense of the poor.

Year I of the Thatcher revolution also saw other moves towards the achievement of economic freedom, notably the abolition of restrictions on the import and export of capital. Although overseas investment was very attractive for the wealthy, its effects were more than counterbalanced by foreigners' desire to buy North Sea oil, the most important new energy resource of the time. James Prior, rather to his surprise confirmed as Secretary of State for Employment, had introduced a new bill to outlaw secondary picketing and restrict the operation of the so-called 'closed shop'. It became the Employment Act (1980) and was roundly criticized by right-wingers, who wanted much more aggressive measures – such as compulsory ballots before strikes could legally be held and the abolition of sympathetic strikes. In coded messages during television interviews and through carefully placed leaks from her private office, Thatcher contrived to convey the impression that she shared their frustrations.[12]

In Year II, the gloves came off. Thatcher learned fast how government works and felt ever more secure of her ground. This security was at least matched by her furious frustration that more had not been achieved during what Keith Joseph called 'the lost year'.[13] The solution was an unprecedentedly fierce attack on public spending. What was mysteriously called the 'Medium Term Financial Strategy' (MTFS) was revealed during the 1980 budget. This set targets to control the growth in the supply of money. Financial journalists had to master new pieces of jargon, M0 through to M3, as various means of calculating the amount of money in circulation. No one could satis-factorily explain how you measured money supply, why one measure should be favoured over any other or indeed whether any measure actually meant very much. Even its main implementor, Nigel Lawson, then a junior minister at the Treasury, soon admitted that 'too much hope was invested in the whole idea and . . . too much . . . claimed for it at the outset.'[14] Monetarism, as implemented, appeared the ultimate triumph of ideology over common sense. It made Ian Gilmour's flesh creep.

While the quality newspapers spread monetarist esoterica lavishly, and sometimes uncomprehendingly, over their financial pages, the thinking behind it was brutally simple: restrict the supply of money and reduce government borrowing needs and you squeeze inflation out of the system. Since inflation was, by 1980, identified as the most potent dragon to be slain, any measures to achieve this, including raising taxes and cutting public spending, could be represented as the lances of St George. In simple terms, Howe and Thatcher were prepared to create an economic slump in order to kill inflation and resurrect the simple notion of 'proper money' for the benefit of the British people.

Howe's 1980 budget, the direction of which was confirmed by its successor the following year, achieved its deflationary ambitions with spectacularly gruesome effect. In 1980–1 manufacturing produc-tion fell by 14 per cent, Gross National Product (GNP) actually con-tracted by 3.2 per cent and unemployment rose to 2.7 million. Adult unemployment rose more rapidly in 1980 than in any single year since 1930, when the world absorbed the consequences of the Wall Street Crash.[15] Britain lost approximately 25 per cent of its manu-facturing production capacity in 1979–81, making the nation ever more dependent upon the provision of services. Had not North Sea oil and gas supplies increased by more than 70 per cent during this very period, it is hard to see how the government could have avoided bankruptcy.

Silver linings could be glimpsed by those intrepid enough to search for them amid the encircling gloom. It was some comfort that the pro-ductivity of those who remained in work during this period increased sharply. This was a key element in the government's drive towards greater international competitiveness. Inflation also began to come down; by the spring of 1982, it was back in single figures. However, this had little to do with monetarism, at least directly. The value of the pound sterling in international markets had appreciated so much in a suddenly oil-rich nation that manufacturers were finding it ever more difficult to sell abroad. The price of imports, which those British who could afford them were still avid to consume, was commensurately low while the huge rise in unemployment was reducing workers' bargaining power and reducing the rate of wage rises.

As ever with the Thatcherite experiment, the effects of the slump were felt unequally across the country. Old manufacturing areas were hardest hit; those which specialized in services, and particularly financial services, got off more lightly. Inequality began to be institutionalized. Meanwhile, despite the government's best endeavours, public expenditure obstinately continued to rise. It reached 44.5 per cent of Gross Domestic Product (GDP) in 1982. An important reason for its growth was the huge increase in unemployment benefit payments. Taxes were also still rising. The overall burden of taxes, direct and indirect, was calculated at 34 per cent of GDP in 1978–9; by 1982/3 this had risen to almost 40 per cent.

The effects of what Denis Healey wryly termed 'sado-monetarism' caused convulsions both within the Conservative Party during 1981 and outside. A number of riots took place in the inner-city areas of London, Liverpool, Manchester and Bristol. The rarity of such events in twentieth-century Britain was another factor which both alarmed the Tory Party and affronted public opinion, which was more inclined to blame hopelessness and despair born of government policy than it was the intrinsic lawlessness and violence of working-class British youth. Thatcher herself saw matters differently. 'Here' she recalled in her Memoirs, 'was the long awaited evidence [for our opponents to argue] that our economic policy was causing social breakdown and violence'. All of this, however, 'rather overlooked the fact that riots, football hooliganism and crime generally had been on the increase since the 1960s, most of the time under the very economic policies that our critics were urging us to adopt'. When she visited the riot area of Toxteth in Liverpool in July 1981, she noted that its housing conditions were not the worst in the city. 'Young people . . . had plenty of constructive things to do if they wanted. Indeed, I asked myself how people could live in such surroundings without trying to clear up the mess and improve their surroundings. What was clearly lacking was a sense of pride and personal responsibility'[16] – and, no doubt, the stern voice of Alderman Roberts to put the fear of God into them.

In January 1981, Margaret Thatcher undertook her first Cabinet reshuffle, promoting bright right-wingers like John Nott and Leon Brittan and either demoting or sacking wits, wets and centre-left intellectuals like Norman St John Stevas and Ian Gilmour. Her changes were characteristically cautious, however. Ministers like James Prior, Francis Pym and Michael Heseltine remained entirely unconvinced about the direction of government policy. What was still a non-monetarist Cabinet was, however, kept largely in the dark. As Pym later complained: 'The 1981 budget was rigidly deflationary and thus highly controversial at a time of deep recession, yet the strategy behind it was never discussed in Cabinet and was only revealed to the full Cabinet on budget day itself'.[17] Thatcher preferred to formulate policy with Treasury ministers she trusted and with economic advisers like Alfred Sherman and a new appointee, Alan Walters. The Cabinet, apparently, let her get away with it.

Later in the year James Prior, who seemed incapable of resigning from the government on principle although he continued to snipe at it covertly, was pushed out to Northern Ireland and as far from Thatcher's sight as could be decently arranged. David Howell, whose tenure at Energy had long seemed a contradiction in terms, moved to Transport. Prior's replacement at Employment was Norman Tebbit, a self-made man with a sharp brain who preferred robust, if sometimes unreflective, conviction to anguished intellectual pretension – and abuse to wit. He was one of the first of the younger group of able Thatcherites to be promoted to Cabinet office because he was of the truth faith. Along with Nigel Lawson who replaced Howell at the same time, he was to make the greatest impact there. His promotion boded ill for the trade unions, just as it symbolized Thatcher's long-delayed feeling that she was at last in control of her government team.

In late 1981 and early 1982, we can now see, Thatcher was at her most formidable, though in considerable adversity. She had now acquired all the experience necessary to exercise powerful leadership. She could clearly see, what fevered speculation in the press about the implications of miserable opinion poll findings and spectacular by-election losses all too readily obscured, that inflation was coming down and productivity going up. There need be no election for more than two years. Meanwhile, she could face down opposition in the Commons. After all, the Labour Party had even greater troubles than the Conservatives. They had lost some of their brightest and best political leaders to the newly formed Social Democratic Party. Worse, they had saddled themselves as leader, in an age when image, appearance and presentation was beginning to matter much more than content argument or debate, with an inveterately scruffy socialist bibliophile. Surely Michael Foot was unelectable? Certainly Thatcher preferred facing him across the despatch box at prime minister's question time to the equally intelligent, and much more brutally effective, Denis Healey. So, although she entered the new year with the lowest approval ratings of any prime minister since opinion polling began, she was confident of her position despite mounting speculation that a fearful Conservative Party would replace her as leader before the next election. As she also knew, things in politics have a habit of turning up to transform the scene utterly. 1982 would prove to be the year when Thatcher discovered popularity to go along with her increasingly formidable sense of destiny.

3   Thatcher triumphant, 1982–8

MRS THATCHER'S CONSTITUENCY

These years saw Margaret Thatcher in her pomp. She achieved absolute dominance within the Conservative Party, which she proceeded to transform (see Chapter 4). Her Cabinet reshuffles in this period were designed to consolidate that dominance. Only those she believed to be true believers of her version of politics were promoted to the highest offices, certainly those concerned with the economy. It is said that the key criterion for promotion from the ranks of the backbenchers was the answer to the simple question: 'Is he one of us?'. The gendered question was doubtless unintentional but significant nonetheless. The first woman prime minister did little to advance the political cause of women. Minimal progress was made during the 1980s. Thatcher did appoint Emma Nicholson, a plummy voiced left-winger who later defected to the Liberals, as Vice-Chairman of the Party charged with advancing the cause of women. Actual advances oscillated between snail-like and imperceptible. Thatcher opposed Nicholson's suggestion that women should be taxed independently. At the 1983 general election, women Conservative MPs numbered thirteen. In 1987, only 46 of the 633 Conservative candidates (7.3 per cent) were women. This paltry proportion – considerably lower than Labour's (14.6 per cent) and the Liberal/SDP alliance (16.6 per cent) – was nevertheless larger than ever before. However, only seventeen Conservative candidates were actually elected. Only 4.5 per cent of the parliamentary party which supported Thatcher's last government were women.[1] Nicholson was bitter: 'Had the Conservative Party really wanted it, the pattern could have been changed. The Conservative Party is . . . an army led from the top'.[2]

Thatcher achieved two successive spectacular election victories. In 1983, the Conservatives won 397 seats to Labour's 209; Labour's share of the popular vote (at 27.6 per cent) was only 2 per cent higher than that of the newly formed Alliance party (an amalgam of defectors from Labour in 1981 – the Social Democrats – and the Liberals). Though Labour, under a new leader – Neil Kinnock – fought a   2 much better campaign in 1987 and succeeded in seeing off the challenge from the Alliance, the Party's recovery against the Conservatives was hardly noticeable. The Conservatives won 376 seats to Labour's 229, and maintained their share of the popular vote at 42.3 per cent.[3] The 1987 election, however, also confirmed the growing trend towards two nations (see Chapter 2). The Conservatives won 227 (87 per cent) of the 260 seats in the south and midlands, with 52 per cent of the popular vote. In Scotland, Wales and much of the industrial north, Thatcher's policies were resoundingly rejected by the electorate.

The system, however, allowed the prime minister to ignore these discordant regional messages. Hers were more than merely large election victories. Since 1945, no party had sustained its majority over three   3 successive general elections. They gave Thatcher unprecedented authority which she clearly intended to use to achieve her vision of change. She was in no doubt about the significance of the sledgehammer blows to Britain's political left which 1983 and 1987 represented. As she wrote, with characteristic trenchancy, about 1983: it was 'the single most devastating defeat ever inflicted upon democratic socialism in Britain'.[4]

Why were the Tories so successful? The so-called 'Falklands Factor'   4 played a huge part in the government's recovery of popularity in 1982–3 (see Chapter 8). Many voters supported the Conservatives in 1983 because they saw in Thatcher a powerful leader who had stood up for Britain against a foreign power. The Conservatives had no compunction about unfurling the patriotic flag. It is worth remembering, however, that the tide of popular opinion was beginning to turn with the economic recovery underway at the beginning of 1982, before the war began. In 1987, the economy – enthusiastically stoked by Nigel Lawson – was roaring away, living standards were increasing rapidly and the great Stock Exchange crash of October was still four months off. The electorate voted for the promise of continued prosperity. The Conservative slogan was simple, mendacious and powerful: 'Britain's Great Again. Don't let Labour   5 Wreck it'.[5]

Other factors also played a part. The election was fought on redrawn boundaries which gave a small, but not insignificant, advantage to the Tories. As commentators have also pointed out, the

Conservatives had the enormous good fortune to be faced by a divided opposition. Labour's appalling disarray in 1980–1 led both to splits and deep unpopularity. The Alliance had enough popular support to come a good second in well over a hundred constituencies – but in a first-past-the-post system this is of no value. Winning a quarter of the popular vote will, if that vote is equally spread, secure less than 4 per cent of the seats while handing the largest party a fair number of seats they would have been unlikely to win in a straight fight. This happened in 1983. The Tory share of the popular vote under Thatcher never exceeded 43 per cent – a substantially smaller proportion than Churchill and Macmillan achieved in the 1950s. Yet this produced two landslides, largely because the anti-Tory vote was so evenly split. There is no doubt that the quirks of the British electoral system favoured the Tories and it is no surprise that Thatcher should be so vehement in her defence of its simple virtue of providing secure majority governments – not least for her!

Fastidious commentators queried the legitimacy of pushing through radical and divisive policies supported by little over two-fifths of those who voted and not much more than a third of the electorate as a whole. Thatcher brushed them aside. She won on the existing rules and could also point out that the Tory lead over their main opponents in both 1983 and 1987 was huge. The populist in her knew perfectly well that the electorate is uninterested in the arcana of constitutional argument, proportional representation and the rest. Such considerations could safely be left to academics, political scientists and the Liberal Alliance. The intelligentsia would, of course, scribble away – but not in the kind of newspapers which Thatcher's new supporters read (see Chapter 6). Thatcher was rightly confident that she was much better at making simple, but powerful, appeals to popular opinion than they. Furthermore, if her opponents chose to split, that was their affair. The Conservative Party would happily harvest the benefits.

There are, however, some more positive points about support for Margaret Thatcher which her opponents make grudgingly, if at all. She appealed to important sections of the electorate which had never voted Tory in such large numbers before. The skilled working classes – bloodlessly called the 'C2s' by the Census office – stand out. In 1987, for example, Thatcher's appeal to their self-interest and their aspirations to self-improvement gave her an 18 per cent lead over Labour among manual workers in the booming south east of England. Those working-class council house tenants who had recently bought their homes under Conservative policy also proved grateful, and loyal. In the 1987 election, 40 per cent of council house *owners* voted Conservative, virtually the same as the Tories' global share of the vote; only 25 per cent of council house *tenants* did. Labour's traditional constituency, the working class, was anyway eroding both in numbers and in loyalty. Social and economic changes, which Thatcherism helped to promote, had seen manual workers shrink to less than one half of the labour force by the late 1980s. The new jobs were predominantly service-sector and middle class – historically Conservative territory. In 1983, only 38 per cent of manual workers and 39 per cent of trade unionists voted Labour.

By contrast, the unskilled, when they bothered to vote at all – which they did less often than the better off – still voted Labour. As Peter Jenkins put it, there was a real danger that Labour was becoming less the party of the working class than 'of the underclass'.[6] Thatcher also gave the working classes, especially in the south and midlands, powerful negative reasons for voting Conservative. Opinion poll surveys in the early 1980s among what proved to be the 'new' Thatcher voters revealed how averse many of them were to the power and restrictive practices of trade unions, and how amenable to the argument that the state had excessive power over people's lives. Their views had changed after a few more years of vigorous Thatcherism, but the prosperity most were enjoying in 1987 kept enough of them loyal.

For some, voting Labour doubtless represented a denial of legitimate hopes of economic improvement. It is interesting also that by the end of the 1980s opinion polls were beginning to understate Conservative support and overstate Labour's. This is difficult to explain but may have something to do with the difference between openly *declaring* that one supported a party which appealed pretty nakedly to self-interest and actually *doing* so in a secret ballot.

The pronounced, and ever increasing regional imbalance in support for the parties also worked in the Conservatives' favour. Labour could count on strong, indeed by 1987 increasing, support in the north of England, Wales and Scotland, but these were areas of economic decline (a decline also accelerated by the application of Thatcherite, monetarist policies). Voters were migrating from these areas towards the more prosperous south and midlands, and as this happened, so the redistribution of parliamentary seats favoured the Conservatives. Paradoxically, however, it also helped to save Labour's bacon. Since the Party could win seats in the more depressed areas almost without lifting a finger, the consequences of Labour's appalling internal mismanagement between 1980 and 1983 were minimized. As Peter

Jenkins has pointed out, Labour contrived to win over 200 seats in 1983 when it had less than 28 per cent of the popular vote. In 1931, after a previous great split, it had won 31 per cent of the vote yet only 52 seats.[7] The impact of the inherent divisiveness of Thatcherite policies in the 1980s was maximized by electoral geography. By the end of the 1980s, it was difficult to argue against the proposition that a 'disunited Kingdom' had emerged, with Labour championing a substantial minority of 'losers' and the Conservatives continuing to appeal to the vested interest of 'winners'.

It was not all one-way traffic. While Thatcher won the Conservatives new working-class voters, her policies, populism and stridency alienated many in the middle classes. For some, though hardly a significant proportion, the opposition was intellectual. They disapproved of what the leading Marxist academic Stuart Hall called Thatcher's 'authoritarian populism' and 'reactionary common sense'.[8] Thatcher could afford to treat left-wing intellectuals with contempt – and relished doing so. For far more, Thatcher's naked dislike of the public sector was the determining factor. It is likely, for example, that more teachers, health-service workers and local government administrators in local government voted against the Conservatives in 1987 than ever before. Their salaries had been squeezed and their contributions to national life constantly belittled by a government which made no secret of its belief that national prosperity depended upon the vitality of the private, not the public, sector.

Only about 55 per cent of the middle classes supported the Conservatives in 1987, the lowest proportion since the end of the First World War. This did not threaten their electoral position. Firstly, a fissure had opened up between the private- and public-sector middle class. The former was growing in wealth and remained overwhelmingly Conservative. Secondly, the numbers of the middle classes were increasing every year and the Conservatives were quite happy to trade a slightly lower proportion of a much larger number – particularly since so many of the disenchanted middle classes voted for the Alliance rather than for what Thatcher called the 'real opposition', Labour. Fairness, of course, did not come into it. The Conservatives got a far larger proportion of the seats in the House of Commons than their share of the popular vote might suggest, and the Alliance far less. But so what? Life, as right-wing ideologues constantly preach, is not fair. Political parties, like individuals, make the most of what they have. In 1983 and 1987, the Conservatives certainly did.

SUPPLY SIDE ECONOMICS

Thatcher used her political dominance to continue her crusade to transform Britain. In these years, she completed the rout of the trade union movement, reduced both the scope and the independence of local government (see pp. 58–64), and subjected many of the professions to the alien rigours of the business ethic (see pp. 65–78). Her economic policies, though subtly changed, continued to dance upon the grave of the Keynesian consensus. Hers remained a formidable agenda, driven on by a women of ferocious energy who knew no life outside politics.

Economic policy was the key. Though the first Thatcher term of office had seen substantial successes, she regarded it as a period of frustration as well as change. She did not have the ministerial team she wanted, and even on the analysis of the true Thatcherite believers, the economic benefits of monetarism were frustratingly slow to appear. As one of Thatcher's most trusted academic advisers, the economist Professor Patrick Minford of Liverpool University, put it: 'In 1979–82 the fight against inflation dominated all else'.[9] As we have seen (see Chapter 2, p. 20), the rate of inflation almost halved during the course of 1982, so Thatcher could justifiably claim victory, at least in the short term. By January 1983 inflation stood at 5.4 per cent, the lowest level since 1970. Norman Tebbit gleefully predicted that Thatcher's government would be the 'first in over twenty years to achieve in office a lower average increase in prices than that of its predecessor'.[10] Inflation would not exceed 7 per cent again until after the 1987 election. The government, keen in this as in so many other matters during the 1980s to present statistics in the most advantageous light, constructed another index, which took the cost of mortgage interest repayments out of the equation. Not surprisingly (since Treasury civil servants had been asked to produce it for precisely this purpose), the alternative measure nearly always showed a lower rate of inflation during this period.

Critics, however, continued to point out that success in the attack on inflation had been partly accidental and anyway won at enormous economic, if not political, cost. Despite the ending of the recession in 1982, unemployment continued to rise. It reached a peak of 3.2 million in 1985 and the cost of unemployment benefit was one important reason why the overall tax burden on those in work continued to increase. Not surprisingly, unemployment statistics were massaged. The government made it less easy to qualify for unemployment benefit and then counted in the official figures only those 'unemployed and claiming benefit'. This reduced the political impact of the monthly figures. Between 1979 and 1996, Conservative governments adjusted the basis upon which unemployment was calculated no fewer than thirty-one times – almost invariably with the objective of reducing the raw figures. Nevertheless, the average unemployment rate in the UK, even according to deliberately doctored statistics, was 9.1 per cent in the years 1979–89, compared with 3.4 per cent in the period 1973–79 and 1.9 per cent during the largely boom period 1960–73.[11] In strictly economic terms, also, it cannot be claimed that the sharp reduction in inflation brought Britain any competitive edge. It was part of a worldwide trend in the early 1980s, and, though the gap had narrowed, other nations within the EEC could still boast both slightly lower inflation rates overall and stronger economies. In the early 1990s, Britain ranked only seventh in the list of the twelve EU countries, measured in terms of their GNP.[12] Only Spain, Ireland, Portugal and Greece – all very late industrializing countries with substantial, inefficient agricultural sectors – ranked lower. Germany (even after absorbing the inefficient and under-productive East in 1990), France and the Benelux countries were much higher.

Most workers – and voters – however, are unaware of comparative international statistics. They are much more concerned with material benefits, and the boom of the mid-1980s brought plenty of these. Real earnings in the 1980s grew by an average of 2.8 per cent. In the 1970s, only a 0.5 per cent increase had been achieved. Even during the latter stages of the post-war boom in the 1980s, real earnings had grown only by 2.1 per cent. Since the boom of the 1980s was accompanied by easy credit which fuelled massive increases in consumer expenditure, it is probable that living standards grew faster under Margaret Thatcher than under any previous prime minister. Certainly what is now called a substantial 'feel-good factor' emerged which Conservative politicians naturally exploited to the full in the run-up to the 1987 general election.

This factor was also successfully manipulated by Margaret Thatcher's ablest Chancellor of the Exchequer, Nigel Lawson. Thatcher described him, with some justice, as 'imaginative, fearless and . . . eloquently persuasive'[13] and quickly promoted him. He first became Chancellor in October 1983 and held the post until a spectacular falling out with his boss over who was in control of economic policy exactly six years later (see Chapter 10, p. 110). During most of this historically long period in office, Lawson played politics and economics more or less equally. He had made his name as the originator of the so-called Medium Term Financial Strategy (see Chapter 2, pp. 19–20) and was expected, therefore, to pursue 'dry' policies such as keeping the money supply tight and reining in any tendency to excessive consumer expenditure, especially on imports. Instead, money targets drifted ever more into the background and had been almost forgotten by the time of the 1987 election. Since he was one of the few ministers on the right of the Party prepared to argue with Thatcher, he got his way more often than most. It later transpired that he was conducting some aspects of government economic policy without informing the prime minister. The 'Lawson boom' was crucial to the Conservatives' election success in 1987, though it stored up enormous problems thereafter when the bills had to be paid during the next economic recession at the end of the decade.

Thatcher and Lawson increasingly disagreed. However, the prime minister entirely approved of her Chancellor's policy on taxation, which continued to stress the virtues of low direct taxation as incentives to effort and entrepreneurial zeal. Lawson both reduced and rationalized the tax structure. The rationalization was completed in March 1988 when Lawson announced an income tax structure comprising only two rates: the standard rate at 25 per cent and a single higher rate of 40 per cent. Tax cuts served their turn as propaganda in the 1987 election as they have in many others, enabling the Conservatives to present themselves as the party of low taxation. Lawson's rationalization was also very astute politically. Since a low top rate affects a large number of only modestly wealthy people as well as the far smaller number of the genuinely rich, any proposal to tinker with the higher rate is open to the charge that it would penalize the middle classes as a whole.

The real irony is the Tories did not succeed in cutting the overall tax burden. Taxation accounted for 38.5 per cent of GDP in 1979 and 40.75 per cent in 1990. The increases were in indirect taxation, particularly VAT, and in compulsory national insurance payments (which are taxes in all but name). Compulsory insurance payments, even more than VAT, are regressive: they take a much larger proportion out of the pay packets of the poor than the wealthy. The consequence of Thatcherite tax policies, as in many other aspects of economic management, was to increase inequality in British society. It is doubtful whether the least wealthy fifth of Britain's population – which of course included the large numbers of unemployed – shared in any of the benefits of the boom of the 1980s. The trend towards greater inequality between rich and poor, which had begun in 1977 under the Callaghan government, increased very substantially under Thatcher, whose policies were widely criticized as having created an 'underclass' not seen since Victorian times. We shall return to Thatcher's view of Victorian values later (see pp. 121–3).

The other major economic success which the government could claim concerned labour productivity. One of the most consistent reasons for Britain's long-run economic decline (which many economic historians would say went back to the last quarter of the nineteenth century) was that productivity per worker in Britain was much lower than in most other developed countries, though not the United States, which historically has a very large proportion of unskilled and recent-migrant workers. Investors get weaker returns from the money they put into low-productivity countries than they do from investment elsewhere. The 1980s saw a dramatic improvement in Britain's relative performance. Whereas in the 1970s Britain had a lower rate of productivity growth (0.6 per cent) than any of the seven largest industrialized economies – the so-called G7 group – during the 1980s the country had moved up to third place, behind only Japan and France. The rate of productivity itself had increased approximately three times.

Critics of Thatcherite economic policy, however, put this apparently glittering success into wider perspective. Had so much of Britain's manufacturing industry (where low productivity was endemic) not been put to the sword during the recession of 1979–81, then the increase would have been more modest. The improvement depended upon massively increased investment in finance and other parts of the service sector; it served to confirm Britain's virtual disappearance as a leading manufacturing economy.

The numbers of workers in manufacturing industry had been falling since the mid-1960s. Between 1966 and Thatcher's coming to power in 1979 it declined by 15 per cent. The rate of decline, however, accelerated after 1979 and the numbers continued to fall during the economic boom of the mid-1980s. In the decade after 1979, 42 per cent more workers disappeared from manufacturing industry.[14] In 1979, manufacturing industry contributed 26 per cent to the gross national product; by 1990, this had declined to 20 per cent.[15] Many new jobs were created to replace them during the recovery of the mid-1980s, of course. The overall labour force grew from 22.5 million to 26.9 million in the decade after 1979. However, the new jobs were disproportionately in those service industries, such as hotel work and tourism, where low rates of pay, part-time working and limited job security all obtained. Highest rewards tended to be earned in the finance sector of the economy, where many of the decade's famous 'Yuppies' (young upwardly mobile professionals) worked. Unsurprisingly, their years of easy wealth coincided with the zenith of Thatcherism.

As critics also pointed out, when the economy began to recover and consumers found more money in their pockets, their preference for imports remained voracious. Indeed, the miserable fate of so much of Britain's manufacturing sector during the first Thatcher government made it even more likely that consumers would look to Japan and, increasingly, elsewhere in the Pacific Rim for their motor cars and electrical goods. In consequence, balance of payments deficits continued to mount. In 1988 they reached the unprecedented level of almost £15 billion.[16]

Britain's emergence from recession in 1982 gave the government an opportunity to present election-orientated budgets. These gave far less prominence to monetarist criteria. They also provide further evidence that, whatever the public image, Margaret Thatcher was practical politician first and economic ideologue a long way second. She was, of course, well aware that her own long-term strategy of turning Britain around was not realizable from the opposition benches. Thus Geoffrey Howe's budget of spring 1982 was intended to give voters more spending money, mostly by increasing personal tax allowances and raising tax thresholds. The dose was repeated in 1983, three months before the election, when the mortgage tax-relief limit was also increased (for the last time, as it turned out) to £30,000. Child benefit was also increased.[17] It is worth noting that revenues from North Sea oil, which were increasing substantially in the early 1980s, also enabled the government to offer inducements to voters. By the mid-1980s, indeed, Britain was an oil-rich nation and the government could use oil revenues to pay for the increased social security and unemployment benefits which the decline of the manufacturing base had necessitated.

Margaret Thatcher's determination to stick to a chosen course is one of the main characteristics which voters identify when (as they invariably do) they call her a strong leader. 'The lady's not for turning' became one of the favourite aphorisms put into her mouth by her speech writers during the deepest days of the recession. Yet, as we have seen, economic policy changed very significantly from 1982–3 onwards. Although a 'medium-term financial strategy' still found a ritualistic place in budget speeches, fiscal targets were regularly loosened. Academic monetarists, angered by this, pressed in vain for policies to remove inflation from the economic equation altogether by maintaining the tightest of controls on the money supply. Having identified one major target – inflation – and having seen it decline to manageable, single-figure, proportions, however, Thatcher was much more interested in the political capital which would accrue from claiming success in this area than she was in pushing right-wing economic theory to its logical limits. Here again, she proved a populist politician of genius, not an ideologue.

PRIVATIZATION

If control of inflation was the key economic objective during the Thatcher's first government, privatization became the central goal during the second. Privatization had three main aspects, all designed to reduce the influence of state regulation and control. There was straightforward denationalization of publicly owned assets, sub-contracting of government-financed goods and services such as refuse collection and hospital meals provision, and reducing or removing state supervision or monopoly in areas such as transport regulation, telecommunications licences and the like.[18] As so often with Thatcherism, the perceived benefits of privatization were at once economic, political and moral.

Compulsory sale of local authority houses to sitting tenants had increased the proportion of owner-occupied homes during the first Thatcher term and had proved enormously popular, especially with groups previously chary of supporting the Conservatives. Fifty-five thousand public-sector houses had been sold in the first year of the Thatcher government and this rose to a peak of 204,000 in 1982/3.[19] Owner-occupation increased from 55 per cent to 63 per cent in the decade after 1979. Opinion polls, meanwhile, also showed a strong preference for private, as opposed to nationalized, ownership of industry.[20]

Privatization of companies promised even richer rewards. Taking major assets, some of which were loss-making anyway, out of public ownership would reduce government debt and raise revenue which could be used for further politically popular cuts in the direct rate of income tax. The sums raised from privatization were substantial. It has been estimated that it raised almost £19 billion in the years 1979–87.[21] Privatization was also broadly popular across the Conservative Party, papering over those damaging splits between 'wets' and 'dries' which had surfaced so prominently during the first Thatcher government (see pp. 21–3). It could also be presented to the electorate as a means of making money easily and with very little risk. The junior minister Richard Needham emphasized privatization's populist appeal: 'The British have always been followers of horse-racing who like to put a few shillings on a winner – privatisation was putting a few bob on a sure winner'.[22] It was a 'sure winner', of course, because the government could set the price of shares in recently nationalized industries and utilities now offered for private ownership and could, therefore, virtually guarantee profits for small investors.

Thatcher emphasized the moral dimension. Her political convictions told her that nationalization was wrong. It burdened the state with ownership which cost the tax-payer money. It was not the job of government to run businesses; businessmen were much better at that. Worst of all, collective ownership was the inevitable adjunct of socialism, and socialism represented a form of enslavement. In her Memoirs, Thatcher considered the political, economic and moral dimensions of privatization as all of a piece:

> Privatisation, no less than the tax structure, was fundamental to improving Britain's economic performance. But for me it was also far more than that: it was one of the central means of reversing the corrosive and corrupting effects of socialism. Ownership by the state is just that – ownership by an impersonal legal entity: it amounts to control by politicians and civil servants. . . . Through privatization – particularly the kind of privatisation which leads to the widest possible share ownership by members of the public – the state's power is reduced and the power of the people enhanced. . . . Privatisation is at the centre of any programme of reclaiming territory for freedom.[23]

Privatization, of course, was underway before 1983. British Petroleum, British Aerospace and the British Sugar Corporation had all been taken into private hands by the end of 1981. Mercury had also been given a licence to compete with the state-owned monopoly British Telecom. Mobile telephone networks, still uncommon enough in the 1980s to be symbols of yuppie lifestyle, had also been licensed. The Conservative Election Manifesto of 1983 made much of the movement towards greater freedom of competition. However, the pace of privatization quickened rapidly after the election. The talisman of wider share ownership was the privatization of British Telecom in 1984 on terms deliberately designed to benefit the small investor. Thatcher's dream was of genuine popular capitalism and she looked forward in her Manichean way to the time when share-holders (good symbols of freedom) would exceed trade unionists (bad symbols of restrictive practice) in number. This was a far from unattainable objective since the government had no qualms about bribing the electorate to participate in share-ownership by rigging the rules of share flotations. Initial purchase prices were invariably set artificially, and attractively, low, virtually guaranteeing quick profits for those small shareholders who chose to sell quickly. Meanwhile, restrictions on trade union activity (see below, pp. 37–9) made membership ever less eligible. The privatization of British Gas in 1986, for example, was accompanied by an almost unbelievably crass advertising campaign based on the creation of 'Sid', the streetwise popular capitalist with simple lessons in share-ownership for the general public. Crassness and successful advertising are, of course, close allies. The Gas flotation was over-subscribed five times and fortunate beneficiaries rejoiced.

Thatcher's campaign for popular capitalism worked extremely well on one level. Shares in going concerns made available at artificially low prices were easy to sell. Important breaches had also been made in the argument that a civilized society should keep those utilities on which all depended in public hands. The very notion of public ownership became deeply unfashionable. The Earl of Stockton, who as Harold Macmillan had been one of the Tories' most successful prime ministers during the period of the Keynesian consensus, attacked privatization as misguided. He spoke to the Tory Reform Group in 1985 about the dangers of getting rid of the Georgian silver before moving on to the furniture and the Canaletto paintings. The press quickly rendered this as 'selling off the family silver'.[24] People appreciated Macmillan's wit, as they had been doing for thirty years. Few however really listened to the serious message behind the *bon mot*. Privatization offered quick and easy rewards. Public ownership by contrast seemed outdated. Perhaps even the metaphor which Macmillan used struck the wrong note; it reminded people that these were the words of a titled gent, born alike to privilege and the exercise of easy power over others.

On another level, however, privatization was less successful. The base of share-ownership did broaden considerably. There were 3 million private shareholders when Thatcher came to office and almost 11 million when she left it.[25] However, the new share-holders were hardly the generation of risk-taking, wealth-enhancing popular capitalists of Thatcher's dreams: doughty class warriors imbued with a hatred of public ownership. Many small share-holders kept their stocks only long enough to realize quick profits and then sold them back again to the large institutions. The long-term financial beneficiaries of privatization were the pension-fund managers. The interest of most ordinary citizens in stocks and shares, if sustained at all, was at one remove – in long-term pension plans which would take twenty years or more to mature. Even among those converted to speculation in equities, the stock market crash of October 1987 provided a harsh lesson in financial realities.

Public support for privatization rapidly dwindled when it was realized that, all too often, its theoretical benefits were belied by dubious, if not downright squalid, practice. Publicly owned monopolies were replaced not by vigorous competition from which consumers benefited in the form of efficient production of high-quality goods at low prices, but by privately owned monopolies, which all too often offered the consumer no better service than before. Chief Executives of these monopolies, or near monopolies (nearly all proven Conservative supporters) paid themselves outrageously high salaries while also taking up share options and pension rights. At the same time, they increased the profit expectations of their share-holders (who, of course, included themselves) by slimming down their workforces and asserting that they had become 'leaner and fitter'. Worse, ministers who had prepared the ground for privatization of particular companies found their way onto the Boards of those companies as soon as they retired, which in some cases, was very quickly after public ownership had been surrendered. Thus, Norman Tebbit, who helped privatize British Telecom, sat on its Board after he retired from the House of Commons. One of the directors of National Freight was Sir Norman Fowler who had been Transport Secretary at the time of its privatization.[26] The reputation for 'sleaze' which has hung unhelpfully around Conservative necks in the 1990s came into sharper focus with the privatizations of the mid- and late 1980s. One did not need to be either a socialist or indeed any kind of anti-Thatcherite to view such developments with distaste. Public support for privatization flagged, and the policy, though certainly not abandoned (there were too many easy financial pickings ahead for that), was no longer marketed as a vote winner.

TRADE UNION POLICY AND THE MINERS' STRIKE

If privatization amply sustained capitalism, and especially those capitalists who helped fund the Conservative Party, then Thatcher showed in these years that she had not forgotten her promise to do more about labour – and specifically the trade unions. Just as she had given ample proof of her belief that managers, at least private-sector managers, should be left to manage free from state interference, so she also demonstrated how effectively the state could intervene by legislation which deprived workers of rights which had rarely been challenged before the 1970s. Strong trade unions threatened the free play of market forces. The trade union legislation of the first Thatcher government (see p. 19) was thus eagerly built upon by the second and third. The Employment Act of 1982 restricted the definition of a lawful strike to one wholly or mainly between workers and their own employers. Strikes in sympathy with other workers became virtually illegal. The Act also contained clauses which made 'closed shops' of exclusively unionized labour more difficult to sustain. Individuals who were dismissed for not joining a union were entitled to high rates of compensation. The Trade Union Act of 1984 required postal ballots at least every five years for all union offices and provided subsidies for holding them. The Trade Union and Employment Acts of 1988 gave individuals greater powers *vis à vis* their unions. They could no longer be disciplined for working during an official strike. Crucially, also, the unions' legal immunity from prosecution for damages sustained during strikes was available only if a secret ballot of its members had been held and had provided a majority for strike action.[27]

Though acutely resented by many, Thatcher's firm stand against the trade unions was generally popular. She succeeded in enacting trade union reform where previous governments had either tried and failed or had not been inclined to try. This had been true of previous Conservative, as well as Labour, governments. Harold Macmillan had asserted, not entirely jocularly, that, alongside the Catholic Church and the Brigade of Guards, the trade union movement was an institution which no Tory government should ever tangle with.[28]

Public support, though by no means uniform across the country, was an important element in Thatcher's important victory in the miners' strike of 1984/5. Coal miners were the traditional elite of the trade union movement and their industrial muscle had become legendary. Thatcher, of course, had been a member of the Heath government which had been brought down by a miners' strike ten years earlier. She would not repeat his mistake. Far from trying to avoid another strike, however, there is considerable evidence that she actively courted a showdown with the miners under their aggressive and charismatic, but vain and politically limited, President, Arthur Scargill. She appointed Ian MacGregor, a trenchant free-marketeer who had been a success at British Steel, as the new Chairman of the National Coal Board in September 1983. Thatcher praised his 'courage' as well as his business sense.[29] The government also prepared carefully for the possibility of conflict, stockpiling coal and trying to ensure that supplies from abroad could be imported at need.

Scargill was quite right to assert, what Conservative ministers throughout denied, that defeat would see the rapid closure of most of Britain's pits and the destruction of the miners' distinctive community and culture. However, he failed to hold a miners' ballot beyond calling the strike. This deprived miners of moral authority for their action, at least in the eyes of public opinion. It also gave the new Labour leader, Neil Kinnock, who was himself MP for a mining constituency and very close to miners' culture – but aware of what a political disaster Scargill was – the excuse to distance himself from the miners' leader. This deprived the miners of wholehearted Labour Party support during their strike. These factors, together with the appearance of a much more conciliatory breakaway union representing the profitable east midlands mining area and an unusually mild winter, led to their eventual defeat in the spring of 1985. Miners and their families had shown enormous courage, resource and self-sacrifice in defence of their pits and their way of life but they fatally misjudged the power which the state, under a determined prime minister, could wield. The bitter irony was not lost on trade unionists who reflected that this same prime minister wished to roll back the powers of the state – in the interests of free-market capitalism.

Defeat was to prove as costly for the miners as victory was sweet for Mrs Thatcher. She mused that the strike had 'established the truth that the British coal industry could not remain immune to the economic forces which applied elsewhere in both the public and the private sectors'. She conceded that the industry then proceeded to shrink 'far more than any of us thought it would at the time of the strike'. Since the reason for this was that the industry had 'proved unable to compete on world markets',[30] however, she appeared to view this dismal outcome with equanimity. The trade union movement, beaten down alike by recession, legislation and industrial defeat, cowered. Another major strike in defence of the restrictive practices of print workers was defeated in 1986. The mine workers' union lost 72 per cent of its members in the years 1979–86. The number of trade unionists as a whole shrank from 13.5 million in 1979 to 10.5 million in 1986, and fell below 10 million by the time she left office in 1990.[31] Margaret Thatcher appeared to have slain another of her dragons.

4 Thatcherism and the Conservative Party

CHANGE AND THE CONSERVATIVE PARTY

It might be thought that the business of the Conservative Party is to conserve. One of the main criticisms of Margaret Thatcher has been that she broke with Conservative traditions by leading the Party in dangerous new directions. One of Thatcher's monetarist gurus, Milton Friedman, asserted – more it has to be admitted on a knowledge of economic theory than of political history – that she is not a true Conservative at all, but a nineteenth-century Liberal.[1] Her misleading assertions about Victorian values (see pp. 121–3) might seem to offer support for this interpretation. The Conservative Party, however, has not historically been a party of narrow reaction. It has usually been receptive to new ideas, whether generated from within or outside. Looked at from this perspective, Thatcher's period in office, however much it shook the country up, hardly represents a betrayal of Conservative values.

Far more often than 'conserving' for its own sake, the Conservative Party in both the nineteenth and the twentieth centuries has been a party of change. When it attempted to defend the old political system against modest proposals for parliamentary reform, in 1828–32, it suffered one of the two largest electoral defeats in its history. Sir Robert Peel nursed the Party back to health during the 1830s by adopting 'necessary reforms' and supporting major changes to legislation on the poor and on prisons, local government reforms, factories and mines as he sought to make the Conservatives responsive to the new industrial age. He then broke it on an issue of reformist economic principle – free-trade generally and the repeal of the Corn Laws in particular – in 1846. The Conservatives have avoided overt splits ever since. It was Disraeli's Tories in the late 1860s and 1870s, rather than Gladstone's Liberals, who placed more trust in working men by giving a majority of them the vote.[2]

In the twentieth century, after internal divisions over tariff reform had caused a catastrophic election defeat in 1906, the Party recovered in the second decade of the twentieth century. During the inter-war period, when it was in office almost continuously, the Conservatives played to what were now its 'traditional' strengths of patriotism and support for reformist policies which united the nation. Both Neville Chamberlain's enthusiastic development of national insurance policies begun by Lloyd George and the Liberals before the First World War, and Tory slum-clearance and housing programmes fitted naturally into this pattern of considered, moderate reform. After the Second World War, as we have seen (see pp. 8–9), so far from the Party attempting to dismantle Labour's welfare state, the Tories participated willingly in the 'Butskellite consensus'. Harold Macmillan, perhaps the outstanding example of a one-nation, reformist Conservative, greatly expanded the house-building programme as a distinctive Conservative contribution to post-war reconstruction.[3]

The Tory Party, therefore, is not averse to change – sometimes radical and dramatic. Nor has it ever denied the existence of internal policy disagreements. Like the Church of England, with which it was for so long associated, though emphatically not under Thatcher, the Conservative Party had always been a broad church and reasonably tolerant of dissenting views. Margaret Thatcher's prescription for change should therefore have occasioned no special alarm. When her first Queen's Speech was presented in 1979, the right-wing journal *The Economist* presented a composite, artificial 'Queen's speech' drawn equally from this and from Heath's in 1970. The exercise convincingly demonstrated how little were the apparent policy disagreements between the two prime ministers who, by this time, were bitter personal enemies.[4] The journal might also have made reference to the distinctive contribution of Enoch Powell. Powell's importance has been obscured by the circumstances of his dismissal from Heath's shadow cabinet over a speech which was widely interpreted as racist. Powell was the first heavyweight politician to mount a coherent attack on the post-war consensus politics from the Conservative right. Many of his ideas anticipated those of Joseph and Thatcher. It is a considerable irony of twentieth-century politics that by the time Thatcher became leader, Powell had left the Conservative Party altogether.[5]

ROUTING THE WETS

Thatcher's period as leader witnessed sharper, and more bitter, disagreements within the Party than at any time since Joseph

Chamberlain's campaigns for tariff reform and imperial preference more than seventy years earlier. Why was this? Two main explanations may be offered. First, Thatcher's style was deliberately confrontational. She made no secret of the fact that she intended to blow apart misbegotten notions of consensus. This was very difficult to square with 'one-nation' ideas which most Tory MPs believed to be the essence of modern Conservatism and also the Party's strongest card at general elections. One-nation Tories had until the mid-1970s controlled the crucial levers of power within the Party, notably Conservative Central Office and the Conservative Research Department. Thatcher had developed or appropriated her own structures – the Centre for Policy Studies, the Institute of Economic Affairs and a possee of academic economists – to challenge those who believed, in the words of Andrew Gamble, that Conservatism 'meant governing a society rather than managing an economy'.[6] She made it clear that hers was a struggle for the soul of the Party.

Second, Thatcher was both a political and social outsider. There was nothing particularly unusual or threatening about this in itself. Historically, the Conservative Party has always been ready to accept, and promote, men of talent from outside the charmed circle of aristocrats, country squires and wealthy bankers. The fact that both Benjamin Disraeli, from a Jewish intellectual family, and Edward Heath, a clever grammar school boy of humble background, could rise to become Conservative prime ministers is sufficient demonstration of this. Thatcher's own lower-middle class background was in some ways surprisingly similar to Heath's. The difference, however, was that Thatcher, having risen within the Party hierarchy and enjoyed its patronage, up to and including a Cabinet post in the Heath government, now aspired not to be absorbed comfortably into that hierarchy but to dismantle it. This was not the Conservative way. Conservatives were expected to work with the grain. Traditional Conservatism was much more comfortable with compromise and consensus than with the conviction and confrontation which Thatcher not so much represented as demanded.

Few in her shadow cabinet understood at the beginning of 1979 how far she was prepared to go to achieve her vision. Her plain, unsophisticated ways were ridiculed in private and she was also the target of that snobbish hauteur which is one of the least attractive features of aristocratic Conservativism. One, who subsequently became a Cabinet minister under Thatcher, revealed his true feelings about her to a journalist in 1978:

She is still basically a Finchley lady. Her view of the world is distressingly narrow. She regards the working class as idle, deceitful, inferior and bloody-minded. And she simply doesn't understand affairs of state. She doesn't have the breadth.[7]

In similar vein, James Prior, her first Employment Secretary, recalled that 'In the early days of Margaret's Cabinet, Ministers often used to pass notes to one another during Cabinet. . . . There were those which were very private, which said: . . . "She's got it all wrong"'.[8] In the early 1980s, Francis Pym offered the revealingly dismissive view that the real problem for the Tories was that 'we've got a corporal at the top not a cavalry officer'.[9]

Cabinet colleagues like Pym and Prior initially assumed that the process of government would soon 'civilize' Thatcher and bring her to see the greater wisdom of doing things in traditional, consensual ways. Some believed her 'conviction' statements to be either mere blustering propaganda or the unsophisticated rantings of a talented woman who lacked the necessary gloss which longer experience of life at the top would eventually provide. The fact that Thatcher's first government contained a significant number of well-bred, one-nation Tories in the most senior positions – including Viscount Carrington as Foreign Secretary, Willie Whitelaw at the home office and Francis Pym at defence – seemed to confirm their beliefs. In the parliamentary party at large, the upper-middle classes and landed 'knights of the shire' still held prominent positions.

As we have seen (pp. 21–2), at no point in the government of 1979–83 did Thatcher's Cabinet have a majority for monetarism. She used a combination of skill and cunning to avoid presenting the centrepiece of her economic strategy before Cabinet for discussion of basic principle. An important element in that cunning was her calculated use of femininity with men, most of whom came from single-sex public-school backgrounds which equipped them poorly to deal on equal terms with a determined, professional woman. One of her most devoted admirers, the aristocratic junior minister Alan Clark, who confessed to finding her physically attractive, nevertheless resorted to stereotypical sexist rant when she successfully argued against one of his schemes:

As the Prime Minister developed her case she, as it were, auto-fed her own indignation. It was a prototypical example of an argument with a woman – no rational sequence, associative, lateral thinking, jumping the rails the whole time.[10]

One of her foreign policy advisers, the Hungarian emigré George Urban, found her on first acquaintance 'much softer and more feminine' than her television image. He believes that her 'perplexing charm' enabled her to be 'getting away with' political ploys and strategems which a man would not.[11]

Certainly James Prior, who found it 'an enormous shock' that the Howe budget of 1979 was 'so extreme', grudgingly recognized the effectiveness of Thatcher's tactics against Cabinet opponents: 'I realised that Margaret, Geoffrey [Howe] and Keith [Joseph] really had got the bit between their teeth and were not going to pay attention to the rest of us at all if they could possibly help it'.[12] As we have seen (p. 22), Francis Pym, then Leader of the House of Commons, thought the 1981 budget an 'awful' piece of work.[13]

The battle within the Conservative Party in the early 1980s is usually described as between 'wets' and 'dries'. 'Wets' were one-nation Tories; 'dries' loyal Thatcherites, most of them conviction monetarists. Inevitably, the distinction is too crude. Some wets, like Prior, Walker and Gilmour, were particularly critical of what they considered unrealistic economic theory. Others, like Heseltine, wanted to use the powers of the state to pursue a more effective industrial strategy. Others again, especially in 1980–1, urged abandonment of monetarist policies on more pragmatic grounds: they feared electoral catastrophe. The 'dries' all shared loyalty – shading into reverence – for Thatcher as a leader, but they were divided also. Howe and Lawson, by different routes, became convinced monetarists; John Biffen, an old ally of Powell, grew increasingly sceptical as the 1980s progressed and was never particularly close to Thatcher personally. Other 'dries', further from the centre of power, were patriots who supported Thatcher because they believed she would revive national fortunes and not to give in to foreigners. Overall, however, the conflict between wets and dries as a whole was what mattered because it was a struggle for the future of the Party, and one which had wider than merely ideological implications.

In 1977, the wets' most articulate spokesman, the old Etonian Sir Ian Gilmour, published *Inside Right*, a book which defended the values of 'old Conservatism':

> British Conservatism is . . . not an '-ism. It is not an idea. Still less is it a system of ideas. It cannot be formulated in a series of propositions, which can be aggregated into a creed. It is not an ideology or a doctrine.[14]

Gilmour also stressed the need for Conservatives to make constructive use of the state:

> if people are not to be seduced by other attractions, they must at least feel loyalty to the State. This loyalty will not be deep unless they gain from the State protection and other benefits. . . . Economic liberalism because of its starkness and its failure to create a sense of community is likely to repel people.[15]

Thatcher never believed that it was any business of government to create 'a sense of community'. Rather it should release the energies of individuals who, one way or another, were imprisoned by the state. Her vision of Conservatism could hardly have been more different from Gilmour's.

Why did the dries win, and with what consequences for Conservatism in the last years of the twentieth century? Perhaps the most important reason was that the wets' tradition of compassionate Conservatism appeared to have failed. They were seen to have been willing accomplices of Keynesian demand management which had weakened the pound, sent inflation soaring and seen responsibility for the government uneasily, and inappropriately, shared between the elected government and a powerful oligarchy of class-obsessed trade union bosses. As one non-Thatcherite Conservative unattributably reported: 'the right wing smelt blood and with Mrs Thatcher they got tacit support from No. 10. Time after time we were told you've had twenty years in charge, now it's our turn'.[16] The wets were never satisfactorily able to combat the argument that a crisis in the nation's affairs had arrived which demanded a radical new approach. Norman St John Stevas, who was to become Thatcher's first sacrificial wet Cabinet lamb at the monetarist feast of the 1980s, told a journalist: 'I don't know whether it [monetarism] will work or not. Why is there no critique of it? Because no one has any alternative. There is nothing else to try'.[17] Thus was TINA delivered into the world. 'There is no alternative' became an acronym which the monetarist right would appropriate for devastating propaganda effect in the first half of the 1980s.

Alternatives did, of course, exist as they always will in politics. The wets did not follow them through partly out of a sense of responsibility for past failures and partly out of that bred-in-the-bone loyalty which Conservatives have for the Party leader except when they fear imminent electoral defeat, or in the aftermath of such a defeat. They could also see the devastating consequences of the blood-letting in the Labour Party and, perhaps too readily, fell back upon overt loyalty to the leader as a better option than fighting for what they believed in. Thatcher ruthlessly exploited what she considered their infirmity of purpose.

The decisive leadership of Thatcher also stood in marked contrast to the pusillanimity of the wets. The anonymous Cabinet minister quoted above praised Thatcher's 'remarkable grasp on government – there was no faltering from day one'. As we have seen (pp. 22–3), Thatcher most impressed friend and foe alike by her decisive handling of crises. Many, including all the wets, were convinced that she was steering the ship directly towards the rocks of electoral disaster but none denied that she was steering it with an unfaltering hand. When Thatcher and her financial advisers responded to the disasters of the slump of 1979–81 with yet more deflation, she left her party opponents with no response except impotent anguish. She believed that they spoke only for a narrow and unrepresentative elite while she was of the firm belief that her constituency was the 'ordinary' England of her own background:

> Deep in their instincts people find what I am saying and doing right. And I know it is, because it is the way I was brought up . . . in a small town. We knew everyone, we knew what everyone thought. I sort of regard myself as a very normal, ordinary person, with all the right, instinctive antennae.[18]

Thatcher was sustained by this inner conviction and used it to extend the limits of prime ministerial power. Another important reason why Thatcher won her battle with the wets was that she was much more ruthless in using the theoretical, but generally underused, powers of the first minister to control agendas and limit discussion of controversial items to those known not to be 'obstructive'. Additionally, she used her press office – and particularly the rumbustious Sir Bernard Ingham – to leak information with the intention of damaging ministers who were falling out of favour. A political press far more interested in personality clashes than in policy discussions could be relied upon to do the rest by talking down, or sometimes up, the prospects of ministers at the next Cabinet reshuffle. Overall, Thatcher exercised more power more directly than any other peace-time British prime minister.[19]

And all the time, and with much greater confidence after the 1983 election victory, she was culling wets from the Cabinet. By 1984, virtually all of the prominent wets – St John Stevas, Gilmour, Prior, and Pym – had been sacked. Of the old Heathite guard only Whitelaw (never an ideas man anyway and supremely loyal to any Conservative leader of any persuasion at any time), Walker (wet but wonderfully efficient and anyway useful as a token gesture towards diversity of opinion) and Hailsham (hardly party political as Lord Chancellor anyway) remained. Howe and Joseph stayed on as old believers of varying temperament and conviction but increasingly the most powerful positions were occupied by Thatcher's own creations, especially Lawson, Tebbit and Brittan. During her second term of office, Thatcher's position was usually unchallengeable. She had achieved a most enviable position. By 1985 she had more experience than almost all of her Cabinet colleagues. She owed no debts of loyalty to those of substantially different political views. She could present herself as a winner – of one war and two general elections – and could look forward to more buoyant economic conditions in which to fight and win another election.

She had two other immense advantages: grass-roots support and a parliamentary party closer than ever before to both her views and her social background. Grass-roots support manifested itself most openly at the annual party conference. Party conferences are ghastly affairs. Ostensibly an opportunity to debate, and even decide, policy, in the late twentieth century they have become synthetic love-ins at which the Party faithful can press the flesh of the great, if not always the good. Television cameras meanwhile obsequiously and redundantly record speeches more likely to have been written by a team of researchers than a senior politician, delivered from an autocue with special attention to the 'soundbites' which will be uncritically broadcast on the 9pm and 10pm television news. Cogent development of either policy or argument has become almost an anachronism. Conference managers also ensure that form triumphs over content as images of cosy unity are presented to the television audience, whatever the reality might be.[20]

Conferences are disproportionately attractive to party activists, and activists tend to be well to the right, or the left, of whichever party they support. Most Conservative prime ministers privately shared the public's view of party conferences: they loathed them. Margaret Thatcher was different. She saw them as an annual opportunity to renew the faith and to re-bond with right-thinking folk. It has been correctly observed that Thatcher was 'the only Tory leader this century to endorse with gusto the prejudices of most conference representatives'.[21] In her own mind, no doubt, she also considered that they represented precisely the kind of public opinion with which the Tory grandees were out of touch.[22] They strengthened her resolve not to compromise or turn back. Her advisers carefully stage-managed party conferences throughout the 1980s to emphasize Thatcher's leadership qualities. The ecstatic and ever longer standing ovations which her annual conference speeches received were given maximum publicity. Under Thatcher the Party conference became almost a populist rally. Debate was shunted off into fringe meetings which usually attracted limited publicity. The embarrassment of many wets at all this vulgar contrivance was as palpable as Thatcher's enjoyment of it. It was an important part of the Americanization of politics which took place in the 1980s and which took the Conservative Party further away from its English, landed roots.

THE CHANGING COMPOSITION OF THE PARLIAMENTARY CONSERVATIVE PARTY

The composition of the parliamentary Conservative Party under Thatcher changed considerably. Larger numbers of MPs were elected who shared Margaret Thatcher's view of the world. Until the late 1970s, about three-quarters of Tory MPs had been educated at public school. The most important changes between the 1920s and 1970s had been in the declining representation of MPs from those schools with the highest social prestige – Eton, Harrow and Winchester.[23] Between 1974 and 1987, the number of Tory MPs educated at any public school declined to about two-thirds. At the same time, Oxbridge-educated Tory MPs declined from 56 to 44 per cent of the total, while those educated at provincial universities doubled to 26 per cent. Even those who represented the ancient universities had previously been educated at grammar or direct-grant schools. Although overwhelmingly university educated, therefore, the Tory Party was becoming less 'posh'.

The professions and business between them continued to provide about four-fifths of Conservative MPs during the 1980s. However, members tended to come either from the humbler sections of the established professions – more ordinary solicitors, fewer high-flying barristers – or from the newer rather than the more established professions – many more accountants, fewer senior bankers. Teachers and lecturers have always provided a considerably smaller proportion of Conservative than of Labour MPs. Among the business interests, the change has been even more dramatic. A larger proportion of the extensive ranks of Tory MPs sitting on the back, and increasingly on the government, benches were self-made businessmen. The motor trade and the housing market were particularly well represented. At the same time, and probably directly related to the ascendancy of Thatcherite Conservatism, the numbers of substantial land-owners (which had been declining for a century) declined even more quickly. Many felt that the times were out of joint. The hard-edged, market-led competitive world of Thatcherism was marginalizing the older traditions of politics as a form of gentlemanly service. Paternalism and deference had been replaced by winners and losers. As one observer put it, the Conservatives were no longer the Party of the estates but of the estate agents. Julian Critchley, the Shrewsbury-educated MP for the army town of Aldershot, talked of a take over by the *garagistes*.

Making every allowance for snobbish exaggeration, the Tory Party under Thatcher was changing more quickly than at any time in the twentieth century. Change in the social composition and political views of parliamentary candidates was mirrored by a decline in political activism at grass-roots level. Thatcherism alienated progressive, paternalist and 'one-nation' Conservatives alike; many of these had been traditionally dominant in rural English seats. Thatcher's attack on local government (see Chapter 5, pp. 58–64) also induced the perception that local politics now offered neither prestige nor such obvious political opportunity for parliamentary candidates. This contributed to a withering of some previously vigorous Tory tap-roots.[24]

The turn-over of MPs, especially on the Conservative side, was also unprecedentedly rapid. Almost three-quarters of MPs returned to the 1987 parliament had been first elected in 1974 or later. This naturally increased Thatcher's authority within the parliamentary party. Since fewer and fewer MPs had known any other leadership, she was seen as the ultimate source of power and patronage. Also, many of the newcomers had been selected by local Conservative associations with a pronounced pro-Thatcher bias. Especially after Thatcher had proved herself as an election winner, the right-wing tendencies inherent in many local constituency parties asserted themselves. In others, the alienation and demoralization of the paternalists gave right-wingers an opportunity to take over. In consequence, fewer and fewer Tory candidates of the old, consensual one-nation school were selected. This change was enthusiastically supported by Tory central office, by the mid-1980s also firmly under Thatcherite control. The trend towards the selection of right-wingers continued after Thatcher left office and shows no signs of abating. Half the Conservative members elected in 1992 had been MPs for ten years or fewer; most of them were right-wingers.

Though many of the new Tory MPs were wealthy, few had inherited their wealth. The emphasis was firmly on self-made success. A new breed of Tories appeared, like David Bevan who had made a fortune as an estate agent and who served a Birmingham constituency from 1979 to electoral defeat in 1992, or Steven Norris, whose money had been made from car dealing and who was an effective transport minister until his retirement in 1997 to resume his business success. Party managers played up this development as a distinctively Thatcherite phenomenon which encouraged merit and individual effort. They conveniently forgot that Thatcher's own upwardly mobile career (impressive enough from grammar school to Oxford and degrees in both Law and Chemistry) had been massively advanced by marrying a millionaire businessman. It is quite likely that the nation owes Margaret Thatcher's appearance as an MP in 1959 to the financial ballast and the influential business connections which Denis Thatcher was able to provide.

The parliamentary party has also become more professional. About half of the increased number of Conservative MPs first elected in 1983 or 1987 had experience as local councillors. To them should be added the growing number who won seats after working in Westminster or in Conservative Central Office as party research assistants or advisers. In consequence, far more MPs now regard politics as a full-time, all-consuming interest. In this, of course, they follow Thatcher's example, although significant numbers have chosen to retire early from parliament in order to take up better paid employment or resume lucrative careers previously held alongside service in local government.

The advantages of these very substantial changes have been much debated. The Tory Party might be thought to benefit from having so many more MPs from relatively humble, lower-middle-class backgrounds who have improved themselves by their own talents and business acumen. Some have a much sharper understanding of the competitive, Thatcherite business ethic than their upper-middle-class predecessors whose experience of wealth had been through gentlemanly capitalism helped along by a privileged education, influential social contacts and inheritance. On the other hand, it is possible to argue that self-made 'winners' too readily assume that their route to success is open to all who work hard and discipline themselves. Faith in the beneficence of the free market often goes hand in hand with both intolerance and even incomprehension of the efforts and needs of those whom life has treated less kindly. It is, after all, of the essence of competition that it produces losers as well as winners.

As even the Victorians, so beloved of Margaret Thatcher, knew perfectly well that lack of success is not always the result of individual failings. In losing its paternalistic ethic, Conservatism in the 1980s became sharper-edged, more strident and less sophisticated.

The Palace of Westminster has, arguably, become both a duller and a less effective place for the presence of so many ambitious full-time politicians. This development is not unique to the Conservative Party, of course, but both the disciplines of government and the substantially larger number of Tory than opposition MPs have ensured that the consequences have been more pronounced on the Tory side. Now that relatively few MPs are elected who are content to remain backbenchers, too few are prepared to say what they really think for fear of having their cards marked as 'troublemakers' by the Whips. Also, the absence of what Denis Healey once memorably called 'hinterland' in so many MPs has contributed to a narrowing of vision and the inability to take a well-informed view on complex matters. As anyone who reads *Hansard* for both the 1880s and the 1980s can readily testify the quality of parliamentary debate has slipped alarmingly. Quality newspapers now report parliamentary proceedings far less extensively than they did. Though some politicians accuse editors of deliberately censoring the wisdom of the nation's elected representatives, the decision owes more to valid editorial judgement that little wisdom – as opposed to repetitive incantations of the Party line – is actually dispensed there.

It is, of course, easy to exaggerate the virtues of the House of Commons in the late nineteenth and early twentieth centuries. Parliament has always contained its quota of the ignorant, the dishonest, the venal and the sleazy. However, recent developments have combined to make the House of Commons a less diverse, less tolerant, less humane and less broadly informed legislature than any of its predecessors. It is not an accident that the changes described here were accompanied by opinion-poll evidence showing sharply declining respect for the honesty, competence and even the value of professional politicians.[25] It would be ludicrous to suggest that these changes can be exclusively ascribed to Margaret Thatcher's leadership. Longer term social, economic and demographic forces were also at work. However, it was a key Thatcherite objective to create a party which was more opportunistic, less deferential and less beholden to an old guard of privileged grandees. In this she succeeded. The extent to which local party organizations followed her preferences and prejudices in the selection of candidates who became MPs in 1987 and 1992 has probably surprised even her. Thatcher transformed the face of modern Conservatism while, in the short term at least, consolidating her party's hold on power. It was a substantial, if not necessarily a beneficial, achievement.

5 The attack on the government ethic

I was determined . . . to begin work on long-term reform of government itself. If we were to channel more of the nation's talent into wealth-creating private business, this would inevitably mean reducing employment in the public sector. Since the early 1960s, the public sector had grown steadily, accounting for an increased proportion of the workforce . . . – about 30 per cent in 1979. Unlike the private sector, it actually tended to grow during recessions while maintaining its size during periods of economic growth. In short, it was shielded from the normal economic disciplines which affect the outside world.[1]

THE CIVIL SERVICE

Though Margaret Thatcher liked, respected and trusted individual civil servants, and was by all accounts a kindly and concerned employer, she hated the civil service. This extract from her memoirs shows why. She considered public-sector employment a necessary evil and was determined to reduce its burden on the state. Civil servants were specially targeted. On Thatcher's analysis, they did not create wealth but reduced it. They took far too long to make decisions, their training inclining them to weigh all evidence carefully. Senior civil servants were a powerful element of the establishment elite, against whom Thatcher was waging *jihad* anyway. They had jobs for life, dispensing lordly advice from the economic consequences of which they were invariably shielded. So attractive and responsible was the life of a senior civil servant that a disproportionate number of the ablest university-trained minds opted to apply for entry to the service rather than take their chance in the rough and tumble of commerce and private industry.

Civil servants were also the permanent professionals. They had an impressive record of persuading ministers, who generally stayed in a particular office for only a couple of years or so anyway, that specific government policies were ill-advised. All of their training disposed them against 'conviction politics' and in favour of smooth administration along broadly consensual lines. They took pride in being able even-handedly to serve both Labour and Conservative administrations. It was easy for someone of Thatcher's background to conclude that these superior, unelected beings needed bringing into the real world. It is not surprising that her favourite television programme in the early 1980s was *Yes, Minister*, a brilliantly witty situation-comedy which turned on the relationship between a malleable, spine-less minister and an effortlessly superior civil service mandarin. The title was itself an irony: the programme invariably ended with the civil servant apparently agreeing – 'Yes, Minister' – when he had in fact manipulated the minister into accepting the approved civil service view. In the normal course of events, Margaret Thatcher did not 'do' humour. In offering a genuine tribute to the all-round usefulness of her deputy William Whitelaw, she asserted: 'I think that everyone should have a Willie' – and had to have the unintended joke explained to her. But she understood the point of *Yes, Minister* and was determined to do something about it.

Attempts to change the ethic of the civil service were by no means new. Both Harold Wilson and Edward Heath in the 1960s and early 1970s had attempted to inject a more managerial tone. Heath, indeed, had produced a portentously phrased White Paper *The Reorganisation of Central Government*, created a Central Policy Review Staff and looked forward to reducing manpower in the civil service.[2] Heath, however, attempted to reform from the inside. He was rapidly ensnared, diverted by other priorities and was anyway prime minister for less than four years. The Wilson and Callaghan Labour governments conducted an extensive review of central administration, which resulted in the reduction of 35,000 administrative posts and savings of almost £140 million.

Characteristically, however, Thatcher's assault in pursuit of her objectives was more tenacious. She came to office having, apparently, given far less thought and preparation to the machinery of government than had Heath. However, unlike him, she instinctively preferred working with 'outsiders' from the business world rather than establishment insiders. Her long period of office gave her the time to overcome resistance to change and enabled her policies to take root.

As so often, Thatcher's policies depended more upon instinct than mature consideration of the issues. As Peter Hennessy put it, 'In 1979 Mrs Thatcher had more a gut-feeling than a game-plan'.[3] She was sure that Britain was overburdened by excessive administration and red-tape. Almost three-quarters of a million civil servants cost every individual £3 a week. The service needed the brisk discipline of the market to eliminate waste and to achieve stated objectives. A leaner and fitter civil service would also give the Conservative Party ample scope for election-winning tax cuts. Thatcher looked to outsiders from the world of business to effect the necessary changes. John Hoskyns, the head of Thatcher's Policy Unit from 1979 to 1982, had made a fortune in the computer business during the mid-1970s and distrusted civil servants and trade unionists equally. His influential policy document *Stepping Stones* (1977) had identified trade unions as the main obstacles to getting Britain moving again. Civil servants were too often pessimistic and cynical: distrustful of, and unsympathetic to, new ideas. He also considered it a bad sign that the civil service unions were doing their best to block change. When examining ways of improving Britain's trading performance in the mid-1980s, Hoskyns was not surprised to find that 'few, if any, civil servants believe that the country can be saved'.[4] Thatcher herself recalled her dismay at the defeatism of a senior civil servant in the 1970s who argued that the height of realistic British ambition should be the 'orderly management of decline'.

Derek Rayner was seconded part-time from Marks and Spencer to set up an Efficiency Unit. His task, as Thatcher herself briskly put it, was to eliminate 'the waste and ineffectiveness of government' and also to encourage civil servants to think more positively. It was Rayner who introduced senior civil servants to the paraphernalia of efficiency audits and management targets. Both he and Thatcher fervently believed in transferring the business ethic into the heart of government administration. As Thatcher put it, 'We were both convinced of the need to bring some of the attitudes of business into government. We neither of us conceived just how difficult this would prove'.[5]

Rayner's strategy was not, however, overly confrontational. He had experience of the workings of Whitehall and had developed from it a subtler understanding than had his political mistress of its strengths as well as its weaknesses. He identified civil servants amenable to the managerial culture and used them to work with, rather than against, the administrative grain. His Unit reported that Whitehall could save as much as £70 million a year and operate with a much smaller permanent establishment. By 1983, the Civil Service had lost 100,000 jobs. By 1987, efficiency savings were calculated to have reached £1 billion.[6] During Thatcher's period as prime minister, the number of civil servants was reduced by 22.5 per cent (from 732,000 to 567,000).[7]

The first Thatcher administration also saw the abolition of the Civil Service Department, which had been established in 1968 to oversee management and conditions in the service. By 1981, it had 5,000 employees though the prime minister was entirely unconvinced of its value. A long-running labour dispute in the civil service and an embarrassing dinner at which heads of civil service departments only succeeded in convincing Thatcher that their main objectives were defensive and negative sealed the fate of the CSD. Its abolition also made it easier for Thatcher to determine appointments to the most civil senior posts. The retirement of no fewer than eight heads of department during 1982 and 1983 ensured that their replacements would be, if not exactly conviction Thatcherites, at least believers in change in general and the managerial approach in particular.[8] From this period dates the increasingly frequent charge that she appointed those known to favour her political views. Opponents have argued that Thatcher's determination to 'get things done' and to make the civil service more accountable led her to compromise its long-established and jealously guarded political neutrality.

Ironically, in view of their later disagreements (see pp. 108–9), Thatcher's closest ally in the managerial revolution at Whitehall was Michael Heseltine. He sponsored a new Management Information System for Ministers in the Environment Department and followed this up with a Financial Management Initiative. These changes saw the introduction of those defined objectives, close financial controls and 'cost centres', already familiar to private industry while making it easier for ministers to impose their will on civil servants. Heseltine explained the rationale:

> A civil servant may tell you that he is responsible for the permissible levels of pollution in the waterways of Britain. That is a worthy activity, but it does not tell you much about what he is doing. I wanted to know what standards had been set; whether higher standards were to be brought in, and when; what this would cost and how the benefits were to be measured.[9]

Heseltine was proud that the development of precise targets enabled both greater productivity and reduced manpower to be achieved. The Department of Environment's establishment was reduced by almost 30 per cent between 1979 and 1983. The number of civil servants attached to the Ministry of Defence, to which Heseltine moved in 1983, was reduced by 20,000 in the years up to his resignation in 1986.

How effective, and how extensive, the imposition of managerialism upon the civil service has been is a matter of considerable debate. It has been pointed out that Thatcher was more concerned with ensuring that she had congenial advisers in place than she was with abstract theories of administration. Likewise, some ex-civil servants have asserted that Thatcher did not defeat the civil service's legendary capacity to absorb change without fundamentally altering either direction or ethos.[10] Even the impact of rapidly declining numbers has been questioned since most of the losses have been either in the highest ranks or in the industrial civil service. The great majority of civil servants remained in secure, pensionable employment unexposed to the rigours of the market place.

Reliance upon the civil service for policy direction, however, certainly diminished during the 1980s. One important consequence of Thatcher's profound dislike of its administrative ethos was that she circumvented it whenever she could. The most obvious indication of this was the number of policy advisers she brought into government who had no previous connection with the civil service. Most, of course, were businessmen. Some however, like Terry Burns or Alan Walters, were right-wing academics – free-marketeers, to her mind refreshingly free from that leftist collectivism and cynicism which Thatcher believed to be the malign legacy of academic elitism. These advisers usually had a much more direct impact on the formulation of policy than did senior civil servants, who were taught to know their subordinate place. Thatcher was less amenable than any earlier prime minister to practised civil service arguments about why new policies could not work.

Thatcher's third government – from 1987–90 – took the most radical decisions in respect of the civil service. Sir Robin Ibbs, yet another business magnate brought in by Thatcher to shake up the mandarins, took over from Derek Rayner. His report *The Next Steps* initiated a major policy shift. It recommended the preservation of only a small core civil service which would continue to run the government machinery. Most civil servants would transfer to new executive agencies charged to 'deliver' specific services. These agencies would not be attached to ministries. The services to be provided covered a wide spectrum – from vehicle licensing to Her Majesty's Stationery Office (the government's publisher) and from tax collection to the management of highways. The common denominator was the provision of services under tight budgetary controls to precise 'targets' and objectives. Thatcher left office before this process accelerated, probably irreversibly. By 1992, no fewer than seventy-two agencies were in place employing almost 300,000 civil servants – roughly half the total.[11] John Major's much lampooned *Citizen's Charter* initiative of 1991 was a logical extension of the philosophy. Government agencies were required to publish targets and to report on how they measured up to them. Throughout, the accent was upon service and account-ability to the public as consumers rather than upon smooth administration. *Next Steps*, and the changed civil service culture to which it gave rise, represented the most radical change in government employment patterns and priorities for almost a century and a half. Not since 1853, when the Northcote-Trevelyan Report presaged the introduction of competitive examinations, rather than patronage, as the means of entry to the civil service, had such a shake-up been attempted.[12]

LOCAL GOVERNMENT

Margaret Thatcher's policies on local government probably repre-sented her sharpest break with the ethos of traditional Conservatism. Historically, the Conservatives were the party of local interests and identities, particularly English ones. Many of its nineteenth- and early twentieth-century MPs saw it as their highest ambition to repre-sent the interests of their constituents. They were sceptical of the influ-ence of central government, preferred to advocate local solutions to local problems and generally agreed with Benjamin Disraeli's dictum that 'Centralisation is the death-blow of public freedom'.[13] Peter Walker's extensive reorganization of English local government, under-taken in 1972 under the Heath government, although politically unpopular, aimed at improving local representative systems not at undermining them.

Thatcher was sceptical of central government if it meant high taxes and control by a self-perpetuating elite. As we have seen, she was very much a provincial outsider from a non-conformist background. Where she most violently disagreed with many old-style MPs, however, was in her attitude towards the integrity and purpose of local government. She did not believe in it as a separate or alternative focus for public politics and she abominated what she saw as its inefficient, wasteful and all too often wrong-headed ways. Collectively, the town halls and municipal ideas of Britain represented yet another dragon that needed to be slain.

In the 1970s, the Heath government had considered drastic action in respect of the Greater London Council, while local government had also been of increasing concern to the outgoing Labour government.

Labour had reduced the level of grant support to local authorities and introduced cash limits on local government spending. Nevertheless, by the time Thatcher took office local government accounted for no less than 28.1 per cent of public expenditure and for 12.4 per cent of GNP.[14] About 60 per cent of its activities were funded by central government anyway and the legitimacy of this was highly questionable. Roughly three-quarters of the electorate voted at general elections while less than a third bothered to turn out for local government elections. If, as frequently happened between general elections, local elections produced anti-government majorities in town halls up and down the land, why should their powers not be curbed by a demonstrably more 'democratic' body – parliament? Kenneth Baker, who was Minister in charge of local government in 1984–5, explained Conservative policy succinctly, if controversially:

> A new generation of hard-left activists replaced old-style Labour moderates and deliberately decided to use town halls as a weapon against the Conservative government. Local government was to become a 'state within a state', the vehicle for delivering Socialism locally in the face of electoral rejection nationally.[15]

Thatcher determined to strip local authorities of many of their powers and to abolish the most troublesome ones. After councils had been instructed by the 1980 Housing Act to sell houses to tenants of three years' standing who wished to buy, the first Thatcher government reduced the grant subsidy to local authorities in the hope that this would restrain their spending. During the years 1980–6 the value of the central subsidy was reduced from 60 per cent of total local authority income to 49 per cent. Local government capital expenditure was, indeed, reduced. In the decade 1977–87 it declined, as a proportion of GDP, from 2.6 per cent to 1.3 per cent, although it should be remembered that this was part of a much longer term development. In 1967, capital expenditure had been 4.1 per cent of GDP.[16] Most authorities initially responded not by slashing expenditure but by increasing rates. These rose by 27 per cent in the year 1980/81 and were still rising substantially after the Conservatives won the 1983 general election. In 1978/79 local authorities raised £23.2 million from rates while receiving £44.0 million in central government grant. Five years later, the figures were £27.0 million and £39.2 million respectively.[17]

Thatcher used her second electoral mandate to reduce local authority powers more directly. The Scots, who were not prone to voting Conservative anyway and so could be safely experimented upon, had already been introduced to the concept of 'rate capping'.[18]

Local authorities who overspent were subject to financial penalties imposed by central government. A prolonged battle over local autonomy ensued which was not a simple matter of left versus right. The respected Birmingham backbench Tory MP, Anthony Beaumont Dark, told *The Financial Times* in January 1984, for example:

> If this [rate-capping] Bill is only to be used against a few admittedly zany authorities, then it is unnecessary. If it is to be used like a gun to demand in the end the unconditional surrender of local powers to central diktat then it is the most retrograde piece of legislation ever introduced by a Conservative government.[19]

In 1985–6, eighteen local authorities (all but two of them Labour controlled) were rate-capped.[20] The government won this acrimonious conflict for three main reasons. First, alongside the now characteristic steely Thatcher resolve on strategy – local government bashing – went an equally characteristic, but far less publicized, willingness to bend on tactics. Thus, in February 1985, the government revised upwards the rate limits of six local authorities (including four particularly troublesome London ones), thus giving their councillors less political leverage to move from opposition to sustained outright defiance. Second, the authorities themselves found it difficult to maintain a united front. Some 'old-Labour' councils were alienated by socialists and left-extremists whose priorities seemed not to be with the mundane issue of local government finance but the heady rhetoric of defiance, law-breaking and even revolution. The particular needs and priorities of local authorities also differed widely. Third, the left-extremists gave the government an immensely valuable propaganda weapon. Liverpool City Council, for example, had fallen into the hands of Militant Tendency, a revolutionary socialist organization. The provocative tactics employed in Liverpool alienated both the Labour Party and other local authorities much more than it annoyed Thatcher.[21] Public opinion, influenced by sensationalist exposure-reporting in the press, veered increasingly to the side of the government rather than the local authorities. What Arthur Scargill had done for the trade union movement in 1984–5 (see pp. 37–9), the equally vain and even more preposterous Derek Hatton did for local government autonomy. When Liverpool, along with Lambeth, became the last councils to agree to set a legal rate in July 1987, Margaret Thatcher could claim another impressive triumph against socialism.

During the second Thatcher government another significant nettle was grasped. The Local Government Act of 1985 proposed to abolish the Greater London Council and six other Metropolitan Authorities entirely and to devolve their responsibilities to thirty-two separate London boroughs and to metropolitan districts. This provoked a spirited and skilful response, especially from the leader of the GLC, the left-winger Ken Livingstone, who had taken over as leader soon after Labour had won London in the local elections of 1981. His decision to reduce London transport fares by 25 per cent was popular in itself but also pointed up the kind of decisions which only an integrated London council could carry through. The effectiveness of the pro-GLC propaganda campaign delayed abolition for a year, but neither it nor the metropolitan authorities could hold out indefinitely against a determined central government with a clear parliamentary majority.

The pro-local government campaigners highlighted an important constitutional issue. The absolute sovereignty of parliament had never in the twentieth century been so nakedly revealed during peace time as during the debates over the abolition of the metropolitan authorities. The absence of a written constitution leaves subordinate authorities without any redress against a decision made in parliament. In theory, the monarch can veto parliamentary legislation but this has not happened since 1708 and the power is effectively extinct. The federal constitutions of Germany, the United States and many other democratic states would have prevented the actions of the Conservative government in 1985/86. It was a Conservative politician, Lord Hailsham, who had coined the term 'elective dictatorship' to describe what he considered the inappropriately extended powers of a Labour government in the 1970s. Yet the term is much more appropriately applied to the Thatcher government in its dealings with local authorities – a government, be it noted, which never gained more than 44 per cent support from the three-quarters or so of those eligible to vote in a general election. From the mid-1980s, local government was directed by central government; only rarely was it consulted and then on issues which central government considered peripheral to its main strategy. Thatcher – who purported to dislike 'big government' – had increased its power more than any prime minister before her.

Having been broken by the first and second Thatcher governments, local government was converted into a competitive 'service enabler' by the third. Drawing upon earlier experiences, notably the deregulation of public transport under the Transport Act (1985) and the activities of the Tory authority of Wandsworth between 1982 and 1987,[22] the Local Government Act of 1988 required local authorities to put most of their existing services out to competitive tender and ensured that only commercial criteria should determine which organizations provided services. Paul Beresford, leader of the Wandsworth council which claimed to have saved £24 million by contracting out services, explained that his strategy was:

> the efficient management of services: to cut waste; to ensure high quality and to test all Council Services, where possible, against the private sector and to contract out, where appropriate.[23]

The operation of a large number of basic services was transferred from local authority to private-sector hands. This policy unfolded under the direction of Nicholas Ridley, a staunch free-marketeer who had taken over as Secretary of State for the Environment in May 1986 and served there until July 1989. It had patchy success. In some places, most services were provided efficiently by the private sector, and more cheaply than before. In others, the cheapest private bid proved anything but the best for consumers who were badly served by new providers who had clearly underestimated, or otherwise miscalculated, the task they were taking on. Overall, it seemed that compulsory competitive tendering had enabled local government to make savings as high as 20 per cent, although more than three-quarters of the new service contracts were won by a unit of local authority-employed staff.[24] Even initially sceptical Labour authorities could see the value of a switch which enabled them both to rethink their service priorities and also to curb trade union restrictive practice.

The integrated package of services previously provided by local government was dismantled by a government utterly convinced that the free-market approach and unbridled competition were the only ways forward. As intended, also, the new policy continued local government fragmentation and enhanced the culture of management rather than that of administration. Along with the granting of new powers to a series of outside agencies, such as the Urban Development Corporations, Inner City Enterprises and the Manpower Services Commission, the Conservatives continued to marginalize local government. These new agencies, furthermore, provided additional opportunities for the deployment of government patronage. Most of their directors were figures well known to hold at least Conservative, if not always Thatcherite, views.

Much the most controversial policy in respect of local government was the introduction of the 'community charge'. Widely known as the poll tax, this was introduced to replace domestic rates. The 1987 Conservative election manifesto promised reformed finance for local government, and, as with rate-capping, new policies were tried out in Scotland first. The burden of rates varied with the size of the property on which they were levied. The new charge for local service would be levied upon each adult. For Margaret Thatcher, the great advantage was 'accountability':

> Of the 35 million local electors in England, 17 million were not themselves liable for rates, and of the 18 million liable, 3 million paid less than the full rates and 3 million paid nothing at all . . . many people had no reason to be concerned about their council's overspending, because somebody else picked up all or most of the bill.[25]

The 'somebody else', of course, was that property-owning group at the heart of Thatcher's support; she empathized with it like no other group in British society. An important sub-set of property owners was small businessmen, from which group Thatcher had herself sprung. The prospect of a uniform business rate, rather than the hugely different burdens which small businesses bore depending upon where they were located, was another part of the package. Accountability was one issue, but the prime minister was anxious to spread the burden of local government more widely. In this policy – perhaps uniquely during her eleven years in power – her political instincts proved disastrously faulty. A poll tax could not be presented to the public as anything other than regressive. It bore more heavily on those with limited incomes and hardly at all (as a proportion of income at any rate) upon the wealthy.

From its inception, the poll tax encountered stiff resistance. Many backbench Conservative MPs – especially those in marginal constituencies – opposed it, feeling it to be a certain vote loser. Some influential voices, not least that of Nigel Lawson, the Chancellor of the Exchequer, were raised against it in Cabinet. Opinion poll evidence told a uniform story: the so-called Community Charge was deeply unpopular. Early projections had suggested to Thatcher that the charge per head would be less than £200 – hefty enough, but supportable. By early 1990, she was receiving revised estimates that it would be about £350, implying a charge for a family with two children of 18 and 20 years of almost £1,500 a year. Meanwhile, opposition to the introduction of the charge was mounting, generating the potential for massive public disorder. Advisers also told Thatcher that many who either moved accommodation frequently or were of no fixed abode would not put themselves onto the voting register, so increasing the likelihood that they would stay beyond the reach of the tax. Such voluntary disenfranchisement was an obvious threat to the democratic process, though how heavily this point actually weighed with Thatcher was debatable, since few of these marginal folk were likely Conservative voters anyway.

The resolution of the poll tax fiasco lies beyond the scope of this book, since it took place after Thatcher left office. Its important contribution to her fall is considered elsewhere (see p. 112). The fact that she continued to press ahead with such a deeply unpopular policy is significant. It emphasizes what a resolute fighter she was. She had fought off severe opposition before and always won. She also knew that many notional party allies would always run for cover at the first sign of danger, or else use that danger to plot against her. The poll tax may also indicate, however, her increasingly insecure grip on political reality in the late 1980s. She seemed to believe that, by appealing over the heads of the political establishment to 'her' people – the ordinary house-owners of rural and suburban England – she would always be vindicated. She was wrong. It is not without irony that Britain's most determined, and most powerful, prime minister since the Second World War should be brought down on a measure concerned with local government – an area on which she had tested constitutional proprieties to their limit and on which she felt that she could mobilize her populist appeal most effectively.

6 The attack on the professional ethic

'All professions are conspiracies against the laity', wrote George Bernard Shaw in *The Doctor's Dilemma* in 1911. Margaret Thatcher would have had very little in common with Shaw, the Irish playwright, lover of music (he was a distinguished, if idiosyncratic, music critic) and socialist moralist who died in 1950 – the year Thatcher fought her first, unsuccessful general election as Conservative candidate for the hopeless constituency of Dartford. On this one point, however, conviction Conservative and garrulous socialist sage were at one. Thatcher, too, was suspicious of professionals. She was irritated by the easy, apparently effortless, expertise many possessed and considered the higher professionals a pampered elite. Professionals regulated themselves. In doing so, she thought that they winked at sloppy practice and casual inefficiency. They were insufficiently self-critical. However finely honed their skills and however much their expertise was valued, Thatcher felt that they were insufficiently responsive to market forces – and thus a collective impediment to the achievement of the kind of world she wished to bring about. Professionals were particularly prominent defenders of that welfare tradition, especially in health and education, which had been inherited from William Beveridge in the 1940s and which had become an increasingly heavy burden upon the tax-payer. Thatcher's radicalism encompassed a critical approach to welfare state. Welfarism, in her view, had spawned a dependency culture; it militated against innovation, risk and economic achievement. It is hardly surprising, therefore, that the professional ethic should be prominently in her sights.

THE NATIONAL HEALTH SERVICE

The National Health Service presented particular problems for an ideologically driven prime minister. On the one hand, the administrative structure of the NHS was widely acknowledged to be both inefficient and wasteful. Some parts of the country were much better served than others. Also its costs were extremely high, not least because universal provision of quality service since the NHS came into being in 1948 had increased life expectancy. More than twice as many people in the United Kingdom (1.6 million) were over 80 years of age in 1981 than in 1951, and the number would increase to 2.2 million by the time Thatcher left office. Also, in 1991 16 per cent of the population was over the male pensionable age of 65, compared with 11 per cent when the NHS was founded.[1] Inevitably, the very old make heavy demands on scarce resources. Economically, the NHS was the victim of its own success. The prime minister's think-tanks devised numerous schemes for reducing costs and introducing more market mechanisms into the service. A Central Policy Review Staff paper in the early 1980s proposed a package of measures – including the promotion of private health insurance, charging for doctors' visits and increasing prescription charges – designed to save between 10 and 12 per cent of the NHS budget.[2]

On the other hand, every opinion poll confirmed the British public's attachment to the NHS. For some it represented almost the only beacon of international excellence amid long-term post-war decline. Any tinkering was bound to be politically unpopular and the radical options presented by right-wing think-tanks could be electorally disastrous. In a widely reported, and by her opponents much derided, statement to the Party Conference in 1982, Thatcher declared: 'The National Health Service is safe with us. . . . The principle that adequate health care should be provided for all regardless of the ability to pay must be the function of any arrangements for financing the NHS. We stand by that'.[3]

Thatcher's policy for the NHS followed a familiar pattern. Always the acute populist, she refused to follow the logic of her right-wing advisers either as far, or as fast, as they wanted. Important changes to the service were undertaken, involving cost-cutting by reducing the length of most hospital stays and the encouragement of 'care in the community' – particularly when that care was provided by the private sector. Health authorities were encouraged to look for efficiency savings; General Practitioners were allocated cash limits which more or less dictated that they prescribe the cheaper of alternative drugs. Some ancillary services were contracted out to the private sector. However, financial commitment to the NHS remained strong. Between 1980 and 1987, the cash made available to it increased by almost 60 per cent while the share of public expenditure directed towards the NHS continued to increase.[4] In statistical terms, the government could make a strong case for saying that it remained committed to the Health Service. Politically, there was every reason for caution. As Thatcher confided in her Memoirs, 'The NHS was a huge organization which inspired at least as much as it exasperated . . . and whose basic structure was felt by most people to be sound. Any reforms must not undermine public confidence'.[5]

Margaret Thatcher's right-wing instincts replaced her electoral caution only after the general election of 1987 when, with spiralling NHS costs threatening almost on their own to destroy the government's commitment to reduced public expenditure, a new review was begun. The Health Service had been under almost constant review by both Labour and Conservative governments, but Thatcher promised that this one would be different. It would inaugurate the most far-reaching review of the service in its forty-year history.[6] She was as good as her word. The NHS White Paper *Working for Patients* (1989) unveiled the principle of the 'internal market' which proposed to separate 'purchasers' from 'providers'. About 300 'Hospital Trusts' would run large hospitals, and health authorities would 'purchase' their services. Money would follow resources. General Practitioners, the first port of call for most NHS users, were brought into the new market system by being given their own budgets. They would thus have choice in where they referred their patients for further treatment. Choice was the carrot, economy the stick: 'Giving GPs budgets of their own also promised to make it possible for the first time to put reasonable limits on their spending – provided we could find ways of having some limit to the number of GPs within the NHS and to how much they spent on drugs'.[7]

Beneath the incentives lay a thinly veiled attack on the medical profession itself. Thatcherism had convicted it of inefficient administration and insufficient contact with her real world – the world of business. Thatcher's view was simple: 'Dedicated its staff generally were; cost conscious they were not'.[8] The management of the new Trusts was to be put in the hands of business, rather than medical, experts and the Conservative Party scoured the business and management world for sympathizers to launch the new system. A predictable, and bitter, battle between the professional and the business ethic ensued. The British Medical Association, which boasts the proud record of opposing every radical health reform of the twentieth century, including National Insurance in 1911 and the National Health Service itself in 1948, spent much more on this anti-government campaign than on any other. The Association met its match in the bluff brutalism of the new Health Secretary, Kenneth Clarke, an overweight cigar smoker who came to his task of government profession-basher with both experience and relish. He was a gift to BMA propagandists: 'Question: What do you call a man who ignores medical advice? Answer: Kenneth Clarke', ran the double-edged joke. But Clarke could take a joke as well as he could dish out punishment. He also knew that he was on to a winner. His department had been given a budget of 'incentives' designed to split the profession and ensure, amid much rancour, that the first, lavishly funded, Trust Hospitals would be established. The first business managers – alert to every cost-cutting opportunity short of their own grotesque salaries – were installed along with them.

Thatcher had left office by the time the NHS reforms were in place but they bore the hallmark both of her preferences and her prejudices. It is, therefore, appropriate to attempt what we might properly call an 'audit' of their short-term effectiveness. Medical anger was slow to abate, though those general practitioners who serendipitously discovered a talent for that financial management which had been no part of their training could see profit, if not objective merit, in the changes. BMA leaders such as John Marks continued to believe the reforms were 'damaging to patients'.[9] Medical practitioners felt that constant financial surveillance impaired their general efficiency by engendering stress. The Durham medical husband and wife team Brian and Margaret Docherty, for example, estimated in 1994 that '80 per cent of GPs are disenchanted with their jobs, feeling increasingly that the new fund-holding powers leave the government with central control, while wasting money on newly created tiers of administration and accounting'.[10]

The most damaging charges were two. First, NHS reforms switched admittedly growing funding away from patient care and towards self-important and overweening administration. Second, the large number of financially independent trusts – all of which needed to show a 'profit on trading' – contributed towards increasingly inequitable treatment opportunities for patients. Structurally, this was always likely since the culture of competition – in this case between Health Trusts – deliberately superseded that of service. The National Health Service was ceasing to be 'national'.

The growth in managerial costs was truly staggering. The Department of Health released figures early in 1995 which showed that the total salary costs of managers in the NHS increased by 283.9 per cent (£158.8 million to £609.6 million) in four years – 1989/90 to

1993/94.[11] This extraordinary development offers further evidence in support of the general observation that – whatever the intention of their begetters – all revolutions beget bureaucracy much more certainly than they beget improvement. In Thatcher's case, the 'culture of audit and financial accountability'[12] assumed a pre-eminence greater even than a prime minister pledged to 'change everything' had bargained for.

Inequality between patients also seems to have increased since Thatcher's NHS reforms were put into operation. Some Trusts have flourished; others are near to bankruptcy – kept afloat more by political than financial considerations. The BMA was reporting by the autumn of 1996 that the treatment of non-emergency patients was now more likely to depend upon whether fund-holding GPs or health authorities had any money left at the end of their financial year than upon how ill, or in how much pain, those patients were. Yet the paradox is that Conservative governments have continued to fund the Health Service more generously than any other element in the public sector. In real terms, funding on the NHS increased by 74 per cent between 1979 and 1995. One has to ask, however, whether misconceived ideology has seen too much of this money spent on the wrong things. It is difficult to dissent from the judgement of the left-wing political philosopher John Gray who concluded that Thatcherite policies

> created a bureaucratic apparatus of internal markets that is both costly and inefficient, diverts scarce resources from patient care and threatens the autonomy of the medical professions. On any reasonable measure this experiment in imposing market forces on the NHS through the agency of a managerial revolution from above has been a ruinous failure.[13]

By the autumn of 1996, no fewer than thirty-four NHS Trusts, statutorily required to break even, were in deficit, and the Department of Health was anticipating that the Health Service as a whole would be £118 million in deficit. Successful Trusts were dealing with more patients than they had budgeted for, so even these were falling foul of unrealistic financial constraints. Meanwhile, between 1990 and 1994 the number of available beds in NHS hospitals had fallen by an average of 2 per cent, this inevitably masking much larger falls in some areas. Barking in East London, for example, had 11 per cent fewer beds available over this period.[14]

EDUCATION

Thatcherite *dirigisme* was not likely to leave the education professionals in peace. Thatcher believed that too much money was being spent to achieve too little: 'increases in public spending had not by and large led to higher standards'. The Inner London Education Authority was singled out for special blame: it 'spent more per pupil than any other education authority and achieved some of the worst examination results'.[15] As with the National Health Service, Thatcher's criticisms went beyond mere prejudice. If, like Thatcher, you believed in the importance both of competition and examination success, then you would readily agree that these attributes were given relatively low priority in many comprehensive schools. If, like Thatcher, you believed that the education profession had not adumbrated a clear set of priorities; if you thought that civil servants in the Department of Education were in cahoots with teacher-trainers to frustrate ministers' policies; if you realized that too many of Her Majesty's Education Inspectors had been 'successful' teachers in schools whose values you deprecated; if you believed that the education establishment was a secret garden of cosy consensuality which valued 'personal development' above measurable attainment, then you would want to dismantle the entire culture. You would also expect fewer heavyweight battles. Parents were, on the whole, less protective of their children's schools than patients were of their doctors' surgeries and the National Union of Teachers carried considerably less clout than the British Medical Association.

As in other areas, notably economic policy (see pp. 8–16) it is important to see Thatcher as a consolidator and an accelerator of change rather than as an initiator of it. As in other areas too, notably health, the most radical changes are 'end-loaded' to the last two or three years of her prime ministership. Debate had raged for at least a century about the alleged inadequacies of the British educational system, widely considered insufficiently 'practical' and catering adequately for only a privileged minority of pupils.[16] The comprehensive experiment of the 1960s rapidly proved as controversial as the '11 +' selection examination, introduced under the 1944 Butler Education Act, had been. It was the Labour prime minister James Callaghan who, in a famous speech at Ruskin College in Oxford in 1976, had called for a Great Debate on the subject. He asked fundamental questions: why were so many pupils leaving school with inadequate levels of literacy and numeracy? Did the secondary curriculum meet the needs of most pupils? Were public examinations fit for purpose?

Callaghan, therefore, wanted to go back to basics, though he was anxious to stress the importance of carrying the teaching professionals with him. Interestingly Keith Joseph, who served as Education Secretary until Kenneth Baker took over in 1986, regretted that he had not followed this advice: 'Don't make the same mistake as I did of attacking the teachers'.[17] Thatcher, as ever, had no compunction about smiting opponents hip and thigh and the educational establishment was certainly considered to be an important part of 'the opposition'. Education was, of course, the only departmental ministry of which she had Cabinet experience and, on the strength of it, roundly informed Joseph that he had 'an awful department'.

As ever, Thatcher also brought passion and conviction to a debate not of her instigation. Her preferred solutions encompassed the usual incompatible objectives of greater central controls on distrusted professionals, increased financial accountability, wider 'consumer' choice in a quasi-free educational market and elements of privatization. Education Acts in 1980 and 1986 extended parental choice of school and gave school governors wider powers which, as it turned out, few of them properly understood or actually wanted to discharge. The government intended school governors to reflect local community interests, and encouraged business interests to get more involved. It also wished Boards of Governors to institute more rigorous checks on complacent or incompetent teachers. Few had any such intention. Many 'governed' consensually and at a distance, if at all, while head teachers 'managed' governors' meetings and hoped to operate much as before. Indeed, it became as difficult to find willing and competent governors for some schools as it had been to find interested or competent overseers in the years before poor law reform in 1834.

The prime minister was, however, able to round up her usual, and usually unloved, suspects in local government. Throughout the 1980s, both powers and funding were systematically withdrawn from local education authorities. LEAs were asked to jump through ever more administrative hoops on lower budgets and with reduced income. Between 1979 and 1986, public spending on schools was reduced by about 10 per cent in real terms.[18] During the period 1984–7, the government fought, and largely won, a number of pay battles with the teacher unions. Education funding was finally increased, by about 4 per cent, in the last years of the Thatcher administration, largely in order to fund the implementation of new departures enshrined in the Education Act of 1988.

This important Act offered the by now characteristically inconsistent Thatcherite mixture of free-market ideology and tighter state control. The management of state schools became concentrated in the hands of head teachers and governors as LEA involvement rapidly waned. Schools were given financial inducements to opt out of LEA control altogether. In most authorities, the professional teacher advisory service was either pared down or withdrawn. Parental choice was to be paramount; theoretically it became easier to choose schools outside an individual's local authority.

Kenneth Baker believed that a large number of comprehensive schools were failing children, and believed that comparisons of educational attainment with other industrial nations were becoming increasingly unfavourable. What nine out of ten German 16-year olds achieved, for example, seemed to be within the compass of only four out of ten English pupils at the same age. For him, 'the key to raising education standards across the country was a national curriculum'.[19] He was not surprised to learn that what he called 'the education establishment in university departments of education were deeply suspicious', although the Inspectorate was considerably less hostile.

Baker decided that only central direction would do. He believed that far too many schools lacked firm direction – 'adrift in a sea of fashionable opinions about what children should not, rather than should, be taught'. Thus, a National Curriculum with compulsory subjects and defined content was imposed on all state schools. The confusingly named 'public schools', which operate in the private sector and to which almost all Cabinet members sent their own children, could adopt the new Curriculum, in whole, in part, or not at all as their governors determined. Thatcher wanted from the National Curriculum a simple, compulsory structure which would provide reliable evidence about school and pupil performance and measurements which could inform parents' choice of schools. The education professionals proved surprisingly resilient in their ability to respond by producing a Curriculum that was neither simple nor easily assessable.

Its design was fatally flawed. No National Curriculum, as such, was ever designed. Instead, work on the ten 'core' and 'foundation' subjects which were supposed to take up 80 per cent of curriculum time was delegated to separate small groups of subject and professional experts. Faced with what they clearly saw as a wonderful, and wonderfully unexpected, opportunity to define their subject they produced intricate and complex structures which – had they ever been implemented – would have taken up about 150 per cent of curriculum time, utterly bemusing most non-specialists in the process. Margaret Thatcher, who kept closely abreast of developments in the secret educational garden, needed her famous ability to survive on four hours' sleep a night as she ploughed through the voluminous complexities which the subject experts devised. History, which she simply considered to be 'an account of what happened in the past' (whose account? one wonders) based upon 'knowing dates', drew her particular anger:

> In July 1989 the History Working Group produced its interim report. I was appalled. It put the emphasis on interpretation and enquiry as against content and knowledge. There was insufficient weight given to British history. There was not enough emphasis on history as chronological study.[20]

Kenneth Baker, a history graduate himself, later commented upon his old boss's simplified views. Thatcher 'saw history as a pageant of glorious events and significant developments, with our small country having given the world parliamentary democracy, an independent judiciary and a tradition of incorrupt administration'.[21] Baker saw the irony in all of this; Thatcher certainly did not. She got the History Curriculum extensively revised, and somewhat simplified, by a National Curriculum Council 'Task Group'. Again, however, the professionals refused to concede lists of dates, the memorizing of factual knowledge at the expense of historical understanding or ritual obeisance before what one then junior civil servant impishly described as 'heroic icons'. Similarly, the Mathematics working party were not to be deflected from their preference for the understanding of concepts over mental arithmetic and the rote-learning of formulae and multiplication tables. In English, battles royal raged over the primacy of literary canon of great works and, in particular, how much Shakespeare it was advisable for 14-year olds to study.

The National Curriculum Assessment Structure, based on complicated attainment targets and a ten-level scale, found little favour with the prime minister. She noted acidly that her Education Secretary had 'warmly welcomed' the Report which recommended this structure whereas she (most unusually!) admitted that she had 'no opportunity' to study it 'having simply been presented with this weighty jargon-filled document in my overnight box with a deadline for publication the following day'. It survived beyond Thatcher's term of office, though her instincts about it proved correct. It had to be considerably simplified once the experts actually tried to *use* it to assess real children.

The National Curriculum, then, lumbered bureaucratically into the 1990s and Thatcher was forced to concede defeat on important matters of detail to the experts. She won, however, on her essentials:

a centralized structure of agreed learning and the means – however crude and flawed – for quantifying school performance. The new General Certificate of Secondary Education, which replaced the old, divided GCE Ordinary Level and Certificate of Secondary Education in 1988, gave even higher-profile measurements of pupil and school attainment. Results showed steady improvement, suggesting that a much larger proportion of 16-year olds were capable of gaining the equivalent of five passes at the old 'O'level under the new system than the old. Professionals seemed to be doing their job. Inevitably, however, critics – mostly from the Tory right – complained about declining academic standards and argued that results had been inflated by excessive reliance upon insufficiently policed coursework. GCE Advanced level, disliked by most education professionals as too narrow, survived as the 'gold standard' of educational attainment. The same critics complained that it had become debased by the examination boards who allowed the pass and high-grade rates to rise for fifteen consecutive years. 'Better teaching', said the professionals; 'easier exams', riposted the critics. Since the examination boards destroy almost all old examination scripts, the issue could not be resolved either way even after a long and frustrating survey undertaken in 1995–6 by the Schools Curriculum and Assessment Authority.

GCSE and A-level results became the crucial variables in new, published school league tables.[22] These the educational professionals criticized as inadequate because they contained no means of assessing either the quality of the intake or the amount of value a school had 'added' to an individual pupil's attainment. Thus a school in a working-class catchment area with few educational traditions might be helping pupils towards high achievement – although it would rank lower (and seem 'worse') than one which selected a large number of very bright pupils for admission and did less with them. League tables, however, could be readily understood by most of those who bothered to read them. The scrutineers' priorities were at least as much social as educational. Many wished to ensure that neither James nor Jocasta went to a 'working-class' school anyway. House prices within the catchment area of 'good schools' tended to increase much more rapidly than those outside them. The National Curriculum did nothing to halt the pronounced trend towards the residential zoning of comprehensive schools and *de facto* selection by area. Parental choice, a central plank of Thatcherite education policy, is of very limited value when many of the 'best' schools are hugely oversubscribed.

CRIME

Crime and criminal policy had surprisingly limited impact on political debate until the 1960s. Criminologists, home office officials and politicians had since 1945 maintained a broad 'Butskellite' consensus on the best means to control crime and to maintain public order. The number of notifiable offences in England and Wales increased steadily but did not exceed 1 million a year until the mid-1960s. The increase of 111 per cent over that decade, however, saw crime emerge prominently in the then Conservative opposition's election manifesto in 1970.[23] Thereafter it remained a significant electoral factor. The Conservative Party appropriated crime as 'its' issue, calling for increased expenditure on police and longer sentences for wrongdoers. Home Secretaries promising tougher action against criminals were guaranteed rapturous receptions at party conference. The disorder associated with strikes and extremist political parties during the 1970s kept the issue in the forefront of debate. Thatcher took it over gladly, knowing crime to be a matter of growing concern amongst 'her' people, particularly the lower middle classes. During the 1979 general election campaign she asserted that 'the demand in the country will be for two things: less tax and more law and order'.[24]

Almost the first action of the Thatcher government in May 1979 was to announce that recommendations for police and army pay rises, due to have been implemented by the outgoing administration in November were to be met in full, backdated to 1 April and paid immediately. It was a symbolic announcement of the government's law and order and defence priorities. In contrast to the severe squeeze on public funding elsewhere, expenditure on the criminal justice system increased from £2 billion in 1979/80 to £3.9 billion in 1984/5.[25] In the first three years of the Thatcher government, almost 10,000 additional police were recruited, bringing the complement to about 120,000. 'Short sharp shock' treatment for young offenders in detention centres was introduced and a major prison-building programme was put in train.[26]

Thatcher's attack on the professionals was much more oblique in the area of criminal policy than it was in the Health Service or education, but her targets rapidly became clear enough. The Thatcher years were notable for a shift in emphasis towards 'community-based' approaches to crime and crime prevention. The Home Office pioneered a 'situational crime prevention' strategy. This relied on making it harder for criminals to attack prime 'targets' and thus reduce the potential for that opportunistic criminal activity which contributed so heavily to recorded crime statistics and which was so common among teenage and young adult working-class males – statistically the most criminally inclined social group. This widely publicized policy had some pronounced successes, notably in the proliferation of Neighbourhood Watch schemes and the development of ever more sophisticated security devices. Not surprisingly, Situational Crime Prevention worked best in prosperous areas. Here owner-occupiers could afford to invest substantial sums in anti-theft devices. Many were also amenable to homilies such as those offered by the Home Office minister John Patten in 1988: 'Individual responsibility for one's own property and responsibility towards the wider community are both important in reducing the opportunities for crime'.[27]

Neither tough Tory stances on crime, nor 'community action', nor substantially increased expenditure on law and order had much impression on the crime figures; rather the reverse. The number of recorded crimes rose by between 5 and 7 per cent per annum during Thatcher's period in government, the number of notifiable offences in Britain increasing from about 2,500,000 a year to about 4,500,000. Motor-vehicle theft, vandalism and burglary increased particularly rapidly during the 1980s.[28] As R. Evans says, 'The enormous costs and limited effectiveness of the criminal justice system became a grievous concern for a Conservative government intent on reducing taxation and promoting policies which deliver "value for money" and "cost-effectiveness"'.[29] Professional criminologists were not slow to offer their explanations for the huge increase in recorded crime during the Thatcher decade. The overwhelming majority of the profession related crime to deteriorating social conditions. Criminologists offered substantial evidence in support of the positive correlation especially between urban deprivation and decay, youth unemployment and levels of recorded crime.

Thatcher was entirely unpersuaded by such professional opinion. She did not trust what was a notoriously left-leaning professional group anyway, of course. More important, she remained convinced that crime was a moral, not a social, issue. Echoing the views of so many party activists, she blamed the decline of authority 'of all kinds – in the home, the school, the churches and the state'. In the wake of the 1981 riots (see p. 21), the media came in for their share of blame too: 'the impression [was] given by television that . . . rioters could enjoy a fiesta of crime, looting and rioting in the guise of social protest'.[30] Her views depressed the professionals. Attempts to put them into practice failed miserably, yet there is no evidence that they did her anything but electoral good. Despite all empirical evidence that Thatcher's policies failed to work, crime remained a 'Tory' issue throughout the Thatcher years. One criminologist summed up the frustrations and bemusement of an entire profession:

> . . . the Conservative party retains its supremacy as the Party of 'law and order'. It has managed to persuade a large section of the electorate that the rising tide of crime is not to be explained by the widened divide between rich and poor, the undermining of public goods and services, the emasculation of local government, and the lauding of competitive individualism to the detriment of collective responsibility. Rather crime is to be ascribed to evil individuals . . . generally young persons, subject to insufficient control by parents who have a duty to police their behaviour.[31]

What is the balance sheet from Thatcher's attack on the professional ethic? Two contradictory conclusions suggest themselves. First, she succeeded in pushing through almost all of her main objectives. In doing so, and again as intended, she shook the professionals up, causing fundamental reappraisals of objectives and values. Most of her changes, furthermore, stuck into the 1990s. Given the virulent opposition they encountered at the time, this represents a substantial achievement. Left to the professionals, few, if any, of the key changes discussed in this chapter would have come about. As with so much of her legacy, flawed and controversial though it has been, few in the 1990s spoke of dismantling it. She reshaped the agenda. Second, however, she seems to have overlooked the crucial point that the service sector of an economy is necessarily labour intensive. The morale of its labour force is, in consequence, crucial. Most of the changes alienated most of the professionals they affected. For those called upon to 'deliver' the new services, the regular consequences were longer working hours and higher stress levels. Even the language has changed. NHS trust managers now routinely 'deliver' health care, while teachers 'deliver' academic or vocational courses – much as milkmen deliver milk. The language of the market place has seeped insidiously, and malignantly, into professional parlance.

Achievement has been less impressive than the scale of innovation. New approaches failed to reduce levels of crime in the Thatcher years. The NHS was fundamentally remodelled along business lines, though neither to its benefit nor to the liking of its users – or 'clients' as they were sometimes called. Surprisingly perhaps, the educational establishment won more battles than the medical establishment, though on matters of detail not broad policy. Schools, encouraged to operate as small businesses, began to advertise their wares in glossy and expensive brochures which, for some, take budget precedence over textbooks. Successful teachers have been encouraged, even required, to enrol on finance and business administration courses. Promotion tends to mean more time selling services or managing budgets and much less time teaching children. Schools increasingly compete with one another over 'intake'. The status of ordinary school teachers, like the real value of their salaries, has declined. As in the Health Service, early retirement packages have been eagerly sought – while a sense of being undervalued has become pervasive. If the professions were tamed by Thatcherism, then this was at substantial cost in both human and economic terms and to little discernible benefit.

7   Thatcher abroad I: Europe

PERCEPTIONS AND CONTEXT

Her own party frequently underestimated Margaret Thatcher in the early years of her leadership (see pp. 42–3). Thatcher's lack of knowledge about the intricacies of foreign affairs was a major cause of this. Though she travelled abroad regularly while leader of the opposition, her background, education and earlier political experience had given her none of the breadth of vision which her Conservative predecessors enjoyed. She was not a linguist and tended to be suspicious of foreigners – first because she did not know them very well and second because she usually could not speak their language. Her simple patriotism was nourished much more in the East Midlands and the Home Counties than through broader imperial contacts.

It is significant that Thatcher wanted to learn about 'abroad' for herself and from her own perspective. She was noticeably cool about foreign office briefings and she did not always trust her Foreign Secretaries to advance British interests. Her first shadow Foreign Secretary was Reginald Maudling who soon complained of being ignored:

> The problem was that contact between us was very little. I asked to go with her on her various visits overseas but I was courteously refused. . . . What was more difficult still was her method of producing speeches on Foreign Affairs. I was not consulted in advance about whether she should make a speech on foreign policy at any given time.[1]

Thatcher took the first opportunity to sack Maudling, whose languid, superior indolence she found as insufferable as his left-centre Conservative views. But even with advisers and ministers in whom she reposed greater confidence she was always likely to announce, or change, policy without consultation. In foreign affairs, much more than in economic policy, she was prone to shoot from the hip.

She also made no secret of the fact that she had little time for the elite corps of the Foreign Office. She believed that the FO too frequently acted as if it were separate from, indeed superior to, other branches of government. Successive Foreign Secretaries, in her view, had been wrapped by their civil servants in a silken bureaucracy. While they were taught the intricacies and mystiques of diplomacy, foreign ministers were too inclined to sell Britain short. Foreign office orthodoxy was temperamentally too inclined to prevarication and to consensus. She thus looked for every opportunity to clip Foreign Office wings. In terms of broad strategy, she was her own Foreign Secretary. Over Anglo-American relations, over the Falklands War (see pp. 90–100) and over negotiation with the EEC she invariably took the lead. During complex negotiations with the EEC in 1980 over a financial rebate, for example, she packed her Foreign Secretary off to Brussels: 'Peter Carrington, having received his mandate from me' was how she later described the incident in a typical passage from her Memoirs. Geoffrey Howe, her Foreign Secretary for six years from 1983 to 1989, both a less confident and, in diplomatic terms, an infinitely less experienced figure than Carrington, also played second fiddle, although it has been suggested that Thatcher lost faith in him because he had become 'a Foreign Office man'.[2]

Thatcher was also averse to working from Foreign Office briefs. One of the most significant foreign policy statements of the Thatcher years – her Bruges speech of September 1988 (see pp. 87–8) – was drafted by Charles Powell, her 'private secretary' from 1984 to 1991, and not by the Foreign Office. The silken skills of Powell were an extraordinarily useful complement to Thatcher's more abrasive style – not least because, whatever he may have thought privately, Powell proved an entirely loyal articulator of her prejudices.[3] The observation that, in foreign affairs at least, he operated more as deputy prime minister than as private secretary had more than a grain of truth.

Margaret Thatcher's objectives and methods in foreign affairs were characteristically straightforward: she put Britain's interests, as she saw them, first, and her ways could be jarringly direct. She noted almost triumphally – concerning one of many fraught negotiations with Common Market partners: 'I know nothing about diplomacy, but I just know and believe that I want certain things for Britain'.[4] The 'certain things' she wanted above all were three: increased respect for Britain as a leading power which still, after all, possessed both nuclear weapons and a permanent (if anachronistic) seat on the

Security Council of the United Nations; a close alliance with the United States; and pretensions to closer European unity put firmly in their place.

The key to understanding Thatcher abroad is that she was prone to regard Americans as honorary Englishmen (*sic*) and Europeans as real foreigners. Her early visits to the United States in 1975 and 1977 had gone down well with hosts who shared her unrestrained free-market ideas. It was characteristic that she immediately broke with the diplomatic convention that leaders of opposition parties do not openly criticize the government when on foreign soil. Thatcher was no diplomat, and when challenged robustly retorted to the then prime minister, James Callaghan that 'It's not part of my job to be a propagandist for a socialist society'.[5] She formed an instant rapport with Henry Kissinger in 1975 and asserted, perhaps prematurely, that 'I feel that I have been accepted as a leader in the international sphere'.

'MY MONEY'

Thatcher had none of Edward Heath's sympathy with the European ideal. Nor did she share his view that Britain's future lay in ever closer contacts with the EEC. She was suspicious of the EEC's tendency to that bureaucratic grandiosity which she knew in her bones was inimical to 'freedom'. This was the central theme of her speeches during the campaign for the first direct elections to the European parliament:

> We believe in a free Europe, not a standardized Europe. . . . We insist that the institutions of the European Community are managed so that they increase the liberty of the individual throughout the continent. These institutions must not be permitted to dwindle into bureaucracy. Whenever they fail to enlarge freedom the institutions should be criticised and the balance restored.[6]

This distinctive critique was something with which her European partners would become all too familiar.

In the first year of government, however, her main priority was not bureaucratic but financial. Ever since joining the EEC in 1973, British contributions to the Community budget had considerably exceeded its receipts and Thatcher was determined to get a large rebate. She set her eyes on an immediate transfer of £1,000 million to the UK exchequer, though how this figure was arrived at – beyond the desire to wave very large round figures in pounds sterling in front of Germans and Frenchmen – was never clear. Her negotiating strategy was alien to the culture of the Community. She set out her stall and defended it, inflexibly and repetitively. She told her European partners in Strasbourg in June 1979 that she could not 'play Sister Bountiful to the Community while my own electorate are being asked to forego improvements in the fields of health, education, welfare and the rest'.[7] A summit at Dublin in November almost broke up in disorder when Thatcher adamantly refused to dance to the weary Community quadrille of coded language and bluff, followed by graceful, mutually anticipated, concession at the fifty-ninth minute of the eleventh hour. When she said she wanted 'my money' back, she meant it, and she did not back down. The German Chancellor, Helmut Schmidt, feigned sleep as she ranted on. The French President, Valéry Giscard d'Estaing was openly contemptuous, describing Thatcher as '*La Fille d'Epicier*' – the Grocer's Daughter.

Neither man realized that insults, both implicit and explicit, were grist to the Thatcher mill. She genuinely *did* believe that national interests came before Community ones. She honestly *did* feel a genuine sense of injustice. Most important of all, she knew that her stand – dismissed throughout Europe as coarse, vulgar and unintelligent – was mightily popular among 'her' people in Britain, the only constituency in which she was truly interested. Aided by the predominantly right-wing tabloid press, she turned European contempt into domestic popularity by employing a calculated measure of xenophobia. It was an excellent example of Thatcherite populism in action. And she could claim reasonable success when she won about two-thirds of 'her' money back. In 1980 the EEC conceded a three-year deal of rebates totalling £1,570 million. Thatcher – wanting the lot – accepted the deal reluctantly and only after considerable persuasion by Viscount Carrington. Her aristocratic and experienced Foreign Secretary was, in fact, privately as aghast at Thatcher's negotiating stance as were Giscard or Schmidt. However, he entrusted to his memoirs only that diplomatic language which came so naturally when he spoke of her 'firmness and intransigence' as the 'key factors in getting us a proper settlement'. He wearily noted: 'I cannot pretend that the resultant atmosphere made all our foreign relations easier to conduct'.[8] His mistress did not give a hoot.

THE COMMON AGRICULTURAL POLICY

Budget grumbles over funding continued until the Fontainebleau summit in 1984, when agreement was reached to reduce the British budgetary contribution to a level broadly related to the country's GNP and not, as before, considerably in excess of it. The most contentious EC issue during the middle years of Thatcher's period in office – and directly related to budgetary rows – was the Common Agricultural Policy (CAP). She called the policy at various times 'wasteful', 'extravagant' and 'Mad-Hatter economics'; it took up almost 70 per cent of the entire EEC budget when she came to power.[9] By the mid-1980s CAP subsidies totalled $22 billion a year.[10] Her criticisms had a point. The CAP had been a foundation stone of the original Common Market and its main purpose was protectionist. The system of guaranteed prices for farmers was designed to ensure continuity of production and stability in food markets. Since there was no prospect of mass starvation in one of the world's richest areas, the CAP represented little more than uncovenanted benefit to often very inefficient small producers, especially (as the Labour intellectual and 1960s minister Richard Crossman tartly pointed out) French peasants. Farmers were subsidized to produce and produced far more than the Community needed. 'Butter mountains' and 'wine lakes' resulted, and surpluses were 'dumped' at rock-bottom prices, often in Communist Eastern Europe. The effect on a vigorous capitalist free-marketeer like Margaret Thatcher of a protectionist system which gave Communists subsidized food can readily be imagined. A further illogicality of the system was that CAP subsidies tended to benefit inefficient farmers more than efficient ones, and British farmers were relatively efficient.

Thatcher wanted to be rid of the CAP, bag and baggage. The policy would never have been put in place had Britain – an industrial nation with a relatively small agricultural sector – been a founder member of the Community. Since it was not, and since farmers were an immensely influential interest group in both France and Germany, there was no prospect of abolition – as Thatcher recognized. One of her main strengths as a conviction politician was the recognition that conviction and practical politics frequently point in opposite directions. When they did, and despite the steely public image, she was a firm believer in Voltaire's dictum: '*Le mieux est l'ennemi du bien*' [the best is the enemy of the good]. She had gained rare approval in Europe in 1986 for signing Britain up to the Single European Act, which would provide a free internal market, involving unrestricted movement of goods, labour and capital by 1992.[11] She wanted to exploit the opportunity to gain further concessions, rather than waste it by tilting at an unchallengeable Community icon. The result was an agreement at Brussels in February 1988 on a package of measures – including automatic price cuts beyond certain production levels – which reduced agricultural surpluses and confirmed substantial rebates to Britain.

The paradox of Thatcher's decision over the Single European Act should not go unremarked. The most stridently anti-European of British post-war prime ministers acquiesced in European legislation which, by qualified majority voting, would override the preferences and policies of democratically elected national governments. Nor was it a dead letter. Numerous European 'directives' followed on a range of economic and social issues, including health, safety, holiday entitlement and the maximum length of the working week. For right-wing 'Euro-sceptics' in the Conservative Party of the mid-1990s, this degree of intervention represented a fatal compromise with the principle of national sovereignty. It is hardly surprising that they were too embarrassed to place the blame for this 'treason' where it properly lay – with Margaret Thatcher.

The last two years of Thatcher's prime ministership were all downhill, in European as in other ways (see pp. 109–14). The enormities of the CAP had spurred a right-wing group of about seventy Conservative MPs to form a 'European Reform Group'. The title was misleading. The Group really wanted to wreck rather than reform. Its profoundly anti-Europeanism re-opened deep wounds within the Party. Temperamentally, Thatcher was as anti-European as most. Politically, she knew that she needed to maintain a party balance, although this was becoming increasingly difficult. Furthermore, during her years in power she had forged useful links within Europe, notably with the Gaullist Prime Minister Jacques Chirac. Personal contact smoothed some of the rougher edges of her anti-Europeanism.

BRUGES AND BEYOND: HOLDING BACK A FEDERAL EUROPE

Many in Europe wanted to use the Single Market as a bridgehead to both closer economic co-operation and political union, culminating in the creation of a fully federal Europe. Thatcher was extremely sceptical of the former and implacably hostile to the latter. It did not help that one of the main supporters of such moves was the President of the EC Commission. Jacques Delors, who held the position from 1985–95, was a cultivated Frenchman, an intellectual and a socialist. In 1988, he chaired a committee which drew up the strategy for European economic and monetary union, immediately dubbed the 'Delors plan'. The strategy had three 'phases': first, movement towards common membership of a European Monetary System; second, a central bank with control over the monetary policy of member states; third, the use of a single currency throughout the Community. Delors showed himself an interventionist in other ways too. He had no inhibitions about involving himself in the internal politics of member states, visiting the British Trades Union Congress in 1988 and – to great acclaim – regaling its delegates with his vision of a federal, socialist Europe.

Thatcher, who recognized Delors' abilities, hated his politics. What Delors welcomed as federalism Thatcher interpreted as 'the erosion of democracy by centralization and bureaucracy'.[12] She was particularly concerned that Commission advice and directives increasingly asserted EC powers to 'interfere' in the affairs of member states on issues as divergent as social security and subsidies for the arts. She believed, against the general view of her European colleagues, that Delors was abusing his powers by issuing directives which lacked the unanimous support of EC member states.

Her response was the Bruges speech of 20 September 1988. It was born of deep frustration that despite her best efforts, Europe was moving in the wrong direction. In it, she declared that nations had, and must retain, distinctive identities. Britain would play no part in fostering 'some sort of identikit European personality'. She resisted any idea of a 'European super-state exercising a new dominance from Brussels' and called instead for 'willing and active co-operation between independent sovereign states' as 'the best way to build a successful European community'. She was careful also to include references to Europe outside the EC. To the frustration of Foreign Office officials, who had wanted a speech which would mend fences and emphasize the government's commitment to the EC as an institution, she gleefully stated: 'We shall always look on Warsaw, Prague and Budapest as great European cities'. One of her key objectives, as she later put it, was a 'wider, looser Europe'.[13]

The Bruges speech has widely been considered 'Gaullist' since it advocated strong government following clearly defined national priorities. There is, indeed, much of the Gaullist heritage in Thatcherism, not least in its invocation of pride and the importance of patriotic resurgence. De Gaulle, however, had the very considerable advantage of being able in the early 1960s to shape early development of the EEC. Much of the EEC was French, as it were, by design. Thatcher, by contrast, was in the late 1980s still the abrasive European outsider and she was unlikely to increase British influence by mere assertion, however eloquently phrased. As always, however, she kept at least one eye on the British electorate. She could also engineer a warm reception for her message in the British press. Especially from 1982 onwards, British newspapers were predominantly Thatcherite on most foreign policy questions, and especially so when she was banging the patriotic British drum. The speech did not, however, prevent substantial Conservative losses in the European parliamentary elections a few months later. Thatcher blamed damaging, and politically significant, divisions within the Party over Europe and not the Bruges speech.

Bruges aimed at putting a brake on any headlong rush towards Euro-federalism. Monetary Union nevertheless proceeded apace. Support grew for an 'Exchange Rate Mechanism' (ERM), whereby interest rates would be allowed to fluctuate only within defined bands. The overall objective was currency stabilization as a basis for more secure investment. It was almost universally supported within the Community. Both the Chancellor of the Exchequer, Nigel Lawson, and the Foreign Secretary Geoffrey Howe, wanted Britain to join the ERM. Thatcher, worried as ever about national sovereignty implications, was hostile. But, by the end of the 1980s, she was both isolated within the Community and increasingly beleaguered within her own party.

After much havering, she eventually agreed to Britain's joining the ERM in October 1990, only six weeks before she lost office. Her Memoirs make it clear that she agreed under duress and against her own better judgement: 'I had too few allies to continue to resist and win the day'.[14] In retrospect, it is clear that Britain went in at far too high an exchange rate, and probably also at the wrong time. The country was anyway forced out again less than two years later by a sterling crisis. The big political and economic battles on currency union remained to be fought. Thatcher had certainly not resolved the internal contradictions of Conservatism over Europe.

THE EUROPEAN RECKONING

Overall assessment of the success of Thatcher's European policy depends upon one's view of the European Community, or European Union as it prematurely and pretentiously called itself from 1994, as a whole. Opponents of closer European unity argue that most of Thatcher's policies were successful. She used her formidable mastery over detail, her cool head for figures and her ability to concentrate for long periods on the most apparently trivial issues to negotiate substantially reduced budgetary contributions for Britain. She firmly rebuffed moves towards greater unity and peeled away some of the woollier idealism of *'l'esprit communitaire'*. One favourable critic called her early achievement 'remarkable' – imposing on the European community 'a Thatcherite interpretation . . . of economic policy [while] manipulating and dominating the community issues'.[15]

In all this, she also rang resonant chords with 'her' people at home. She believed that most of the French and German ministers, with or against whom she worked, had agendas just as narrowly nationalist as her own. Only their longer membership of the Community, which had enabled them to incorporate their countries' own priorities into its structure during the 1950s and 1960s, made them seem more pro-European. Blatant rudeness and disdain for the conventions of diplomacy she excused as bringing welcome directness and honesty to the negotiating table. A senior French diplomat dismissed Thatcher thus:

> That woman is an old-fashioned nationalist with no feeling for the European ideal. She reckons merely in terms of accountancy, not the broader political vision that is needed. . . . Seen from Paris, the British government appears to express little belief in the need to develop the Community's institutions.[16]

Thatcher saw what the diplomat clearly intended to be a stinging rebuke in quite different terms. The 'European ideal' she regarded as humbug; 'accountancy' is crucial to good management, in the nation state just as naturally as in the home; too many of the 'Community's institutions' – not least the appalling CAP – needed deracination rather than 'development'. As for 'political vision', Thatcher thought one person's vision another's impractical idealism. She presented herself as realist, albeit one with firm convictions. Her Bruges speech offered an alternative, and more practical, vision of European development:

> Let Europe be a family of nations, understanding each other better, appreciating each other more, doing more together, but relishing our national identity. . . . Let us have a Europe which plays its full part in the wider world, which looks outward not inward, and which preserves the Atlantic Community – that Europe on both sides of the Atlantic – which is our noblest inheritance and our greatest strength.[17]

The speech demonstrates that this most 'practical' of prime ministers could waffle with the best of them, but the specific message indicates how much she differed from the pro-Europeans. Insidious reference to Europeans 'on both sides of the Atlantic' reminded critics where her true loyalties lay.

The main criticisms of Thatcher's European policy are two. First, she failed to realize what she was signing Britain up to in the Single European Act. Her natural sympathizers had greatest reason to rue this spectacular piece of political naivete. Second, she frequently wasted important opportunities by aggressive posturing. Such posturing was – more often than she allowed – followed by a standard 'Euro-fudge' anyway. Britain, largely because of the dominant perception in the 1950s that both its Empire and its US alliance were more important, had been a late entrant to the EEC. When it joined in 1973, the British economy was far weaker *vis à vis* the major nations of the Community than it would have been in 1957. Britain did, however, have both a longer-established political democracy and at least as substantial a tradition of worldwide influence. These assets could have been used to build up a position of political equality, if not leadership, especially since the British economy, boosted by North Sea oil, recovered quickly in the early 1980s giving the country more opportunity to pull its weight co-operatively within Europe. In short, Britain had assets which the Community needed. Thatcher withheld them in a sustained orgy of spleen, scepticism and penny-pinching precision. Any vision she had was all too clearly non-European. The close relationship she built with President Reagan suggested that Thatcherite Britain remained both strategically and emotionally much more attached to an Atlantic than to a European axis.

The long-term danger remained that the United States – by the early 1990s the world's only superpower and one which was becoming less 'European' not only in temper but in ethnic composition with every passing year – had less interest in Britain than Britain had in the United States. A grossly unequal, if not sentimental, American alliance, anachronistically buffed as a 'special relationship' seemed a perverse preference over growing influence in a self-confident and economically advanced European power bloc. The assertion that close links with the United States were not incompatible with constructive membership of the EC cut little ice.

The European Community in the 1980s too often saw a once-powerful, but now substantially diminished and geographically pretty remote state, on the north-west fringes of Europe, trying to relive past glories under a formidable, but formidably wrong-headed leader, who refused to accept that medium-sized European nation states could make effective and constructive contributions only through close collaboration with each other. Critics of Thatcher's EC policy bemoaned a decade of fractious wasted opportunity. In the late 1980s and early 1990s Britain hedged, remained 'difficult' and negotiated opt-outs from measures designed to improve intracommunity trade, banking and social conditions. All too often the constituency being addressed was not the Community but a disunited parliamentary Conservative Party. As Glynn and Booth have put it, Britain 'faced the prospect of continued relative decline on the fringes of a European community moving towards ever closer integration'.[18]

8 Thatcher abroad II: defence and The Americas

ANGLO-AMERICAN CONTEXT

The Americas were crucial to Margaret Thatcher during the 1980s. She looked most naturally for support and friendship to Ronald Reagan, US President from 1981 to 1989, a like-minded right-winger, though the mind at his disposal was a good deal less powerful than hers. Her political fortunes were rescued from what seemed terminal decline in early 1982 by a brief and successful war with Argentina over sovereignty in the Falkland Islands. She is both temperamentally and materially drawn to the United States, as her phenomenally lucrative and empathetic lecture tours there during the 1990s has demonstrated. 'Atlanticism' was a key element in British foreign policy during the 1980s.

Thatcher acknowledged its importance in a typically grandiose assessment made soon after she left office: 'The United States and Britain have together been the greatest alliance in the defence of liberty and justice than the world has ever known'.[1] Ignoring the fact that alliances are almost invariably made for far more pragmatic reasons than these, it is easy to see why the two countries had developed a long-term empathy. Most of the US's early leaders were of British origin, and once the new state's independence was conceded by Britain in 1783, there was far more to bring them together than keep them apart: ethnicity, mutually beneficial trading relations and separate non-competing spheres of territorial influence were three which held good for most of the nineteenth century.

In the twentieth century, the United States fought two wars alongside the United Kingdom, though in both cases only eventually. In the Second World War, the US contribution was decisive when Britain, alone of Hitler's European opponents, survived to carry on the fight after 1940. Britain entered the Second World War as one of the leading imperial powers; the United States ended it as one of two antagonistic 'super-powers'. Its determination to build up Western Europe as a geopolitical counterpart to the evil Soviet empire brought the United States more decisively into European affairs than ever before. Britain was seen as the mainstay of that European policy. Winston Churchill, whose own mother had been American, deliberately delivered his famous 1946 'Iron Curtain' lecture in a US institution with an apposite name – Westminster College, Fulton, Missouri.

The two nations have been sufficiently close allies since 1945 to warrant the frequently used description 'special relationship'. However, it was not an alliance without strain. Quite apart from specific, short-term disagreements – most notably Eisenhower's feeling that he had been maliciously mislead by Eden over Britain's aggressive intentions at Suez in 1956 – longer term tensions were never far from the surface. The United States wanted Britain to take the lead in a strong Western-European phalanx against the USSR. At least until the late 1950s, Britain continued to see itself as a nation, if not as powerful as the two super-powers, then clearly more powerful than the rest. Its worldwide interests were, therefore, too important to risk dilution by membership of the Common Market. The United States (albeit usually privately) considered this self-perception unrealistic. Britain's relative economic decline became ever more apparent. Its worldwide role was also enormously diminished as it quit most of its old imperial possessions between the late 1940s and the early 1960s. Dean Acheson's observation in 1962 that 'Great Britain has lost an Empire and has not yet found a role' was more than a neat aphorism. It conveyed in code widespread US frustration with its ally's pretensions. Britain's independent nuclear status was both a costly piece of self-advertisement for a declining power and a further source of US annoyance. Britain could exert massive influence in an important, but precisely defined, sphere – Europe – but chose instead to posture as a great power to embarrassingly limited effect. US frustration was only increased by the fact that de Gaulle vetoed British membership of the EEC in the early 1960s on the grounds that Britain was too 'American' and insufficiently 'European'.

The 'special relationship' in the years before Thatcher, therefore, was often more a matter of style than substance. It benefited both sides to assert its indissoluble existence and, indeed, genuinely warm relationships developed between national leaders. Kennedy and Macmillan in the early 1960s, Carter and Callaghan in the later 1970s stand out. Beneath the surface, however, relationships were not as 'special' as they seemed and were becoming less close anyway. Heath's Europeanism saw him support the EC over the United

States during the trade protection squabbles of the early 1970s, for example. The reality was that Britain wanted a relationship more 'specially' than the United States. Yet Britain had less to offer an increasingly multi-cultural nation with important Pacific defence and economic interests with every year that passed.

AMERICAN LOVE AFFAIR ↘

What the United States had for Margaret Thatcher, of course, was both impeccable free-trade credentials and a down-to-earth 'can-do' mentality. Culturally, she was always much closer to the United States than to Western Europe. The US contained, so she believed, far more people with a practical business approach and far fewer intel-lectuals, theorists and ironists who presumed to tell her – in elegant, superior tones and at great length – what was not possible. Her love affair with the country was reciprocated, with characteristically Amer-ican interest. Each of her many visits was accompanied by fawning attention, not least from the White House, and by a series of soft-centred, high-profile television interviews designed to show Thatcher as the quintessence of strong leadership, though loyally pro-American.

It seemed that Britain had finally delivered to the United States the true successor to Winston Churchill. Thatcher, the consummate poli-tician, never lost an opportunity to quote from the 'Winston' she hardly knew – except in his stroke-diminished dotage. Indeed, in 1983 she was in the United States to receive the 'Winston Churchill Foundation Award'. The citation read 'Like Churchill, she is known for her courage, conviction, determination and willpower. Like Churchill she thrives on adversity'.[2] It was a good job that no one told the Awarders that much of Churchill's 'adversity' derived from political failure and from his frequently appalling relations with the Conservative Party, from which he was semi-detached for most of the 1930s. It is not clear, either, whether Thatcher knew that, during his period as a successful Liberal minister in an Asquith government which massively increased income taxes on the wealthy, Churchill enthusiastically increased the power of the state over people's lives. By the 1980s, however, these historical inconveniences could be swept under welcoming red carpets. The fact that Thatcher was a woman provided that essential 'human interest angle' without which the domestic US market could not be captured. Margaret Thatcher, no less than Grace Kelly or Katharine Hepburn, was a star – and she loved it.

Not surprisingly, Thatcher considered Ronald Reagan her kind of ally. She enthused:

> He was a buoyant, self-confident, good-natured American who had risen from poverty to the White House – the American dream in action – and who was not shy about using American power or exercising American leadership in the Atlantic alliance. In addition to inspiring the American people, he went on later to inspire the people behind the Iron Curtain by speaking honest words about the evil empire that oppressed them.[3]

Thatcher saw close Anglo-American relations as the key to safeguarding the interests of the free world against mounting challenges. The 'evil empire' had confirmed its true nature when it invaded Afghanistan in 1979. The outbreak of war between Iran and Iraq in 1980 indicated how Islamic fundamentalism could further destabilize the Middle East – since 1945 a notoriously volatile area anyway. Israel's invasion of Lebanon in 1982 only confirmed the pattern. Thatcher also believed that the maintenance of Britain's independent nuclear deterrent was the most effective contribution Britain could make to the 'special relationship'. She authorized replacement of the now ageing Polaris submarine with first Trident I, and in 1982, the updated and more expensive Trident II, purchased from the US government. Although Trident II was acquired on particularly generous terms – a consequence, it was said, of Thatcher's ability to charm Reagan[4] – it still cost £9 billion.[5] Meanwhile, the armaments industry in both countries anticipated substantial profits from sub-contracts.

The closeness and interdependence of US and British defence policy was emphasized by the stationing of US Cruise missiles in British bases from 1983 to 1988. In April 1986 Thatcher permitted the United States to launch bombing attacks against Libya in 1986 from bases in Britain. No other EC leader allowed the United States similar licence. Throughout the 1980s, European statesmen criticized the British government for taking an insufficiently critical or independent stance in its relationship with the United States. It was a major cause of tension with EC partners (see pp. 81–2, 86–7).

Defence policy was a priority for Thatcher and arms dealers enjoyed a bonanza during the 1980s. The prime minister's son, Mark, was one of many to benefit. As so often, politics and populism went hand in hand. Defence was usually a 'Conservative' issue but it had a much higher political profile during the 1980s for two reasons. The first was 'the Falklands factor' (see below), and the second the collective lunacy which afflicted the Labour Party for much of the decade.

Michael Foot fought the 1983 election on a self-indulgent parade of socialist conscience; nuclear disarmament was a key feature. Neil Kinnock's usually deft footwork deserted him on defence during the 1987 campaign. Thatcher, never one to miss an easy target, savaged Labour's defence policies on both occasions. At the last Tory conference before the 1987 election, she told adoring delegates that 'A Labour Britain would be a neutralist Britain. It would be the greatest gain for the Soviet Union in forty years. And they would have got it without firing a shot'. Both opinion polls and post-election analyses confirmed that the public shared Thatcher's view that it had been 'the balance of nuclear forces which had preserved peace for forty years'.[6] Defence was a major vote-winner for the Tories in the 1980s. Opponents could debate both the validity and the morality of the *policies*, but the *politics* she got incontestably right.

TENSIONS IN THE SPECIAL RELATIONSHIP

Although Reagan's Presidency inaugurated a period of close, even suffocating, personal warmth between the two national leaders, the United States never remotely regarded Britain as an equal partner in the alliance. Important defence and foreign policy initiatives were announced without consultation. In 1983, for example, Reagan announced a radical new Strategic Defence Initiative (SDI). Since this depended on the use of complex anti-ballistic missile systems, the new policy was rapidly christened 'Star Wars', following the title of the immensely successful science-fiction film released six years earlier. SDI was a source of particular worry for Europe. If its use (as the boffins claimed) could render the United States impregnable against any nuclear attack, why should the United States continue to spend huge amounts of money via the North Atlantic Treaty Organisation in defence of Western Europe?

Thatcher shared European concerns. She used her influence with Reagan to ensure that what was clearly one of his major enthusiasms was placed in broader context. This objective, it has to be said, was shared by some of Reagan's own advisers who were well used to blunting what they saw as impractical initiatives from the Pentagon. At a meeting in Camp David just before Christmas in 1984, Thatcher stressed that Britain had no desire to stifle research into Star Wars but insisted that the new strategy be seen alongside, and not as a replacement for, nuclear deterrence. This accommodation survived to the end of Thatcher's prime ministership, by which time the imminent collapse of the 'evil empire' was changing all defence perspectives anyway. Thatcher's business antennae were alive to the commercial benefits of SDI. In 1985, she ensured that British firms were the first in NATO to participate with the Americans in research and development contracts associated with the project.[7]

The US invasion of the Caribbean island of Grenada in October 1983 was another important initiative taken without consultation. The United States moved in response to requests from other Caribbean islands fearful that events in Grenada, where a Marxist regime had been toppled and replaced by another extreme leftist group, would destabilize the whole region. Two crucial points arise. Grenada was a member of the Commonwealth. Irrespective of any special relationship, therefore, Britain might have been expected to be consulted. Certainly, the Queen, who was Grenada's Head of State, thought so. She was 'reported to be furious – as much with Mrs Thatcher as with . . . the Americans about being deliberately or carelessly ignored'.[8] Second, since Britain had intervened to such effect over the Falklands, why was it so supine over Grenada eighteen months later?

Thatcher, naturally, concentrated on the consultation element. Probably without intending it, Reagan's action humiliated the British government. Only the day before the invasion, the Foreign Secretary, Geoffrey Howe, had told parliament that he knew of no American invasion plans. Thatcher noted that 'I felt dismayed and let down by what had happened. At best the British Government had been made to look impotent; at worst we looked deceitful'.[9] It was clear to most observers that the United States was no less likely to intervene in an area of the world where it considered its interests directly affected than was the USSR. The parallels with Afghanistan in 1979 were much closer than either Thatcher or Reagan were prepared to admit. The Grenada invasion was naked power politics; the diplomatic niceties of consultation did not come into it – British Commonwealth or no British Commonwealth.

It was a Conservative journal, *The Spectator*, which pointed out the weakness of Thatcher's position on Grenada:

> During the Falklands War, Mrs. Thatcher very unwisely chose to generalise her justification for recapturing the islands as a vindication of the principle that aggression should not pay, whereas the sensible argument was simply that Britain would not allow British land and people to be taken over by a foreign power. Now the United States has been thoroughly aggressive and of course there is nothing that Mrs. Thatcher can do and very little that she can

say about it. It serves her right for always being high-falutin about the cause of liberty, instead of practical about the defence of Britain.[10]

THE FALKLANDS ✕

For many, the reconquest of the Falkland Islands in May 1982, after their brief occupation by Argentinian troops under the direction of a recently established military junta, represents the high-watermark of Thatcherism. The military expedition roused fierce passions but success was swift, and, as these things go, relatively painless. About 250 British and 2,000 Argentinian troops lost their lives in a conflict which lasted only three weeks and which demonstrated both the skill and efficiency of the British military and naval machine – at any rate against a demonstrably weaker opponent. The logistical problems encountered in waging a war 8,000 miles distant were also triumphantly overcome.

Thatcher won high praise in the country for steering a straight, nononsense course against a clear aggressor who had invaded British territory. The British victory raised the nation's prestige internationally and enhanced the national sense of self-worth. For some romantics, it was long-delayed retribution by the British for the fiasco of Suez. Its political benefits for Thatcher were immense and she capitalized on them to brilliant effect. Her populist genius was seen at its height during her speeches in the immediate afterglow of victory:

> We have ceased to be a nation in retreat. We have instead a newfound confidence – born in the economic battles at home and tested and found true 8,000 miles away. . . . We rejoice that Britain has rekindled that spirit which has fired her for generations past and which today has begun to burn as brightly as before. Britain found herself in the South Atlantic and will not look back from the victory she has won. When we started out there were the waverers and the faint-hearts, the people who thought we could no longer do the great things we once did, those who believed our decline was irreversible, that we could never again be what we were, that Britain was no longer the nation that had built an empire and ruled a quarter of the world. Well they were wrong.[11]

'Winston' could hardly have done better; indeed, he did not. He lost the election of 1945, whereas the 'Falklands Factor' was the single most important factor in the large Conservative election victory of

1983 (see pp. 24–5). The Falklands War was overwhelmingly popular in Britain, as a genuinely national struggle with the lives of British troops at stake. Public opinion polls suggested an 80 per cent approval rating of the British response to send a task force to reconquer the islands. The Tory Cabinet minister James Prior found 'incredible support for Margaret in the pubs' of his constituency, Lowestoft.[12] Of the political parties, only *Plaid Cymru* (the Welsh Nationalists) opposed going to war, probably because of the long-established Welsh contingent in the Argentinian region of Patagonia. Labour MPs quickly expressed their support. The few open doubters, mostly from professional and intellectual backgrounds, were quickly made to feel the strength of popular support, especially in the working men's clubs.

The press, as so often with Thatcher, was mostly on the loyal side of triumphalist. The *Sun* consolidated its already substantial hold on the popular market by conducting a war campaign of unprecedentedly crass and distasteful xenophobia. The *Daily Mail* and *Daily Express* offered less strident, but equally unswerving, support. Most of the quality newspapers argued that 'freedom was indivisible' and that unprovoked aggression compelled a military response. *The Financial Times*, invoking cost–benefit analysis, was more sceptical. Outright opposition came, as expected, from the left-centre quality newspapers *The Guardian* and *The Observer*. Thatcher probably calculated that their small-circulation, hand-wringing opposition was an advantage. Almost none of 'her' people read them anyway. Those who did were disproportionately well informed and articulate but, politically, they were of no account. Their opposition showed that the British press was free to say what it liked; Britain was, after all, going to war to preserve freedom.

The overwhelming victory justified what was actually a considerable gamble. Few other leaders would have taken it. Having taken it, furthermore, she was determined to see things through to their conclusion and to ensure that both she, and the British people as a whole, took pride in a remarkable achievement. She recalled the reaction of the Soviet military: 'years later I was told by a Russian general that the Soviets had been firmly convinced that we would not fight for the Falklands, and that if we did fight we would lose. We proved them wrong on both counts and they never forgot the fact'.[13]

After the heady rhetoric, and after noting both a huge military triumph and a brilliantly orchestrated propaganda coup, it is worth recalling at this distance of time what Britain was fighting *about*. The Falklands were a remote group of islands in the far South Atlantic, of no strategic significance on which lived 1,800 mostly British subjects. The islands had been acquired by Britain in 1833 in somewhat dubious circumstances and Argentina had long laid claim to them. Most in the Foreign Office recognized that the Falklands were an anachronistic imperial burden. Frequent attempts were made to broker a peaceful resolution of the disputed claims. These had continued throughout the years 1979–82.

It is hardly surprising, therefore, that others – far less hostile to Thatcher than Soviet generals – should have wondered whether Britain had taken leave of its senses in the spring of 1982. The US Secretary of State, Alexander Haig, for example, reported on the reaction in the State Department:

> In the early hours of the crisis, most of the staff shared the amusement of the press and public over what was perceived as a Gilbert and Sullivan battle over a sheep pasture between a choleric John Bull and a comic dictator in gaudy uniform.[14]

The Europeans were no more flattering. The French and German governments gave guarded support but could not understand why Britain was committing itself to the huge expenditure of a war – and the indefinite expense of maintaining a deterrent presence thereafter almost within shouting distance of the South Pole – in such circumstances. The French newspaper *Le Monde* was ruder, likening Thatcher's adventure to the famous French satire *Clochmerle*, where local dignitaries lose all their dignity over something entirely trivial – the siting of a public lavatory.

Rational, and longer term, calculations might be made by those not directly involved. Thatcher had to take immediate decisions and sell them to a British audience. She did so quite brilliantly, emphasizing the moral dimension. British military intervention was right; not to intervene would be cowardly; Britons never would be slaves. She cut through awkward questions about whether the conflict could have been honourably prevented. She ignored the clear evidence of inadequate policy-making on the Falklands in the years before 1982. In her view, she was faced with a crisis and dealt with it by invoking British patriotism. She knew in her bones that she was right, but she was equally aware of the immense political value of success. She understood that intangibles like 'freedom' and 'patriotism' are more politically charged than desiccated calculations of strategy. In the Falklands War, her leadership gave the British people a success which most of them rejoiced at, while raising the country's stock internationally.

The Argentinian occupation provoked the resignation of the Foreign Secretary. Lord Carrington denied that he misread the signals about an imminent invasion but decided to go anyway as the ranking minister. He had, as he put it,

> a sympathetic understanding that the whole of the country felt angry and humiliated. . . . Inhabitants of a British colony – men and women of British blood – had been taken over against their will. Diplomacy had failed to avert this. Military reinforcement had not been tried. Deterrence had been exposed as a bluff.[15]

Carrington's was one of the very last examples of unprovoked ministerial resignation on grounds of principle when the minister concerned had no immediate responsibility for proven incompetence and wrongdoing.

Many aspects of the Falklands War have remained extremely controversial. Pertinent questions have been raised to which ministers have never satisfactorily replied: Did the government exhaust all diplomatic avenues before ordering the task force into action? Was it motivated by the desire to teach a demonstrably weaker regime a sharp lesson? Was the prime minister motivated more by the lure of glory than the need to save lives? The playwright and diarist Alan Bennett dwelled sardonically upon this last aspect when he read in June 1982 that the Argentinians had capitulated:

> A cease fire with 250 of our forces dead, one for every twenty civilians in the Falklands Islands – the price, Madam says, of freedom.[16]

It will not be possible to provide authoritative answers until all the official documents are released, which will not be until 2012 at the earliest. Meanwhile, however, controversy over the Argentine cruiser *The Belgrano* must suffice to suggest that the Falklands affair is not a simple matter of truth, justified retribution, and a demonstration of the virtues of the British way. It is now clear that Michael Heseltine, who became Defence Secretary in January 1983, colluded with officials in his ministry to conceal the truth about the circumstances in which *The Belgrano* was sunk – with the loss of more than 300 lives. A civil servant in the Ministry of Defence, Clive Ponting, was prosecuted under the Official Secrets Act for leaking accurate, but classified, information to the Labour MP, Tam Dayell. Ponting revealed that the 'official' version of the reasons for sinking the *Belgrano* was, quite simply, untrue. The decision to sink the cruiser had not been taken, as both prime minister and Defence Secretary, John Nott, had continuously asserted, by a British submarine captain in the South Atlantic who feared that *The Belgrano* represented an immediate and direct threat to the British task force. At the time it was sunk, *Belgrano* was not even sailing towards the task force. The decision was taken by a War Cabinet aware of a great deal more than it admitted at the time – not least that, during furious diplomatic endeavours, Peru had fashioned a peace plan which could have averted the war entirely.

Heseltine pressed vigorously, but unavailingly, for Ponting's conviction. Ponting did not deny what he had done, but claimed in court the higher duty to reveal the truth rather than conceal it to preserve embarrassing fact that the public had been consistently and intentionally lied to, not only during the war (which might have been excusable) but for as long after it as ministers could get away with. Despite the strongest possible hint from the judge that Ponting should be convicted, twelve arbitrarily selected members of the public ignored his advice.

Ponting's acquittal did Thatcher no political damage. Detailed raking over the embers of what the overwhelming majority of the British public wanted to consider an unalloyed triumph was of interest only to political opponents, pedants and those intellectuals whose faint-hearted equivocations she so despised. Her Memoirs on the subject are characteristic. She vaporized about the 'large amount of dangerous and misleading nonsense [which] circulated both at the time and long afterwards about why we sank the *Belgrano*'. She asserted that the government was responding to a 'clear military threat' and that the decision to sink was accordingly military, not political. This may well be true; we still await the full evidence. However, it is significant that she made no reference to the elaborate government cover-up of 1982–4 and did not reflect on how that cover-up might impugn the image she so skilfully cultivated for honesty and plain speaking. The name of Clive Ponting makes no appearance in Thatcher's full and scholarly index.[17] Heseltine, whose bluff had been called and whose behaviour had been far less honourable than Carrington's, never apparently considered resignation himself.[18]

9 Thatcherism abroad: influence and prejudice

'Dealing with Margaret Thatcher was like taking alternate hot and cold baths'.[1] Helmut Kohl's assessment gives some idea of the personal impact Thatcher had on other world leaders. She could be personally charming and she grew to enjoy international diplomacy as she gained in experience, but she was never a comfortable colleague. In European diplomacy her substantial specific achievements were of limited general importance because it was clear to fellow leaders that her priorities lay elsewhere. Being alternately wheedling and strident, therefore, was of little use. International leaders dislike being lectured or harangued and Thatcher's diplomatic style incorporated too much of both.

Appearances, however, can be deceptive. Thatcher was a more cautious, and certainly more temporizing, world leader than the strident image implies. She also developed a perceptive understanding of what was achievable. When she came to power, she wanted a resolution of the long-running dispute over the independence of Southern Rhodesia which since 1965 had been governed by white colonials led by Ian Smith, in what the Foreign Office prissily told the BBC to refer to as 'the illegal Smith regime'. Among the nationalist leaders queuing to take over when negotiations brought 'majority rule' Thatcher much favoured Abel Muzorewa, a moderate black bishop she trusted, over Robert Mugabe, a black Marxist she did not. Additionally, Muzorewa had been the only senior black politician to stand in an election arranged by the Smith government in April 1979. Mugabe, who had been leading a civil war against Smith, had boycotted the elections.

Lord Carrington was able to persuade Thatcher that endorsing Muzorewa would be interpreted internationally as 'a device to perpetuate the white man's rule behind an amenable and unrepresentative black front'.[2] Thatcher, recognizing that 'unpleasant realities had to be faced', opted for all-party talks to be held in London. From these, a peaceful transition to majority rule ensued and it was Mugabe who became the independent Zimbabwe's democratically elected leader. Rather against the steely image, the prime minister understood the need for compromise on what was widely considered a sensitive human-rights issue. Unlike the Queen, she was never a great admirer of the Commonwealth, not really seeing what such a polyglot organization was *for*. She also felt that it also contained too many uncouth leaders and too many uncongenial and ideologically unsound regimes. Nevertheless, she understood that settling the Rhodesia issue would smooth Commonwealth relations at the beginning of her term of office. It would also win international approval. Her summary was characteristically crisp and simple. It also demonstrates why the raging internal struggle between practical politician and ideologue was almost invariably won by the former:

> It was sad that Rhodesia/Zimbabwe finished up with a Marxist government in a continent where there were too many Marxists maladministering their countries' resources. But political and military realities were all too evidently on the side of the guerilla leaders.[3]

Pragmatism tempered principle in other high-profile foreign policy issues too. As we have seen, she could afford to stand up to Argentina over the Falklands (see pp. 96–100) in 1982 because she was secure in the support of the United States. She was, however, in no position to stand up to China in 1984 – a far more powerful and even nastier regime – over the handing back of Hong Kong. Thatcher had gone to Peking in the autumn of 1982 hoping to do a deal on the basis of which Britain would concede sovereignty to China in 1997, according to the terms of the ancient Treaty of Nanking signed in 1842. In return, she hoped that the Chinese would permit indefinite continuance of the British administration in one of the liveliest and most profitable money markets in the Far East. The Chinese, who did not recognize the validity of the Treaty anyway, saw no reason to concede anything.

The final agreement that Hong Kong should become Chinese in 1997 was signed in 1984. It included statements recognizing that different economic systems might co-exist in a single state. 'One country, two systems', the Chinese called it. In reality, however, the Chinese had entered no binding commitments to preserve capitalism in Hong Kong; Thatcher could offer no guarantees to its citizens that their economy, still less democracy, would survive. She acknowledged that the deal, though eventually reached with sufficient overt expressions of Anglo–Chinese goodwill to send the Hong Kong stock exchange soaring, made only the best of a bad job. Crudely, she had caved in to what she called 'an intransigent and overwhelmingly superior power'.[4] By 1987, Alan Clark, the romantic imperialist and indiscreet junior minister at the Department of Trade and Industry, was remarking that British influence in Hong Kong was already severely reduced: 'One more piece of wealth and real estate that has been allowed just to run through our fingers'.[5] The crackdown on dissidents in China after June 1989 confirmed Thatcher's own fears and emphasized the fragility of the assurances made only five years earlier.

Thatcher had few successes with the Communists of the Far East. Her influence, however, became substantially greater in Communist Eastern Europe. Here she showed both prescience and prejudice. She did not foresee the collapse of her 'evil empire'; indeed, she substantially miscalculated both the speed of the collapse and its implications. In June 1990, for example, on a visit to the Ukraine, she looked forward to that state's continued contribution to the development of the Soviet Union and asserted that London and Kiev would never exchange ambassadors.[6] Nevertheless, she more shrewdly assessed the internal contradictions of Communism before the disintegration of the Soviet Union in 1991 than did most of her contemporaries. The conviction politician in her also reinforced her perception: something as unnatural and inhumane as Communism *could not* survive. From the mid-1980s, she made a point of going to Eastern Europe as often as she could. When relations with the Soviet Union were frosty in 1984, she made a well-publicized visit to Hungary – which had made a number of small-scale market-led reforms. She was gratified at the warmth of the reception she received during a walkabout in a Budapest street market. She attributed this to her 'reputation as a strong anti-communist political leader'. Her visit also confirmed her view that there were no Communist people, only Communist regimes. The people in them 'retained a thirst for liberty'. In September 1990, only two months before her fall, she revisited Hungary and also Czechoslovakia, both of which had by then cast off the Soviet yoke and were 'coming to grips with the communist legacy of economic failure, pollution and despondency'.[7]

Thatcher visited the East in part because she enjoyed preaching the superior virtues of capitalism and being received by ordinary people either as a liberator or sage. But she was influenced by more hardheaded calculations also. As the Soviet Empire lurched towards collapse, Thatcher became more concerned to ensure that the resultant fragmentation would not work to Germany's advantage. During the major defence review of 1981, an exercise designed to cut costs and whose structure was in the event distorted by the consequences of the Falklands War (see pp. 96–100), the British army on the Rhine was largely exempt from change. Thatcher's abiding suspicion of Germany was one reason why the British defence budget in the second half of the 1980s was comparatively large: 5.5 per cent of GNP compared with only 3.8 per cent for Britain's European allies in NATO.[8]

It has recently been suggested by one of her erstwhile foreign policy advisers that an important element in Thatcher's foreign policy thinking was anti-German prejudice:

> She didn't hide her cordial dislike of all things German (forgetting, it seemed, the Teutonic descent of the English nation, of the English language and of the royal family) aggravated by her distaste for the personality of Helmut Kohl. . . . The contrast between herself as a visionary stateswoman with a world-view and Kohl the wurst-eating, corpulent, plodding Teuton, has a long history in MT's imagination'.[9]

She seemed to share the unreasoned views of many British people of her generation that Germany, which during the twentieth century had 'caused' two world wars, could never be trusted. She is said to have confided to one of her foreign policy advisers in 1989, as the Berlin Wall collapsed and as Helmut Kohl placed German reunification at the centre of his policy:

> You know, there are things that people of your generation and mine ought never to forget. We've been through the war and we know perfectly well what the Germans are like and what dictators can do and how national character basically doesn't change.[10]

She refused to accept the overwhelming view of both the other EC members and the Americans that Germany had been a model liberal democracy since 1945 and that the much larger and richer West could safely be trusted to absorb East Germany into an effective and representative regime which would add to the stability of Europe rather than detract from it. Not surprisingly, this was also the view of the Foreign Office. As we have seen (pp. 80), Thatcher's initial, and visceral, position on the Foreign Office was that whatever they advised was likely to be wrong.

Confirmation of what might be termed Thatcher's 'Germano-scepticism' comes from her own Memoirs:

I do believe in national character, which is moulded by a range of complex factors: the fact that national caricatures are often absurd and inaccurate does not detract from that. Since the unification of Germany under Bismarck . . . Germany has veered unpredictably between aggression and self-doubt. . . . The true origin of German *angst* is the agony of self-knowledge . . . a reunited Germany is simply too big and too powerful to be just another player within Europe. Moreover, Germany has always looked east as well as west, though it is economic expansion rather than territorial aggression which is the modern manifestation of this tendency. Germany is thus by its very nature a destabilizing rather than a stabilizing force in Europe.[11]

Her campaign to delay, if not halt, German Unification, however, had little chance of success; indeed, it was probably counterproductive. In the late 1980s the Russians were too preoccupied with their own internal crises to pay heed to Thatcher's warnings. Within the EC, Thatcher's unique diplomatic style (see pp. 81–2) militated against the formation of an anti-German alliance. President Mitterand of France, whom Thatcher anyway distrusted as an urbane but slippery Socialist, was hardly likely to be deflected by any intervention of hers from the Franco-German axis which had provided the motive force of Europeanism for much of the decade. If Helmut Kohl wanted a united German state, then Francois Mitterand would not stand in his way. To the frustration of diplomats and the Foreign Office, therefore, Thatcher's stance only increased British isolation in Europe.

Visits to Eastern Europe, however, continued to sustain both her self-regard and her sense of mission. She had developed a useful personal relationship with Mikhail Gorbachev, Soviet leader from 1985 to 1991, famously declaring after their first meeting in 1984 that she could 'do business' with him.[12] She found him, as indeed he was, a far more flexible and intellectually stimulating figure than the frozen Marxist stereotype. She deliberately chose a visit to the Soviet Union in the spring of 1987 as a launching pad for her successful re-election campaign. She used her good relations with Gorbachev to demonstrate to the British public that she was a key player on the world stage, able to move easily between the super-powers. Pompously, however, she slapped down a British reporter who asked about the significance of her visit for the domestic political scene: 'I am on a historic mission representing my country'.[13] Again she rejoiced at the 'rapturous' reception she received both in Moscow and in Tbilisi

(Georgia). An interview on television also reinforced the image of a strong, but compassionate, leader who had come to the heart of the evil empire to speak directly to its good, but downtrodden, people and offer them hope. She later stated that she could sense 'the ground shifting underneath the Communist system. . . . The West's system of liberty which Ronald Reagan and I personified in the eastern bloc . . . was increasingly in the ascendant'.[14]

The dose was repeated during a visit to Poland in November 1988 in which she spoke freely with the Solidarity leaders, visited the Gdansk shipyard which had seen the rebirth of the Polish liberation movement in 1980 and whose workers now cheered her to the echo. She also spoke plainly to the Communist leader General Jaruzelski about the need for change. Once more, she noted the essentially non-Communist 'spirit' of an enslaved people yearning for freedom, and offered them hope. Once more she found what she was programmed to find: socialism was 'doing its usual work of impoverishment and demoralization'.[15]

It would be easy to dismiss Margaret Thatcher's frequent Eastern forays as pandering to little more than the lady's self-regard and love of flattery. That there was an element of both is beyond dispute, as anyone reading the unintentionally revealing sections of her Memoirs will immediately see. However, there was more to it. First, she had a long-term objective, unrealistic, no doubt, but far removed from mere ego-massaging. She wanted to see the liberated countries of Eastern Europe assimilated rapidly into an expanded European Community. None was more devoted than she to the idea of a genuinely Europe-wide comity of independent nation states. Few feared more the domination of Western Europe by an aggressive, expansionist Germany. Hungary, Poland, Czechoslovakia – perhaps even Romania as it emerged from the dark tunnel of brutality, waste and corruption constructed by the Ceausescus – might act as a collective counterweight to this possibility.

Second, Thatcher's example genuinely *was* influential in the East. The image of the 'Iron Lady', which a Soviet newspaper had helpfully conjured for her as far back as 1976 and which she sedulously cultivated thereafter, was extremely useful. For many struggling against Communism, Thatcher was an inspiring figure. She had won a war; she was not afraid of speaking her mind; she had been more forthright than any Western leader in voicing their own hatred for the evil empire which oppressed them. Is it any wonder that Thatcherism mattered there? Even in the West her political leadership could be inspirational, as was instanced in Spain by the election in March 1996 of a

Thatcherite free-marketeer, Jose Maria Aznar, who became the first right-wing leader of that country since the long rule of Generalissimo Franco. To most EU diplomats, however, Thatcher seemed capable only of boring on about British interests, narrowly and perhaps wrong-headedly conceived. In the East, her reception was quite different. Thatcherism championed the values of the free-market. Thatcherism supported national self-determination. Thatcherism inspired visions of the triumph of liberty over the darkness of socialism. Thus what at home too often symbolized high unemployment, rising inequality and the excesses of vulgar capitalism, meant something altogether more benign in the tottering and ramshackle Soviet empire of the 1980s.

Thatcher's prescriptions were eagerly absorbed as the necessary medicine to destroy the dark contagion of Bolshevik tyranny. Thatcher herself might posture almost as a new Alexander II, not Tsar- but capitalist-Liberator. Only cynical Western eyes (and perhaps not many of them in 1990), could see the newly independent Eastern states as lurching from one extremism to another. The reckoning came only after she had left office when it became all too clear that Thatcherism was hardly better at generating instant prosperity – except for the privileged and sharp-shouldered few. Only time could teach the follies of excessive reliance upon entirely unregulated markets. Only experience could demonstrate how seamless could be the transition from party apparatchik to capitalist spiv. Disillusion did set in, of course, as is indicated by the remarkable successes of Communist candidates in free elections held in Eastern Europe during the 1990s.[16] As we have seen, even a mature political democracy adapts to the kind of shock which Thatcherism administers to the body politic only with difficulty. Its impact on states with little or no such tradition is much more intoxicating and the full effects cannot yet be assessed. That Thatcherism had a huge impact, however, is undeniable. Thatcher herself raised Britain's profile, and probably its status, in the world. Even outside the Soviet Empire, Thatcherism became widely valued as a valid set of precepts to halt the long and sterile march of state authority and influence. For a time, at least, it seemed to have the measure of the internal contradictions of Keynesian demand-management: a growing state, printing money and rising inflation. Thatcherism may have beguiled more than it benefited, but it certainly mattered.

10 The fall

During her long prime ministership, Margaret Thatcher's political demise was frequently prophesied, and, by her many critics, eagerly awaited. It was widely felt that she could not survive the desperate economic depression of 1980–1, for which her government's economic management was directly responsible. Many in her own party hoped that she would not. Her recovery after the Falklands campaign and her substantial election victory in 1983 silenced Tory doubters for a while. However, it is reasonable to date the background to her eventual fall to 1986, the year of the Westland Affair and the resignation of Michael Heseltine.

Westland was, in one sense, a political storm in a teacup. The financial difficulties of an ailing west of England helicopter company would not normally be the stuff of Cabinet crisis, but they were portents of something much bigger. Westland gave an early indication of the deep divisions within the Conservative Party over Europe and it was not coincidental that it would eventually be the challenge to her leadership of strongly pro-European Michael Heseltine which brought the prime minister down. Westland is also a useful place to begin because its effects brought Thatcher herself to doubt, for the first time, her own political indestructibility. She confided in her memoirs that, at the height of the crisis, 'I was considering my own position', knowing perfectly well that 'there were those in my own Party and Government who would like to take the opportunity of getting rid of me'.[1]

Heseltine, as Defence Secretary, wanted to mount a defence of the Westland Company based on a European consortium, whereas Leon Brittan, the Industry Minister, backed by No. 10, favoured a rescue bid from the US company Sikorski. The disagreement assumed critical proportions for two reasons. First, Heseltine was becoming increasingly alienated both by Thatcher's authoritarian style of government and her evident preference for US links over European ones.

Second, what might – and should – have remained a battle within Cabinet became a public scandal because of leaked confidential material clearly aimed at discrediting Heseltine. Though a specific leak was traced to Brittan's department, there had clearly been collusion with No. 10, possibly orchestrated by Thatcher herself. Brittan was forced out of office. Thatcher's own position might have become parlous had a forensic parliamentary debater like the young Robin Cook been in charge of the Labour assault rather than Neil Kinnock – all passion but no precision when presented with the rare opportunity of a prime minister lacking confidence and actually prepared to admit mistakes.[2]

Westland raised important doubts about the Thatcher government's style and policy. It also left Heseltine, much the most ambitious rival to the prime minister, out of office and with time to plan future strategy from the back benches. The large election victory of 1987 removed any immediate threat to Thatcher's position. Beneath the surface, however, it soon became clear that all was not well. Thatcher's government style seemed to become even more personal and less accountable. Ministers complained privately that she trusted unelected advisers more than she did them; she also set up *ad hoc* groupings of personal advisers on important policy matters rather than have them discussed at Cabinet in their formative stages. Generally she honoured the conventions of Cabinet government more in the breach than in the observance. This had been the cause of Heseltine's departure.

The contrast between the first and second halves of her prime ministership is striking. In the earlier phase, she was generally able to choose when to remove ministers she did not trust. By the mid-1980s, she appeared to have fashioned a Cabinet with as many sympathetic and well-disposed ministers as it is feasible to secure in that diverse coalition of interests which every major political party must comprise. In the last three years of her prime ministership, however, she regularly lost ministers to resignation at times that were often highly embarrassing.

The resignation of Norman Tebbit immediately after the 1987 election set a doleful pattern. There were strong compassionate reasons for his departure. His wife had been crippled by an IRA bomb during the Tory Party conference of 1984 and Tebbit wanted to devote more time to her care. Thatcher preferred to believe – at least for public consumption in her Memoirs – that this was Tebbit's sole reason for going: 'his reasons were as personal as they were admirable. I did bitterly resent his decision. I had too few like-minded supporters in the Government, and of these none had Norman's strength and acumen'.[3] The truth was not so simple. Behind the scenes, the 1987 election campaign had been a divisive one for the Tories. Tebbit, as Party Chairman, bringing Thatcher news about how her personality grated with the public, found himself the archetypal messenger being blamed for the message. In a characteristic gambit, the prime minister took her own initiative, employing a different advertising agency who, not surprisingly, presented less personally wounding findings.[4] This was one incident among several as a previously close relationship became decidedly frosty. Tebbit went in 1987, at least in part because he felt his authority being undermined. His shrewdness, intelligence and plain, thuggish ability to intimidate were much missed by Thatcher.

Allegations of excessive power from No. 10 was also the central reason for the yet more damaging departure of the Chancellor of the Exchequer, Nigel Lawson, in October 1989. He and Thatcher fundamentally disagreed about entry to the European Monetary System (EMS) and about the exchange rate policy to be followed before entry. Considerable evidence also exists to suggest that the prime minister resented Lawson's increasing tendency to push his independent opinions while on overseas trips. Lawson was much the most economically literate of Thatcher's Chancellors, a forceful personality anyway and well able to punch his then considerable weight.[5] When Thatcher made it clear that she favoured the advice being given to her by her economic adviser, Alan Walters, to that of her own Chancellor, Lawson responded that either Walters went or he did. In the event, both departed. Substantial damage was done by this evidence of public disaffection. Thatcher could hardly afford to lose someone of Lawson's quality anyway while complex financial negotiations over Europe were in train (see Chapter 7, p. 86). The already prevalent reputation was strengthened of a prime minister who traded on the strength of conviction leadership yet who could not tolerate equally strong opinions in others.

Downing Street influence was not restricted to the prime minister. Ministers either temporarily or permanently out of favour tended to be 'talked down' in unattributable briefings held by Sir Bernard Ingham, Thatcher's Chief Press Secretary throughout her premiership. Ingham, a Yorkshireman of Labour origins, with a temperament which veered uncertainly between the bluff and the brutal and a highly developed sense of his own importance, delighted in passing political black-spots onto lobby journalists, knowing that they would be written up eagerly for the next day's quality papers. Thatcher probably never understood how much resentment the Ingham press machine caused. In her last years of office, it almost certainly worked against her since it gave Conservative politicians of much greater significance than Ingham a lingering sense of resentment. When it comes to their own careers, politicians, like most people, have long memories.

During the leadership crisis of November 1990, Thatcher was evidently as bemused as she was resentful about the 'disloyalty' which she believed destroyed her. As a prime minister of eleven years' standing she felt that she should have been able to draw on a much greater fund of loyalty, especially from ministers most of whom owed their careers to her preferment. Now, one by one, in a lachrymose parade to her private room in the House of Commons they told her she must go. Though her fall was the result of a complex interaction of factors, she should certainly have been asking sharper questions of Sir Bernard as to its cause. Too few ministers in November 1990 felt that they could rely enough on her loyalty to them in the long term for them to pledge it to her in the short. They had observed how many of their predecessors had been treated.

Six weeks after the Lawson resignation, Thatcher faced her first leadership challenge, from an obscure left-wing Tory backbencher Sir Anthony Meyer. She won it easily but that was not the point. The *contest* was the point. It gave sixty Tory MPs the opportunity of a secret ballot to demonstrate that the prime minister did not have their confidence. In a party whose two rationales sometimes appear to be loyalty to the leader and election victory, this was deeply significant. Thatcher had won the Conservatives three successive elections, given them a lease on power for a generation and yet a backbencher of whom almost no one outside Westminster had heard could demonstrate her vulnerability. As she knew only too well, her real opponent was not Sir Anthony Meyer but Michael Heseltine. Over the next twelve months, while all Westminster insiders realized that the next year would see another, and much more threatening, challenge, Heseltine fixed on a mendacious mantra which he solemnly intoned to enquiring political journalists. He 'could foresee no circumstances' in which he would oppose Thatcher in a leadership contest. No one, least of all Thatcher, believed him. Heseltine, she knew, had many faults: lack of a sense of political opportunity was not one of them.

The actual contest of November 1990 was precipitated by two factors. The first stemmed from several causes and was ultimately the more important. A large number of Tories felt that the next election was unwinnable under Thatcher's continued leadership. 1990 was a very difficult year for them. Partly because of Lawson's earlier policies to prepare Britain for ERM membership, interest rates had soared to 15 per cent, making the home owners' mortgages ruinously expensive while the value of their houses was also tumbling. Inflation – the key evil of Keynesianism in Thatcher's eyes – had recently risen above 10 per cent again. Whatever its economic merits – and few were prepared to back it even on these grounds – the poll tax (see pp. 62–4) was proving a public-relations disaster. At the end of March, a demonstration against it in London's Trafalgar Square degenerated into rioting and 400 policemen were injured. Thatcher, preferring as ever to recall the horrors of public disorder rather than the depth of feeling to which it had given rise, stated simply: 'I was appalled at such wickedness'.[6]

Two more of Thatcher's long-serving ministers, the shrewd Norman Fowler and Peter Walker, that long-preserved yet entirely symbolic proof of the prime minister's tolerance to wets, chose to resign early in 1990. A third, the clever but unguarded Etonian right-winger Nicholas Ridley, was forced out for telling a journalist (actually Nigel Lawson's son) even more prejudiced things about Germany than Thatcher privately believed: 'I'm not against giving up sovereignty in principle, but not to this lot [meaning a German-led federalist European community]. You might just as well give it to Adolf Hitler, frankly'.[7]

The Cabinet seemed to be falling apart. Those few experienced ministers who were left openly and embarrassingly, squabbled on another key European issue – the EMS. Opinion poll findings were dismal, confirming that 1989 losses in the European elections were no flash in the pan. The newspapers talked up the prospects of a Labour victory, perhaps soon. Backbenchers need the electorate to sustain their pension contributions and their often profitable links to private industry at least every five years. Many – not all in marginal constituencies – were decidedly jumpy by the summer of 1990. By early November, one of the most besotted of all Thatcherite loyalists, Alan Clark, was recording in his diary:

> The papers are all very bad. Tory Party falling apart, the death blow, that kind of thing. Something in it, I fear, unless we can get a grip on events.[8]

The second precipitating factor in Thatcher's departure was the resignation of Sir Geoffrey Howe on 1 November 1990, or more accurately the resignation speech which he made in the Commons twelve days later. Howe was by a considerable stretch the most senior minister in the conservative government after Thatcher. He alone had a record of continuous Cabinet service under her since 1979 and he had held the two most senior offices of state below the premiership – Chancellor of the Exchequer and Foreign Secretary – for four years and six years respectively. He was not, however, a high-profile minister. People tended to remember not him, but what was said about him – most notably Denis Healey's wounding jibe that being attacked in parliament by Sir Geoffrey was like being savaged by a dead sheep. Howe had, however, left his best for last and was determined to prove that the old bruiser's famous put-down was somewhat less than the whole truth.

He was no longer Foreign Secretary, having been removed much against his will from that office in July 1989 for excessive Europeanism and possibly also for excessive deference to the hated Foreign Office official line. He had insisted on the honorary title of Deputy Prime Minister but took little comfort from it; his star was clearly on the wane. Thatcher's ever more strident anti-Europeanism chafed with him throughout 1990 but he was goaded to resignation by some spectacular words on the subject in answer to a question from the leader of the opposition. He believed that Thatcher's stance on Europe was diminishing the nation's influence where it mattered.

His resignation speech was as action packed as anything in his political life. It contained a cogent recantation of monetarist policy, which he himself had implemented as Chancellor a decade earlier, and the accusation that Thatcher's dithering about entering the EMS had caused the recent damaging increase in inflation. He also included a withering denunciation of the prime minister's 'nightmare image' of a European Community stalked by malevolent anti-democrats who wanted to destroy national sovereignty. He had already said enough to earn a place in the pantheon of twentieth-century parliamentary political speeches. But he had not quite done. His final sentence was dynamite:

> The time has come for others to consider their own response to the tragic conflict of loyalties with which I have myself wrestled for perhaps too long.[9]

Michael Heseltine had been presented, gift-wrapped, with just the opportunity he said he could not foresee, but for which the last four years of his life had been a preparation. The very next day he announced that he would be a candidate for the leadership of the Conservative Party.

Only during the last ten days of an eleven-and-a-half-year premiership did both luck and political judgement desert Margaret Thatcher at the same time. She did most things wrong from the day she knew she must fight another leadership battle until she emerged, tear-stained, from the steps of No. 10 Downing Street to return her seals of office to the Queen. And yet she so nearly won. She chose the wrong team and was rewarded with an appallingly mismanaged campaign, which ended up underestimating Heseltine's support by about seventy votes.

She also decided to be prime ministerial and represent her country at a European Security and Co-operation Summit in Paris rather than bargain or wheedle for Tory backbench votes in London. This was in its way fitting. Europe had brought her low and it was appropriate that her prime ministership should effectively end there with the news, telephoned through to the British Embassy in Paris on 20 November, that she had failed, by a mere four votes, to obtain the required majority over Heseltine to be declared winner on the first ballot: 178 Conservative MPs had failed to back her and most insiders calculated that existing support would haemorrhage away in any second ballot. And yet she initially opted to fight on, barging a surprised BBC reporter out of the way to seize a microphone within minutes of hearing the result and announce that she intended to contest the now necessary second leadership ballot. It looked rude and it sounded impetuous. The real calculations were being made that Tuesday evening not by her (she was fulfilling a diplomatic engagement at the opera) but by her ministers in London. Only their procession to her Commons office more than twenty-four hours later finally persuaded her to release her grip.

The deed done, a feistily de-mob happy performance in the House of Commons may have induced a retrospective sense of guilt in some Tory deserters. At all events, enough rallied around Thatcher's own chosen successor, John Major, to ensure that he comfortably defeated Heseltine in the second round from which she was now an enforced absentee. Because a third candidate, the Foreign Secretary Douglas Hurd, had also entered the contest Major polled fewer votes in winning the leadership than Thatcher had done in – effectively – losing it. This reflection did not ease her often graceless retreat to the fringes of political life. No matter; she was gone. *The Guardian*, never a friend to Thatcher, published a one-word reader's letter which recalled, with savage irony, the lady's response to success in the Falklands almost a decade earlier. The letter read: 'Rejoice!'.

11 The legacy

ECONOMY AND SOCIETY

Enough time has passed since the fall to make at least a preliminary evaluation both of Thatcher and of the legacy of Thatcherism. This separation is inevitably crude, but it may help to make two distinctions: between Thatcher and Thatcherism on the one hand, and between short-term, political effects and longer term economic and cultural ones on the other. Thatcher proved more successful than Thatcherism. Her short-term political successes stand in stark, almost embarrassing, contrast to the damaging and divisive failure which Thatcherism now appears to have been.

Thatcher was uncomfortable with intellectual abstractions, her instinct being to doubt their relevance and utility. The notion of 'society' – the working laboratory of social scientists, a key professional group for whom she had little time – clearly worried her. In 1987, she was famously reported in the popular magazine *Woman's Own* as holding the view that there was 'no such thing as society'.[1] Her later Memoirs attempted to clarify her meaning that:

> there are individual men and women and there are families. And no government can do anything except through people, and people must look to themselves first. It's our first duty to look after ourselves first and then to look after our neighbour.[2]

However, even the clarification suggested a clear order of priority and the 'society statement' was frequently quoted as evidence of her selfishness and heartlessness. Abundant evidence exists of her personal kindnesses but there is little doubt of her belief both that charity began at home and that people were, to a very large extent, masters of their own fate. As she acidly remarked: 'When I heard people complain that "society" should not permit some particular misfortune, I would retort, "And what are you doing about it, then?"'. Her perception of society was competitive not collaborationist. It was held more from prejudice tempered by personal experience and it did immense damage – largely because, unlike most other powerfully simple statements which issue from the mouths of politicians – she actually – indeed, fervently – believed in it.

Whatever the cultural overlay and the economic dogma which suffuse 'Thatcherism', politics were what Margaret Thatcher knew about and she practised them with enormous skill. Not only did she win three successive general elections for the Conservatives and, arguably, laid some of the foundations for John Major's fourth, but she also changed the nature of her own party (see pp. 40–52) and the face of political debate. A decade of Conservative dominance inevitably altered the agenda of the other political parties. One of her major objectives was to destroy Socialism. In the short term, at least, she succeeded. Her triumph should, however, be set in the context of Labour politics. The Labour Party is the only significant political organization in Britain which, since its foundation in 1900, has been remotely interested in promoting socialist policies, and for the most part, its leaders have avoided them like the plague. We might, therefore, legitimately wonder whether Thatcher's anti-socialist crusade was against a real, or an imaginary, dragon.

Nevertheless, the Labour Party emerged from the splits and ideological traumas of the early 1980s a distinctively different party. The few remaining real socialists – to use a term much favoured by Thatcher – either put up or shut up in the approach to the 1997 general election. Meanwhile Labour leaders and spin doctors either expunged the 'S' word from the political vocabulary or played around with a kind of 'ethical socialism'. This was meant to square internal political circles rather than to convey any kind of socialist message to the electorate at large. Ironically, a most significant achievement of Thatcher is one she would be horrified to claim. She provoked a major reassessment within the Labour Party, thus helping to make 'New Labour' not only electable but electorally dominant – albeit more than six years after her own political demise.

In economic terms, the legacy is much more mixed. One central objective of Thatcherism was to reduce the burden of taxation. This failed. At the end of 1996, taxation accounted for 37.2 per cent of a taxpayer's annual income; in 1979 it had been only 31.1 per cent.[3] Characteristically, though, this strategic failure was masked by tactically significant political success for Thatcher the politician. The burden of *direct* taxation in the same period went down from

19.9 per cent to 17.7 per cent and the Labour Party has proved unable to shed its unwelcome image as 'the party of high taxation'. Thatcher well knew that the public perceive taxation as being those amounts which are taken directly from their pay packets in PAYE. They do not think of the high levels of tax which they pay every time they buy a gallon of petrol or eat a meal in a restaurant.

Britain's relative economic decline has not been halted since 1979. It is true that annual growth rates in the years 1979–88 and 1988–97, at 1.9 per cent and 1.5 per cent respectively, were considerably higher than those of the period 1973–9. However, these relative successes stand out as failures in comparison with other developed economies, especially those of Germany, Japan and the United States. Also, growth rates in the hated years of 'Butskellite Consensus' were much higher than in the Thatcher years. Again, however, strategic failure needs to be set against some high-profile tactical successes. The British inflation rate, which stood at 22 per cent at the end of Thatcher's first year, came down dramatically during most of the Thatcher years. The early 1980s and early 1990s were periods of spectacular falls and over the last decade the British inflation rate (a crucial blip in 1990 apart) has kept in reasonable balance with those of the other main industrialized countries.[4] In all years but two, however – 1984 and 1995 – the British rate has been higher than those of G7 comparator countries.

By design, Britain became a more unequal society under Thatcher. Incentives for high-earning risk-takers were supposed to help them create more jobs, thus increasing overall national prosperity. As we have seen, tax cuts for the better off were real and the Lawson boom (see p. 31) did bring widespread economic benefits. General consumption levels increased sharply during the decade 1978–88. The proportion of families with telephones increased from 62 per cent to 85 per cent, and with central heating from 54 per cent to 77 per cent for example.[5] Those at the bottom of society, however, failed to benefit. If an unofficial 'poverty line' is drawn at half the average national income, the numbers in poverty increased from 5 million in 1979 to 14.1 million in 1992.

The changing balance of work towards part-time opportunities, especially for women, also disadvantaged the poor. While the proportion of families in which both adults worked rose during Thatcher's term of office, the proportion of families with no full-time worker also rose – from 29 per cent to 37 per cent. This was only partially due to the increased number of pensioners in an ageing society. Inequality was the inevitable result, with the sharpest anomalies at both the top and bottom of the scale. Thatcherite Toryism brought overall prosperity. After deducting costs of housing, the average real income of British families rose by between 1979 and 1992 by 37 per cent. However, the real incomes of the poorest 10 per cent declined by 18 per cent, while that of the richest ten per cent increased by 61 per cent. In 1979, the richest 10 per cent of the population held 20.6 per cent of the nation's wealth and the poorest 10 per cent 4.3 per cent. In 1991, the proportions were 26.1 per cent and 2.9 per cent respectively.[6]

Thatcher's personal success is beyond dispute. However, Thatcherism also had more short-term successes than its detractors like to pretend, and those successes were presented in an extremely favourable light by a generally sympathetic press. Thatcher's image, except with relatively small minorities – including the highly educated professional middle classes and left-wing political activists – remains that of a strong, successful leader who 'turned Britain around'. Perhaps, in a depressingly post-modernist age, the fact that she did not matters less than the fact that she is widely perceived to have done so. She did, however, bring about substantial changes. Britain was indoctrinated to consider material success the main, if not the only, goal and to embrace the so-called 'enterprise culture'.

LEARNING AND THE ARTS

The contempt with which Thatcherism is regarded by many in the intellectual elite and the professional classes is understandable, even if their manner of expressing it is not. Intellectuals and creative artists derided the economics of the corner shop and discerned in Thatcher the cultural sensitivity of a Philistine with learning difficulties. Intellectuals were also profoundly uncomfortable with someone who experienced none of the exquisite mental stimulation afforded by either doubt or alternative views. The language used about her by the rationalists was quite irrationally intemperate, owing at least as much to social and intellectual snobbery as to political antagonism. Baroness Warnock, incongruously for a philosopher, found much to criticize in her dress sense: 'packaged together in a way that's not exactly vulgar, just *low*'.[7] Dr Jonathan Miller, polymathic intellectual and aesthete rolled into one (and satirized by *Private Eye* as the Dr Samuel Johnson *de nos jours* for his pains), deplored her 'odious suburban gentility and sentimental, saccharine patriotism, catering for the worst elements of consumer idiocy'. He found her 'loathsome, repulsive in every way'.

Intriguingly, however, Miller's productions for English National Opera during the 'powerhouse years' of the 1980s contributed much to the substantial creative renaissance which took place there under the direction of the Earl of Harewood (the Queen's cousin) while state funding for the arts was being cut back. 'Harewood's boys' offered to a predominantly young, and growing audience, experimental and challenging music theatre. Inevitably, some productions offered only silly and self-indulgent examples of 'producer-licence'. One such, *Orpheus in the Underworld*, guyed Thatcher as a morally censorious 'Public Opinion'. More, however, used art creatively to illuminate and examine life. There was no cause and effect relationship between state parsimony and artistic creativity – though much high-quality art was fuelled by anger and frustration. British opera and British film were two cultural forms which attracted worldwide critical admiration in the 1980s. Artistic managers discovered unsuspected entrepreneurial and marketing talents as they attracted sponsorship from private industry, especially during Lawson boom. Meanwhile, Andrew Lloyd Webber's apparently limitless supply of saccharine melodies allied to the talents of managers like Cameron Mackintosh attracted unprecedentedly large numbers to the commercial musical theatre. Tourism boomed in Thatcher's Britain and *The Phantom of the Opera* was one of the things the tourists came to see. Out of its profits, and those of their musical clones, Lloyd Webber, a man of considerable cultural sensitivity, accumulated one of the most impressive private art collections in the world.

Universities, almost all of which were more than 80 per cent government funded, were likewise unfamiliar with the disciplines of the market place. Most initially derided these as uncertain guides to quantity and utterly irrelevant to their overriding concern for quality. Academic tenure encourages a critical independence of view which short-term contracts do not. It is not surprising that tenured professors should use their independence, while it survived, to lambast a prime minister who rejected their values and who, in 1981, instituted an 18 per cent cut in funding over three years.[8] Famously, Oxford University refused her an honorary degree in 1985, arguing that her education policies were doing 'deep and systematic damage to the whole public education system in Britain'. Right-wing supporters of Thatcher the universities did produce, if in small numbers. Ironically, if their expertise lay in economics or business, they tended to be scooped up to work in government 'think tanks' or as special advisers to the prime minister. Some, like Patrick Minford and Alan Walters, on occasion exercised greater influence even than Cabinet ministers (see p. 110).

Were the academics right to be so censorious? Thatcher presided over a substantial expansion in higher education. Student numbers increased from 535,000 to 710,000 during the 1980s, leading to even more rapid expansion to 1.25 million by the early 1990s. At the same time, ferociously tight controls were maintained over spending. Universities became more productive but hardly *better*. Students were taught in larger classes, scrabbled for library books whose number had certainly not increased *pro rata*, and had less personal contact with their tutors whose research and administrative performance, as well as their teaching skills, were now being measured. The universities successfully defended the concept of peer-review but the criteria handed down to the academic peers required quantitative as well as qualitative measurement. The need to ensure that public money was being properly spent was entirely laudable, and should have been instituted long before. The *means* of measurement, however, were both bureaucratic and labour-intensive. The resources channelled to those institutions which showed themselves most adept at form-filling, self-promotion and presentation were inadequate to sustain the quality they claimed. All too often, inappropriate 'performance indicators' were instituted to gauge success against value-for-money criteria. Too many either failed to work at all or measured the wrong things. More, but not necessarily better, research papers and books were written to meet the requirements of regular 'research assessment exercises'. A distressingly frequent ailment in the academic world of the 1990s was premature publication.

Thatcher bamboozled those on the intellectual left as much as she antagonized them. Academic Marxists in particular, always a more numerous group than any other kind, thrashed about trying to explain why simplification, homily, insistence and repetition delivered in a manufactured voice should have so much more persuasive power over working people than their own intricately argued hypotheses about consciousness, solidarity, hegemony and the rest. Some grudgingly conceded the attractions of what was dubbed her 'authoritarian populism'.[9] Language was one thing, of course. Even allowing for the wide disparity in relative resources, Thatcher was far more effective than the intellectual left at getting her message across. She paid attention to effective, accessible communication.

Patriotism, however, was more important. Most people, though perhaps not most intellectuals, love their country. They respond to assertions about, and some promise of, national revival. They tend, as Margaret Thatcher told them in 1982 they should, to 'rejoice' at victory. Too many intellectuals forgot the vigorous patriotic tradition which characterized radical politics in the later eighteenth and nineteenth centuries. Reformist radicals identified with their country against their government in a pre-democratic age.[10] This lost tradition has weakened the left. Patriotism became appropriated by the right wing of the political spectrum during the imperialist expansion of the late nineteenth century and the left has forgotten its patriotic heritage. In the 1980s a populist of genius drew upon it to devastating effect. For some left-wing intellectuals, it was the last straw. Unhinged from the old certainties, they sank without trace – though not without noise – into that huge, relativist black hole of intellectual vacuity known as post-modernism. Margaret Thatcher did not notice their passing.

IMAGES AND VALUES

The unintended by-products of Thatcherism defined late twentieth-century British society unflatteringly. It became less tolerant, more greedy and far less humane. It elided the socially critical distinction between selfishness and self-interest. Three dominant symbols of materialist Britain in the late 1980s and early 1990s stand out. Harry Enfield's brilliant comic parody 'Loadsamoney' offered a coarse stereotype of 'wad-wielding' vulgarity, judging everything in terms of immediate material gain. Striped-shirt yuppies, the complacent beneficiaries of deregulated, booming finance capitalism, noisily swigged lunchtime champagne in City wine bars just before the Stock Exchange crash of 1987. Privatization also produced spectacular winners with rewards out of all proportion to both their efforts and their entrepreneurial talents: Chief Executives of recently privatized utilities, like Cedric Brown of British Gas, who used what remained of monopoly positions to award themselves huge salaries supplemented by share options, and outgoing directors of state-owned companies who saw privatization through and who collectively pocketed almost £27 million as 'compensation'.[11]

In the wake of these excesses it is almost too painful to recall Thatcher's stated objective to recover what she variously called 'Victorian virtues' and 'Victorian values'. Her own narrow conception of these tells us much:

> The Victorians . . . had a way of talking which also summed up what we were now rediscovering – they distinguished between the

'deserving' and the 'undeserving poor'. Both groups should be given help: but it must be help of very different kinds if public spending is not just going to reinforce the dependency culture. . . . The purpose of help must not be to allow people merely to live a half-life, but rather to restore their self-discipline and their self-esteem.[12]

Here we encounter the cultural essence of Thatcherism: make people stand on their own feet and replace a dependency with an enterprise culture. This presents two problems. First, it rests on a spectacularly narrow, and atypical, perception of what Victorian values actually were. Second, it has distorted both policy and public attitudes. Thatcher's briskly confident assertions on subjects about which she knows little – and nineteenth-century British history certainly falls into that category – are frequently not made for political effect but as statements of deeply held belief.

In reality, although the Victorians distinguished between the deserving and the undeserving poor they did so within a clear *social* context. Those same Victorians who believed in *laissez-faire* as a guiding principle of economic policy also produced substantial amounts of state intervention, in the form of Factory, Mines and Employment legislation and of government agencies to administer poor law and education. These were – in some senses – the precursors of the welfare legislation of the twentieth century. They believed such 'social legislation' to be an essential element in an emerging ethic of public service rooted in social, as well as individual, improvement.[13] The Victorians also had a developed civic ideal, manifest in the promotion of local government to administer a wide range of services. Administrative experts in Victorian Britain – men like Edwin Chadwick in public health or James Kay-Shuttleworth in education, for example – would have described policy-making on the basis of inadequate knowledge as government rooted in prejudice rather than principle. For these reasons, it is difficult to accept the recent judgement of one political scientist that Thatcherism can be explained 'as a reassertion of nineteenth-century liberalism'.[14] Another, David Marquand, was much nearer the mark when he pointed out that the 'vigorous virtues' of the nineteenth-century market economy were themselves nourished by 'a stock of moral capital accumulated over long generations to which the norms of the market place were at best alien and at worst anathema'.[15]

A major defect of Thatcher's view of the world, in short, was that it lacked historical sense and perspective. This had important political and moral consequences. It was an entirely unintended malevolence

of Thatcherism that it saw Britain become more corrupt and its
political leaders less accountable as, intentionally, it became ever
more centralized. The drive against the local authorities, which
mostly rejected the Thatcherite message, concentrated power at the
centre. One distinguished commentator believed that political centralization 'has so strained the conventional limits of the British constitution that the constitution became a part of party politics, rather than a
set of rules lying above politics'.[16]

Perhaps the greatest paradox of the 1980s is that a regime which
came to power vowing to get the state off people's backs ended up substantially increasing the power of central government. Its enthusiastic
henchmen were highly politicized 'political advisers', chairmen of
quangos appointed on grounds of political sympathies rather than
administrative abilities, and a civil service whose political neutrality
was tested to destruction by managerialist ministers. Some civil
servants, like Clive Ponting (see pp. 99–100), responded by leaking
government secrets. One distinguished journalist recently noted the
changing culture:

> Until Mrs Thatcher took the stage, leaks from career civil servants
> (as opposed to so-called ministerial 'advisers' from outside White-
> hall) weren't just rare; they were almost unthinkable. So why the
> change? One reason is the sheer shabbiness of what . . . government
> is doing under the cloak of confidentiality. Another is the steady
> and intentional mix of politicisation and deliberate destabilisation
> which has been government policy ever since 1979.[17]

Another political commentator asserted that officials' role as givers
of objective advice and askers of inconvenient questions has been
battered into submission. In its place has grown a system and practice
of surrender to ministerial imperatives'.[18] Too many MPs, especially
but by no means exclusively on the Conservative side, cut corners.

Thatcher's policies were driven by conviction rather than insight
and sustained against both common sense and the conclusion of
rational debate. Thatcherism at the end of the century was, in its
way, as insensitive and 'driven' an ideology as Bolshevism had been
at the beginning. Despite its political successes, the overall impressions
left by the turbulent Thatcher decade are negative. True, Thatcherism
believed in the beneficence of market forces, using these, in some
inchoate way, to 'turn Britain around' and re-establish an era of
national greatness. But not in much else. The list of those things
Thatcherism attacked or demeaned is far longer: welfare, the power
of the state to improve people's lives, the professional ethic of service,

local government, trade unions, the notion of community, Europe. Margaret Thatcher's 'conviction politics' led her more readily to destroy than to create, and her abiding narrowness of vision prevented her from seeing the likely medium- and long-term consequences of her policies. She entirely failed to notice, for example, that what might be termed the long century of growing state responsibility, dating roughly from 1830 to 1970, was fuelled in significant part by the need to control and moderate brute capitalism which, for all its wealth-creating potential, contained what Bernard Porter has recently termed 'inexorable . . . self-destructive tendencies'.[19] In using the power of the state negatively – to resurrect as much unbridled capitalism as a decade of power in an elective dictatorship could encompass – Thatcherism morally impoverished and desensitized a nation.

Ideology is a reasonable servant for politicians, but in most cases, a disastrously bad master. Too much of Margaret Thatcher's regime vindicates the rhyming couplets written during Robert Walpole's prime ministership:

> For forms of government let fools contest;
> Whate'er is best administered, is best:
> For modes of faith, let graceless zealots fight;
> His can't be wrong whose life is in the right:
> In faith and hope the world will disagree,
> But all mankind's concern is charity.[20]

That Margaret Thatcher's regime placed too much emphasis on forms and faiths – monetarism, privatization and the rest – and too little on charity is perhaps its greatest indictment. Despite, or perhaps because of, the extraordinary political triumphs of Margaret Thatcher, Britain by the late 1980s had become a more grasping, greedy and mean-spirited society. Hers is a legacy to be lived down.

Notes

1 THE 1970s: EXPLANATIONS AND ORIGINS

1 Patrick Cosgrave, *Thatcher: The First Term* (Bodley Head, London, 1985), pp. 26–7.
2 Margaret Thatcher, *The Downing Street Years* (HarperCollins, London, 1993), p. 38.
3 J. Bulpitt, 'The Discipline of the New Democracy: Mrs Thatcher's Domestic Statecraft', *Political Studies*, 34 (1986), pp. 19–39; *Daily Telegraph*, 23 November 1990, quoted in J. Charmley, *A History of Conservative Politics, 1900–96* (Macmillan, London, 1996), p. 236; S. Letwin, *The Anatomy of Thatcherism* (Fontana, London, 1992). A useful summary of the arguments about Thatcherism as an ideology can be found in B. Evans and A. Taylor, 'The Debate about Thatcherism' in *From Salisbury to Major: Continuity and Change in Conservative Politics* (Manchester University Press, Manchester, 1996), pp. 219–40.
4 I. Gilmour, *Dancing with Dogma* (Simon & Schuster, Edinburgh, 1993); Francis Pym, *The Politics of Consent* (Hamish Hamilton, London, 1994).
5 This is a line which initiates will recognize as deriving from Gramsci and is reliably rendered in S. Hall, *The Hard Road to Renewal: Thatcherism and the Crisis of the Left* (Verson Books, London, 1988).
6 Quoted in P. Riddell, *The Thatcher Government* (Blackwell, Oxford, 1985 edn), p. 7.
7 Quoted in K. Harris, *Thatcher* (Fontana, London, 1989), p. 250.
8 R. Skidelsky (ed.), *Thatcherism* (Blackwell, Oxford, 1989), p. 14.
9 The ideas of Friedman and Hayek were not identical. Friedman was a more thorough-going monetarist, while Hayek placed greater stress upon the supremacy of markets over all other kinds of organization, political and social. See F. A. Hayek, *Denationalisation of Money* (Institute of Economic Affairs, London, 1978); Milton Friedman, *Inflation and Unemployment* (IEA, London, 1977) and Norman Barry, *Hayek's Social and Economic Philosophy* (Macmillan, London, 1979). Monetarism and the new right in the 1970s is accessibly discussed in A. Gamble, *The Free Economy and the Strong State* (Macmillan, London, 1988), pp. 27–60.
10 A. Gamble, *Britain in Decline* (Macmillan, Basingstoke, 1985), pp. 13–15; J. F. Wright, *Britain in the Age of Economic Management* (Oxford University Press, 1979), p. 21.

11 Gamble, *op. cit.* note 10, p. 16; S. Pollard, *The Wasting of the British Economy* (Croom Helm, Beckenham, 1982), p. 11.
12 Keith Robbins, *The Eclipse of a Great Power: Modern Britain, 1870–1992* 2nd edn, (Addison Wesley Longman, London, 1994), p. 429.
13 Bernard Porter, *Britannia's Burden: The Political Evolution of Modern Britain, 1851–1990* (Arnold, London, 1994), p. 343.
14 Cosgrave, *op. cit.* note 1, p. 42.
15 Gamble, *op. cit.* note 10, pp. 90–5.
16 M. Pugh, *State and Society: British Political and Social History 1870–1992* (Arnold, London, 1994), p. 298.

2 ELECTION AND DEPRESSION, 1979–81

1 Margaret Thatcher, *The Downing Street Years* (HarperCollins, London, 1993), pp. 4–5.
2 Kenneth Harris, *Thatcher* (Weidenfeld & Nicholson, London, 1988), p. 71.
3 Quoted in Andrew Gamble, *The Free Economy and the Strong State: The Politics of Thatcherism* (Macmillan, London, 1988), p. 140.
4 Ian Gilmour, *Inside Right* (Hutchinson, London, 1977), pp. 96, 121.
5 Harris, *op. cit.* note 2, p. 82.
6 Quoted in S. Edgell and V. Duke, *A Measure of Thatcherism* (HarperCollins, London, 1991), p. 3.
7 Cited in Gamble, *op. cit.* note 3, p. v.
8 D. Kavanagh (ed.), *The Politics of the Labour Party* (Allen & Unwin, London, 1982), pp. 9–45.
9 For development of this point see E. J. Evans, *The Forging of the Modern State: Early Industrial Britain, 1783–1870* (Addison Wesley Longman, London, 2nd edn 1996), pp. 261–2, 367–70, and Martin Pugh, *The Making of Modern British Politics, 1867–1939* (Blackwell, Oxford, 2nd edn 1993).
10 Peter Jenkins, *Mrs Thatcher's Revolution: the Ending of the Socialist Era* (Jonathan Cape, London, 1987), p. 95. For a detailed analysis of the 1979 election see D. Butler and D. Kavanagh, *The British General Election of 1979* (Macmillan, London, 1980).
11 Thatcher, *op. cit.* note 1, p. 43.
12 Martin Holmes, *The First Thatcher Government, 1979–1983* (Harvester, Brighton, 1985), p. 133.
13 P. Cosgrave, *Thatcher: The First Term* (Bodley Head, London, 1985), p. 94.
14 Quoted in Harris, *op. cit.* note 2, p. 103.
15 P. Riddell, *The Thatcher Government* (Blackwell, Oxford, 1985), pp. 64–8; Will Hutton, *The State We're In* (Vintage edn, London 1996), p. 70; Martin Pugh, *State and Society: British Political and Social History* (Arnold, London, 1994), p. 304.
16 Thatcher, *op. cit.* note 1, pp. 144–5.
17 Harris, *op. cit.* note 2, p. 109.

3   THATCHER TRIUMPHANT, 1982–8

1 Calculations from Bryan Cribble, 'Candidates' in D. Butler and D. Kavanagh, *The British General Election of 1987* (Macmillan, London, 1987), pp. 197–205. See also D. Butler, *British General Elections since 1945* (Blackwell, Oxford, 2nd edn 1985), pp. 81–4.

2 Emma Nicholson, *Secret Society: Inside and Outside the Conservative Party* (Indigo Books, London, 1996), pp. 89, 96.

3 The core reference points for British general elections since 1951 are the studies by the psephologist David Butler. Those which cover the Thatcher period are D. Butler and D. Kavanagh, *The British General Election of 1979* (Macmillan, London, 1980), *The British General Election of 1983* (Macmillan, London, 1984) and *The British General Election of 1987* (Macmillan, London, 1988).

4 Margaret Thatcher, *The Downing Street Years* (HarperCollins, London, 1993), p. 339.

5 Ivor Crewe, 'Has the Electorate Become Thatcherite?' in R. Skidelsky (ed.), *Thatcherism* (Blackwell, Oxford, 1988), p. 32.

6 Peter Jenkins, *Mrs. Thatcher's Revolution* (Jonathan Cape, London, 1987), p. 166.

7 *Ibid.*, p. 169.

8 S. Hall and M. Jacques (eds), *The Politics of Thatcherism* (Lawrence & Wishart, London, 1983), p. 30.

9 Patrick Minford, 'Mrs Thatcher's Economic Reform Programme' in Skidelsky (ed.) *op. cit.* note 5, p. 96.

10 Cited in M. Holmes, *The First Thatcher Government, 1979–83* (Wheatsheaf, Brighton, 1985), p. 67.

11 Figures from HMSO *Economic Trends* and OECD *Labour Force Statistics* and collected in L. Hannah, 'Crisis and Turnaround? 1973–1993' in Paul Johnson (ed.), *20th Century Britain* (Addison Wesley Longman, London, 1994), p. 347. For changes in unemployment calculations, see the *Guardian*, 22 October 1996.

12 Harold Perkin, *The Third Revolution: Professional Elites in the Modern World* (Routledge, London, 1996), p. 59.

13 Thatcher, *op. cit.* note 4, p. 308.

14 Leslie Hannah, 'Mrs Thatcher, Capital Basher?' in D. Kavanagh and A. Seldon (eds), *The Thatcher Effect* (Oxford University Press, Oxford, 1989), p. 39.

15 Lesley Hannah, 'Crisis and Turnaround? 1973–1993' in Johnson, *op. cit.* note 11, p. 345.

16 Samuel Brittan, 'The Government's Economic Policy' in Kavanagh and Seldon, *op. cit.* note 14, p. 13.

17 Holmes, *op. cit.* note 10, p. 68.

18 M. Dunn and S. Smith, 'Economic Policy and Privatisation' in S. P. Savage and L. Robins (eds), *Public Policy under Thatcher* (Macmillan, London, 1990), p. 34.

19 S. Edgell and V. Duke, *A Measure of Thatcherism* (HarperCollins, London, 1991), p. 140.

20 Ivor Crewe, 'The Values that Failed' in Kavanagh and Seldon, *op. cit.* note 14, pp. 248–9.

21 Figures quoted in M. Holmes, *Thatcherism: Scope and Limits, 1983–87* (Macmillan, 1989), p. 60.
22 Quoted in *ibid.*, p. 61.
23 Thatcher, *op. cit.* note 4, p. 676.
24 'Famous' quotations are often attributed to politicians, rather than to the news editors who 'translated' them from the politicians' first thoughts in order to fit on the tabloid page. I am grateful to Alan Watkins, *A Conservative Coup* (Duckworth, London, 2nd edn 1992) pp. 105–6 for going back to the original text of Macmillan's speech.
25 ProShare statistical information, quoted in the *Observer*, 13 October 1996.
26 Perkin, *op. cit.* note 12, p. 69.
27 On trade union law in the 1980s, see D. Farnham, 'Trade Union Policy' in Savage and Robins, *op. cit.* note 18, pp. 60–74.
28 K. O. Morgan, *The People's Peace: British History, 1945–90* (Oxford University Press, Oxford, 1990), p. 472.
29 Thatcher, *op. cit.* note 4, p. 342.
30 *Ibid.*, p. 377.
31 C. Cook and J. Stevenson, *The Longman Companion to Britain Since 1945* (Addison Wesley Longman, London, 1996), pp. 98–9.

4   THATCHERISM AND THE CONSERVATIVE PARTY

1 A. Sked and C. Cook (eds), *Post-war Britain: A Political History* (Penguin, London, 2nd edn 1984), p. 329.
2 For the Conservative Party in the nineteenth century, see R. Stewart, *The Foundation of the Conservative Party, 1830–67* (Longman, London, 1978). A useful brief assessment is found in B. I. Coleman, *Conservatism and the Conservative Party in Nineteenth-century Britain* (Arnold, London, 1988). See also R. Blake, *The Conservative Party from Peel to Thatcher* (Fontana, London, 1985).
3 John Ramsden, *The Age of Balfour and Baldwin, 1902–40* (Longman, London, 1978) and Anthony Seldon, 'Conservative Century' in A. Seldon & S. Ball (eds), *Conservative Century* (Oxford University Press, Oxford, 1994), pp. 17–65. For a briefer account of early twentieth century Conservatism, see Stuart Ball, *The Conservative Party and British Politics, 1902–51* (Longman, London, 1995).
4 D. Kavanagh, *Thatcherism and British Politics* (Oxford University Press, Oxford, 1987), p. 183.
5 Powell put a distinctive gloss on his own contribution to the conversion of the party to monetarism in 'The Conservative Party' in D. Kavanagh and A. Seldon (eds), *The Thatcher Effect* (Oxford University Press, Oxford, 1989), pp. 80–88. See also R. Shepherd, *Enoch Powell* (Hutchinson, London, 1996).
6 Andrew Gamble, *The Free Economy and the Strong State: The Politics of Thatcherism* (Macmillan, London, 1988), p. 150.
7 Quoted in Hugo Young, *One of Us* (Pan Books, London, 1990 edn), p. 127.
8 Jim Prior, *Balance of Power* (Hamish Hamilton, London, 1986), p. 117.
9 Young, *op. cit.* note 7, p. 331.

10 Alan Clark, *Diaries* (Weidenfeld & Nicholson, London, 1993), p. 215.
11 George R. Urban, *Diplomacy and Disillusion at the Court of Margaret Thatcher* (I. B. Tauris, London, 1996), pp. 17, 183.
12 Prior, *op. cit.* note 8, p. 119.
13 Quoted in Kenneth Harris, *Thatcher* (Weidenfeld & Nicholson, 1988), p. 109.
14 Quoted in Peter Jenkins, *Mrs Thatcher's Revolution* (Jonathan Cape, London, 1987), p. 97.
15 Quoted in Sked and Cook (eds), *op. cit.* note 1, p. 330.
16 Martin Holmes, *The First Thatcher Government, 1979–83* (Harvester, Brighton, 1985), p. 74.
17 Young, *op. cit.* note 7, p. 205.
18 Margaret Thatcher, *The Downing Street Years* (HarperCollins, London, 1993), p. 207.
19 This point is developed by Vernon Bogdanor 'The Constitution' in D. Kavanagh and A. Seldon (eds) *The Thatcher Effect* (Oxford, 1989), pp. 133–42.
20 For a more charitable view, see R. N. Kelly, *Conservative Party Conferences* (Manchester University Press, Manchester, 1989).
21 Richard Kelly, 'The Party Conference' in A. Seldon and S. Ball (eds), *Conservative Century* (Oxford University Press, Oxford, 1994), p. 251.
22 On grass-roots Conservative Party support, see P. Whiteley, P. Seyd and J. Richardson (eds), *True Blues: The Politics of Conservative Party Membership* (Clarendon, Oxford, 1994), especially pp. 150–60 where it is argued that Thatcher assimilated and reflected existing grass-roots attitudes at least as much as she pulled the Party to the right, especially on social issues.
23 For this section, see Anthony Adonis, 'The Transformation of the Conservative Party in the 1980s' in A. Adonis and T. Hames (eds), *A Conservative Revolution: The Thatcher–Reagan Decade in Perspective* (Manchester University Press, Manchester, 1994), pp. 159–65.
24 Whiteley, Seyd and Richardson (eds), *op. cit.* note 22, pp. 231–3.
25 An opinion poll held in the autumn of 1996 discovered that two-thirds of respondents believed that corruption was endemic among politicians of all parties, the *Guardian*, 19 October 1996.

5 THE ATTACK ON THE GOVERNMENT ETHIC

1 Margaret Thatcher, *The Downing Street Years* (HarperCollins, London, 1993), pp. 45–6.
2 K. Theakston and G. Fry, 'The Party and the Civil Service' in A. Seldon and S. Ball (eds), *Conservative Century* (Oxford University Press, Oxford, 1994), pp. 394–5.
3 P. Hennessy, 'The Civil Service' in D. Kavanagh and A. Seldon (eds), *The Thatcher Effect* (Oxford University Press, Oxford, 1989), pp. 115. See also Hennessy's more extended study, *Whitehall* (Fontana, London, 1989).
4 Quoted in P. Jenkins, *Mrs Thatcher's Revolution* (Jonathan Cape, London, 1987), p. 261.
5 Thatcher, *op. cit.* note 1, p. 30.

6 Hennessy, *op. cit.* note 3, p. 117.
7 C. Cook and J. Stevenson, *The Longman Companion to Britain Since 1945* (Addison Wesley Longman, London, 1996), p. 87.
8 Hugo Young, *One of Us* (Pan Books, London, 1990), pp. 230–2, 336–8. Thatcher, *op. cit.* note 1, pp. 46–9.
9 M. Heseltine, *Where There's a Will* (Hutchinson, London, 1987), p. 21.
10 See e.g., Clive Ponting, *Whitehall: Tragedy and Farce* (Sphere, London, 1986). The extent of change is debated in R. Atkinson, 'Government During the Thatcher Years' in S. P. Savage and L. Robins (eds), *Public Policy under Thatcher* (Macmillan, London, 1990), pp. 8–16 and Theakston and Fry *op. cit.* note 2, pp. 398–9.
11 Theakston and Fry, *op. cit.* note 2, pp. 399–400.
12 E. J. Evans, *The Forging of the Modern State: Early Industrial Britain, 1783–1870* (Addison Wesley Longman, London, 2nd edn 1996), p. 301.
13 Quoted in Peter Jenkins, *Mrs Thatcher's Revolution* (Jonathan Cape, London, 1987), p. 178.
14 Sylvia Horton, 'Local Government 1979–89: A Decade of Change' in S. P. Savage and L. Robins (eds), *Public Policy under Thatcher* (Macmillan, London, 1990), pp. 172–86.
15 Kenneth Baker, *The Turbulent Years* (Faber & Faber, London, 1993), p. 112.
16 H. Butcher, I. Law, R. Leach and M. Mullard, *Local Government and Thatcherism* (Routledge, London, 1990), p. 64.
17 G. Stoker, *The Politics of Local Government* (Macmillan, Basingstoke, 2nd edn 1991), p. 13.
18 Rate-capping was the term used to describe the powers taken by central government to limit the revenue which local authorities could raise from the rates. It was introduced in Scotland in 1982 and in England and Wales by the Rates Act of 1984.
19 Quoted in Butcher *et al.* (eds), *op. cit.* note 16, p. 71.
20 Stoker, *op. cit.* note 17, pp. 169–74. See also M. Goldsmith (ed.), *New Research in Central–Local Relations* (Gower Press, Aldershot, 1986).
21 On Liverpool in the context of broader local government concerns, see Stoker, *op. cit.* note 17, pp. 45, 102, 135. For a sympathetic appraisal of Liverpool's position, see M. Parkinson, *Liverpool on the Brink* (Policy Journals, Hermitage, Berkshire, 1985) and for the Militant defence, see P. Taafe and A. Mulhearn, *Liverpool: A City that Dared to Fight* (Fortress Books, London, 1988).
22 Stoker, *op. cit.* note 17, pp. 216–19.
23 From *Good Council Guide: Wandsworth, 1982–87* and quoted in J. A. Chandler, *Local Government Today* (Manchester University Press, Manchester, 2nd edn 1996), p. 235.
24 The *Guardian*, 18 July 1990, quoted in Stoker, *op. cit.* note 17, p. 221.
25 Thatcher, *op. cit.* note 1, p. 645.

6 THE ATTACK ON THE PROFESSIONAL ETHIC

1 *Social Trends, 1992* (HMSO, London, 1993), Table 1.5.
2 P. Riddell, *The Thatcher Government* (Blackwell, Oxford, 1985), p. 134.
3 *Ibid.*, p. 137.

4 Charles Webster, 'The Health Service' in D. Kavanagh and A. Seldon (eds), *The Thatcher Effect* (Oxford University Press, Oxford, 1989), p. 171. The NHS share of public expenditure increased from 12 to 15 per cent in the years 1979–96: the *Guardian*, 4 November 1996.

5 Margaret Thatcher, *The Downing Street Years* (HarperCollins, London, 1993), p. 607.

6 Ian Kendall and Graham Moon, 'Health Policy' in S. P. Savage and L. Robins (eds), *Public Policy Under Thatcher* (Macmillan, London, 1990), p. 112.

7 Thatcher, *op. cit.* note 5, p. 615.

8 *Ibid.*, p. 607.

9 Interview in the *Guardian*, 21 January 1995.

10 Interview in *The Sunday Times*, 26 June 1994.

11 Quoted in the *Guardian*, 6 February 1995.

12 The phrase is Ian Hargreaves' in a review of Simon Jenkins, *Accountable to None: The Tory Nationalisation of Britain* (Hamish Hamilton, London, 1995). Jenkins' book discusses the paradox of the Thatcher revolution. Pledged to liberate the individual from the burden of the state, it produced a central government exercising greater powers than any before it.

13 John Gray, 'The Reinventing of the NHS' in the *Guardian*, 3 January 1995.

14 Information from report in the *Independent*, 4 November 1996.

15 Thatcher, *op. cit.* note 5, p. 590.

16 The literature on this subject is vast. For a brief selection, see M. J. Wiener, *English Culture and the Decline of the Industrial Spirit, 1850–1980* (Penguin, London, 1985); M. Sanderson, *Educational Opportunity and Social Change in England* (Faber & Faber, London, 1987) and A. P. Summerfield and E. J. Evans (eds), *Technical Education and the State* (Manchester University Press, Manchester, 1990).

17 Quoted in Kenneth Baker, *The Turbulent Years* (Faber & Faber, London, 1993), p. 161.

18 Malcolm McVicar, 'Education Policy' in Savage and Robins (eds), *op. cit.* note 6, p. 133.

19 Baker, *op. cit.* note 17, p. 189.

20 Thatcher, *op. cit.* note 5, p. 595–6.

21 Baker, *op. cit.* note 17, p. 206.

22 Means of quantifying attainment in higher education also became fashionable in the later stages of the Thatcher era. See pp. 119–21.

23 D. Downes and R. Morgan, 'Hostages to Fortune? The Politics of Law and Order in Post-War Britain' in M. Maguire, R. Morgan and R. Reiner (eds), *The Oxford Handbook of Criminology* (Clarendon Press, Oxford, 1994), pp. 183–232. For criminal statistics, see M. Maguire, 'Criminal Statistics' in *ibid.*, pp. 233–91. On notifiable offences, see C. Cook and J. Stevenson (eds), *Britain Since 1945* (Addison Wesley Longman, London, 1996), p. 140.

24 Stephen P. Savage, 'A War on Crime? Law and Order Policies in the 1980s' in Savage and Robins (eds), *op. cit.* note 6, pp. 89–102.

25 R. M. Evans, 'Situational Crime Prevention in Late Twentieth-century Britain – A Critique', BA Dissertation, Dept of Criminology, University of Hull, 1996, p. 8.

26 Riddell, *op. cit.* note 3, pp. 196–7.

27 On Situational Crime Prevention see Evans, *op. cit.* note 25. The protagonist of SCP was R. V. G. Clark, 'Situational Crime Prevention: Theory and Practice' *British Journal of Criminology* (1980): 136–47. Patten's advice is quoted in Savage, *op. cit.* note 24, p. 98.
28 G. Laycock and K. Heal, 'Crime Prevention: The British Experience' in D. J. Evans and D. T. Herbert (eds), *The Geography of Crime* (Routledge, London, 1989); Maguire, *op. cit.* note 23, p. 251–62.
29 Evans, *op. cit.* note 25.
30 Thatcher, *op. cit.* note 5, p. 143.
31 Maguire, *op. cit.* note 23, p. 206.

7　THATCHER ABROAD I: EUROPE

1 Reginald Maudling, *Memoirs* (Sidgwick and Jackson, London, 1978), p. 225.
2 Hugo Young, *One of Us* (Pan Books, London, 1990), p. 557.
3 *Ibid.*, pp. 551–2. Extracts from the Bruges speech can be found in Margaret Thatcher, *The Downing Street Years* (HarperCollins, London, 1993), pp. 744–5.
4 Quoted in Kenneth Harris, *Thatcher* (Weidenfeld and Nicholson, London, 1988), pp. 99. For the Carrington incident, see Thatcher, *op. cit.* note 3, p. 86.
5 Hugo Young, *One of Us* (Macmillan, London, 1989), p. 121.
6 Thatcher, *op. cit.* note 3, pp. 60–1.
7 Quoted in Patrick Cosgrave, *Thatcher: The First Term* (Bodley Head, London, 1985), p. 86.
8 Lord Carrington, *Reflect on Things Past* (Collins, London, 1988), p. 319.
9 Thatcher, *op. cit.* note 3, pp. 62, 313, 733.
10 Martin Holmes, *Thatcherism: Scope and Limits, 1983–87* (Macmillan, London, 1989), p. 77.
11 Keith Robbins, *The Eclipse of a Great Power: Modern Britain, 1870–1992* (Addison Wesley Longman, London, 2nd edn 1994), pp. 381–2.
12 Thatcher, *op. cit.* note 3, p. 742.
13 *Ibid.*, pp. 741–6, 759.
14 *Ibid.*, p. 722.
15 Bruce Arnold, *Margaret Thatcher: A Study in Government* (Hamish Hamilton, London, 1984), pp. 200–1.
16 Quoted in Holmes, *op. cit.* note 10, pp. 75–6.
17 Thatcher, *op. cit.* note 3, p. 745.
18 S. Glynn and A. Booth, *Modern Britain: An Economic and Social History* (Routledge, London, 1996), p. 240.

8　THATCHER ABROAD II: DEFENCE AND THE AMERICAS

1 From a speech made in New York in August 1991. Quoted in Tim Hames 'The Special Relationship' in A. Adonis and T. Hames (eds), *A Counter-Revolution? The Thatcher-Reagan Decade in Perspective* (Manchester University Press, Manchester, 1994), p. 114.
2 Quoted in Hugo Young, *One of Us* (Pan Books, London, 1990), p. 396.

3 Margaret Thatcher, *The Downing Street Years* (HarperCollins, London, 1993), p. 157.
4 Hames, *op. cit.* note 1, p. 128. For Thatcher's account of the negotiations see Thatcher, *op. cit.* note 3, pp. 244–8.
5 Fergus Carr 'Foreign and Defence Policy' in S. P. Savage and L. P. Robins (eds), *Public Policy under Thatcher* (Macmillan, London, 1990), p. 236.
6 Quoted in Martin Holmes, *Thatcherism: Scope and Limitations, 1983–87* (Macmillan, London, 1989), p. 80.
7 *Ibid.*, p. 85.
8 B. Pimlott, *The Queen: A Biography of Elizabeth II* (HarperCollins, London, 1996), p. 497.
9 Thatcher, *op. cit.* note 3, p. 331. For an alternative account of the prime minister's incandescent rage over the Grenada incident, see Young, *op. cit.* note 2, pp. 345–8.
10 *The Spectator*, 29 October 1983, quoted in Bruce Arnold, *Margaret Thatcher: A Study in Power* (Hamish Hamilton, London, 1984), p. 255.
11 Thatcher, *op. cit.* note 3, p. 235 and quoted in Eric Hobsbawm, 'Falklands Fallout' in S. Hall (ed.), *The Politics of Thatcherism* (Lawrence and Wishart, London, 1983), p. 260.
12 Jim Prior, *A Balance of Power* (Hamish Hamilton, London, 1986), p. 148.
13 Thatcher, *op. cit.* note 3, p. 174.
14 Alexander Haig, *Caveat*, quoted in Peter Jenkins, *Mrs Thatcher's Revolution* (Jonathan Cape, London, 1987), p. 161.
15 Lord Carrington, *Reflect on Things Past* (Collins, London, 1988), p. 370.
16 Alan Bennett, *Writing Home* (Faber & Faber, London, 1994), p. 123.
17 Thatcher, *op. cit.* note 3, pp. 215–16.
18 David Hooper, *Official Secrets: The Use and Abuse of the Act* (London, 1987). The specific incident is discussed in Bernard Porter, *Plots and Paranoia: A History of Political Espionage in Britain, 1790–1988* (Routledge, London, 1992), p. 215. Ponting's own defence is told in his two books *The Right to Know* (Sphere, London, 1985) and *Whitehall: Tragedy and Farce* (Sphere, London, 1986).

9 THATCHERISM ABROAD: INFLUENCE AND PREJUDICE

1 Helmut Kohl's view of Thatcher's diplomatic methods, quoted in the *Independent*, 5 October 1996.
2 Lord Carrington, *Reflect on Things Past* (Collins, London, 1988), p. 290.
3 Margaret Thatcher, *The Downing Street Years* (HarperCollins, London, 1993), pp. 73, 78.
4 For Thatcher's own account of the discussions in 1982 and the 1984 agreement, see *ibid.*, pp. 259–62, 487–95. See also Hugo Young, *One of Us* (Pan Books, London, 1990), pp. 397–8 and B. Porter, *Britannia's Burden* (Arnold, London, 1991), p. 376.
5 Alan Clark, *Diaries* (Phoenix Books, London, 1994), p. 160.
6 George R. Urban, *Diplomacy and Disillusion at the Court of Margaret Thatcher* (I. B. Tauris, London, 1996), p. 167.
7 Thatcher, *op. cit.* note 3, pp. 454–8, 808–9.

8 Tim Hames, 'The Special Relationship' in A. Adonis and T. Hames (eds), *A Special Relationship? The Thatcher-Reagan Decade in Perspective* (Manchester University Press, Manchester, 1994), pp. 133–4.
9 Urban, *op. cit.* note 6, p. 131.
10 *Ibid.*
11 Thatcher, *op. cit.* note 3, p. 791.
12 Thatcher, *op. cit.* note 3, p. 463; Young, *op. cit.* note 4, p. 393.
13 Young, *op. cit.* note 4, p. 514.
14 Thatcher, *op. cit.* note 3, pp. 478–85.
15 *Ibid.*, p. 779.
16 R. Crampton, *Eastern Europe in the Twentieth Century* (Routledge, London, 1994), p. 410–15.

10   THE FALL

1 Margaret Thatcher, *The Downing Street Years* (HarperCollins, London, 1993), p. 435.
2 The Westland affair is discussed in detail in Peter Jenkins, *Mrs Thatcher's Revolution* (Jonathan Cape, London, 1987), pp. 185–204, and Hugo Young, *One of Us* (Pan Books, London, 1990), pp. 435–57.
3 Thatcher, *op. cit.* note 1, p. 587.
4 Young, *op. cit.* note 2, pp. 508–12.
5 Alan Watkins, *A Conservative Coup* (Duckworth, London, 2nd edn 1992), pp. 108–23. The contrasting accounts by the protagonists of Lawson's departure can be found in Thatcher, *op. cit.* note 1, pp. 713–18 and N. Lawson, *The View from Number 11: Memoirs of a Tory Radical* (Corgi, London, 1993), pp. 960–8.
6 Thatcher, *op. cit.* note 1, p. 661.
7 The interview appeared in the *Spectator* on 13 July 1990.
8 Alan Clark, *Diaries* (Phoenix Books, London, 1993), p. 341.
9 Howe's speech can be savoured in full in *Hansard*, vol. 180, for 13 November 1990. Extracts are widely quoted in recent political studies. See, e.g. Watkins, *op. cit.* note 5, pp. 152–4.

11   THE LEGACY

1 *Woman's Own*, 31 October 1987.
2 Margaret Thatcher, *The Downing Street Years* (HarperCollins, London, 1993), p. 626.
3 House of Commons Library Research Paper, quoted in the *Independent on Sunday*, 6 October 1996.
4 OECD Economic Outlook Statistics, July 1996.
5 *Social Trends* (HMSO, London, 1988).
6 Material compiled from *Households below Average Income* (HMSO, London, 1996) and government statistics in Charles Leadbeater 'How Fat Cats Rock the Boat', the *Independent on Sunday*, 3 November 1996.
7 Quoted in Hugo Young, *One of Us* (Macmillan, London, 1989), p. 411.
8 Young, *op. cit.* note 7, p. 414. See also M. Holmes, *Thatcherism: Scope and Limits, 1983–87* (Macmillan, London, 1989), pp. 122–37 and Kenneth

Minogue, 'The Emergence of the New Right' in R. Skidelsky (ed.), *Thatcherism* (Blackwell, Oxford, 1988), pp. 125–42.

9 The phrase is Stuart Hall's. The debate may be followed in Bob Jessop, Kevin Bonnett, Simon Bromley and Tom Ling (eds), *Thatcherism: A Tale of Two Nations* (Polity Press, Oxford, 1988), esp. pp. 57–124. See also S. Hall, 'Popular-democratic Versus Authoritarian Populism' in Alan Hunt (ed.) *Marxism and Democracy* (Lawrence & Wishart, London, 1980) and S. Hall and M. Jacques, *The Politics of Thatcherism* (Lawrence & Wishart, London, 1983).

10 E. J. Evans, 'Englishness and Britishness, c1790–1870' in Alexander Grant and Keith J. Stringer (eds) *Uniting the Kingdom: The Making of British History* (Routledge, London, 1995), pp. 223–43. See also R. Samuel (ed.), *Patriotism: The Making and Unmaking of British National Identity* (2 vols., Routledge, London, 1989); H. Cunningham, 'The Language of Patriotism, 1750–1914', *History Workshop Journal* XII (1981), pp. 1–30, and E. J. Hobsbawm, *Nations and Nationalism Since 1780: Programme, Myth and Reality* (Cambridge University Press, Cambridge, 2nd edn 1992).

11 Accounts of privatized utilities recorded with Companies House in 1996 and reported in 'The Power Game Millionaires', the *Guardian*, 15 November 1996.

12 Thatcher, *op. cit.* note 2, p. 627.

13 For further development of this point, see Eric J. Evans, *Social Policy, 1830–1914* (Routledge, London, 1978), pp. 1–18, 110–36, and Harold Perkin, *The Third Revolution: Political Elites in the Modern World* (Routledge, London, 1996), pp. 70–1.

14 M. Garnett, *Principles and Politics in Contemporary Britain* (Addison Wesley Longman, London, 1996), p. 95.

15 D. Marquand, 'Moralists and Hedonists' in D. Marquand and A. Seldon (eds), *The Ideas that Shaped Post-War Britain* (Fontana, London, 1996), pp. 25–6.

16 V. Bogdanor in D. Kavanagh and A. Seldon (eds), *The Thatcher Effect* (Oxford University Press, Oxford, 1989), p. 142.

17 Ian Aitken, 'Civil Service Leaks Lead to Corrosion', the *Guardian*, 21 November 1996.

18 Hugo Young, 'RIP – an Inconvenient Civil Service', the *Guardian*, 14 November 1996.

19 Bernard Porter, 'Thatcher and History', *The Durham University Journal* LXXXVI (1994): 1–12.

20 Alexander Pope, Epistle No. 3.

Guide to further reading

PRELIMINARY NOTE

A detailed archival study of the Thatcher years will not be possible until the release of key government sources. These will not become available for the whole period until 2020 at the earliest. The student is, therefore, dependent upon material published either at the time, or very soon afterwards. Much of it comes from politicians themselves and, vital though they are, all such evidence needs to be treated with caution. Most politicians, especially if they remain active in public life, are desperate to have their actions viewed in a favourable light and keen to ensure that the policies for which they were responsible are understood from their own perspective.

Despite its recent provenance, the available literature is huge. It is of very variable quality and not all of it takes the story down to 1990. Many works which are cited in the footnotes do not appear here. What follows represents a highly selective, but not – the author hopes – arbitrary guide to the most useful, and most accessible, works written by politicians, historians, political scientists, economists and sociologists.

GENERAL HISTORIES:

K. O. Morgan   *The People's Peace: British History, 1945–90* (Oxford University Press, Oxford, 1990) – an authoritative account.

B. Porter   *Britannia's Burden: The Political Evolution of Modern Britain, 1851–1990* (Arnold, London, 1990) – a much longer perspective, but very good, if waspish, on Thatcher.

P. Clarke	*Hope and Glory: Britain, 1900–1990* (Allen Lane, London, 1996) – a useful account, which puts Thatcher into the overall perspective of Britain's decline.
B. Harrison	*The Transformation of British Politics, 1860–1995* (Oxford University Press, Oxford, 1996) – a distinguished study which offers valuable insights on 'Victorian values'.
J. Charmley	*A History of Conservative Politics, 1900–96* (Macmillan, London, 1996) – generally sympathetic but well aware of the diversities which characterize twentieth-century Conservatism.
A. Seldon and S. Ball (eds)	*Conservative Century* (Oxford University Press, Oxford, 1994) – massive collection of authoritative essays on twentieth-century Conservatism, with useful comment on Thatcherism.

BIOGRAPHIES AND STUDIES OF THE THATCHER GOVERNMENTS

Kenneth Harris	*Thatcher* (Weidenfeld & Nicholson, London, 1988) – accurate and well-organized but lacking a cutting edge.
Hugo Young	*One of Us: A Biography of Margaret Thatcher* (Pan Books, London, 1990) – a long, but consistently engaging, read from a distinguished journalist. Especially strong on how the specific details illuminate the overall picture.
Peter Jenkins	*Mrs Thatcher's Revolution: The Ending of the Socialist Era* (Jonathan Cape, London, 1987) – well-written and adopting a stance broadly critical of Thatcher.
Bruce Arnold	*Margaret Thatcher* (Hamish Hamilton, London, 1984) – a highly critical view of Thatcher's 'totalitarian' methods. Deals with the first government only.
Patrick Cosgrave	*Thatcher: The First Term* (Bodley Head, London, 1983) – Cosgrave was one of Thatcher's political advisers and provides some significant 'insider-comment'.
Martin Holmes	*The First Thatcher Government, 1979–83: Contemporary Conservatism and Economic Change*

	(Wheatsheaf, London, 1985) – a sympathetic assessment.
Martin Holmes	*Thatcher and Thatcherism: Scope and Limitations, 1983–87* (Macmillan, London, 1989) – in essence a sequel to the volume cited above.
Peter Riddell	*The Thatcher Government* (Blackwell, Oxford, 2nd edn 1985) – another high-class journalistic study of the first government.
S. Edgell and V. Duke (eds)	*A Measure of Thatcherism* (HarperCollins, London, 1991) – strongly sociological perspective in a disparate collection of essays.
S. P. Savage and L. Robins (eds)	*Public Policy under Thatcher* (Macmillan, London, 1990) – useful collection of essays on the implications of specific policies.
K. Minogue and M. Biddiss (eds)	*Thatcherism: Personality and Politics* (Macmillan, London, 1987).
R. Skidelsky (ed.)	*Thatcherism* (Chatto & Windus, London, 1988) – an eclectic set of essays with a cerebral introduction by the editor.
Peter Riddell	*The Thatcher Decade* (Blackwell, Oxford, 1989).
Peter Riddell	*The Thatcher Era and its Legacy* (Blackwell, Oxford, 1991).
Dennis Kavanagh	*Thatcherism and British Politics: The End of Consensus?* (Oxford University Press, 1987).
D. Kavanagh and A. Seldon (eds)	*The Thatcher Effect* (Oxford University Press, 1989) – a very variable collection of brief essays, but the best are excellent.
Alan Watkins	*A Conservative Coup: The Fall of Margaret Thatcher* (Duckworth, London, 2nd edn 1992) – the title is somewhat misleading. The focus is on why, and how, she went but there are many longer term references. Particularly strong on political gossip and sharp, precise constitutional references.

MAINLY POLITICAL, ECONOMIC AND THEORETICAL ANALYSES

Andrew Gamble	*The Free Economy and the Strong State* (Macmillan, London, 2nd edn 1994).

Will Hutton	*The State We're In* (Vintage edn, London, 1996) – deservedly a best seller. Accessibly written, but a tough-minded Keynesian critique of monetarist theory and its political practitioners.
Mark Garnett	*Principles and Politics in Contemporary Britain* (Addison Wesley Longman, 1996) – useful brief introduction to the main issues.
David Willetts	*Modern Conservatism* (Penguin, Harmondsworth, 1992) – a thoughtful interpretation from a Tory politician, arguing, not always convincingly, the case for continuity in Conservative principles from Disraeli through to Thatcher and Major.
David Marquand	*The Unprincipled Society: New Demands and Old Politics* (Fontana, London, 1988) – another attack on Thatcherism, from a political scientist with a social-democratic, ethical perspective.
Harold Perkin	*The Third Revolution: Political Elites in the Modern World* (Routledge, London, 1996) – written by a social historian, the title notwithstanding. Lucid and vigorous, with a trenchant line on Thatcher's attack on the professionals.
Andrew Adonis and Tim Hames (eds)	*A Conservative Revolution: The Thatcher-Reagan Decade* (Manchester University Press, Manchester, 1994) – brings a useful comparative perspective and attempts to show why right-wing ideas were dominant in the West throughout the 1980s.
Peter Hennessy	*Whitehall* (Fontana, London, 1990) – unrivalled study by a professor of Contemporary History of how the government machine actually works. Draws heavily on the experience of the Thatcher years.
G. Stoker	*The Politics of Local Government* (Macmillan, London, 2nd edn 1991) – a very valuable introduction to the often complex – and during the Thatcher years immensely controversial – world of local government responsibility.
Christopher Johnson	*The Economy under Mrs Thatcher, 1979–90* (Penguin, London, 1991).
Alan Walters	*Britain's Economic Renaissance: Mrs Thatcher's Reforms, 1979–84* – the tendentious title betrays

the book's origins. Walters was a key economic adviser to Thatcher. The book is skilfully argued.

Bob Jessop, K. Bonnett, S. Bromley and T.Ling (eds)
: *Thatcherism: A Tale of Two Nations* (Polity Press, Oxford, 1988) – another tendentious title which indicates its political provenance. The unwieldy practice of the editorial 'collective' is a strong clue.

S. Hall and M. Jacques (eds)
: *The Politics of Thatcherism* (Lawrence & Wishart, London, 1983) – another collection of essays from the left, some of them theoretical.

AUTOBIOGRAPHIES AND STUDIES BY PRACTISING POLITICIANS

Margaret Thatcher
: *The Downing Street Years* (HarperCollins, London, 1993) – absolutely essential, not because it's a brief or a specially good read, but because it contains so many insights into both government and the workings of a highly political mind. Many of the insights are unintentional, which adds to the book's value.

Margaret Thatcher
: *The Path to Power* (HarperCollins, London, 1995) – 'prequel' to the above and written in a very similar style.

Nigel Lawson
: *The View from Number 11* (Bantam, London, 1993) – equals Thatcher's books in length and in its penchant for self-justification; comfortably exceeds it in readability. This is the book of a strong-minded politician only rarely visited by doubt.

Ian Gilmour
: *Dancing with Dogma: Britain under Thatcherism* (Simon & Schuster, London, 1992) – a graceful attack by Thatcher's ablest 'wet' opponent in Cabinet. Also brings a useful historical perspective to bear.

Kenneth Baker
: *The Turbulent Years* (Faber & Faber, London, 1993) – anodyne in places but useful as the memoirs of a wet who – as Chairman of the Party – was one of Thatcher's loyalist Cabinet supporters at the end.

Alan Clark

Diaries (Phoenix, London, 1993) – Clark wasn't an important politician, though he desperately wanted to become one. He rates a single entry in the index of Thatcher's big book. However, he was close to many people who *were* politically important and writes about them in a wonderfully uninhibited manner. Much the best diary of the Thatcher years and one of the best of the 'political' contributions.

Norman Tebbit

Upwardly Mobile (Futura, London, 1989) – a visceral right-winger who was close to the centre of power in the middle years of Thatcher's ascendancy. His view would have been more enlightening if it had been as indiscreet as Clark's.

James Prior

Balance of Power (Hamish Hamilton, London, 1986) – a reasonably frank account of the difficulties of a left-wing Conservative in a right-wing government.

Index

academics, influence of, 29, 57, 119–21

Acheson, Dean, 91

Afghanistan, 93, 95

Alliance (of Social Democrats and Liberals), 25, 26, 28

Argentina, 96–100

Arts, the, 118–19

Asquith, Herbert H. (Prime Minister, 1908–16), 92

Aznar, Jose Maria, 107

Baker, Kenneth, 59, 72–3, 141

balance of payments, 33

Baldwin, Stanley (Prime Minister, 1923–4, 1924–9, 1935–7), 14, 16

Bank of England, 10

Barber, Anthony, 5

Beaumont-Dark, Anthony, 50, 60

Belgrano, The (Argentinian warship), 99–100

Bennett, Alan, 99

Beresford, Paul, 62

Bevan, David, 50

Beveridge, William, 65

Biffen, John, 13, 44

Bristol, 21

British Medical Association, 67–9, 70

British Gas, 36, 121

British Telecom, 35, 37

Brittan, Leon, 21, 47, 108

Brown, Cedric, 121

Bruges Speech, 80, 85–6

Burns, Terry, 57

business interests, 6, 35, 48–51, 53, 63, 77–8, 92, 112

Butler, R.A., 14, 41, 70, 75, 117

Cabinet, 22, 24, 42, 45, 46, 47, 108–9, 111–12, 114

Callaghan, James (Prime Minister, 1976–9), 9–11, 13, 15–16, 18, 31, 54, 70–1, 81, 91

Carrington, Peter, (Viscount), 43, 80, 82, 99–100, 101

Carter, James Earl (President of the USA, 1977–81), 91

Central Policy Review Staff, 66

Centre for Policy Studies, 13, 42

Chamberlain, Neville (Prime Minister, 1937–40), 41

Chamberlain, Joseph, 42

child benefit, 33

China, 102–3

Chirac, Jacques, 84

Church of England, 41

Churchill, Winston (Prime Minister 1940–5 and 1951–5), 14, 26, 91, 92, 96–7

Citizen's Charter, 58

Civil Service, 1, 4–5, 7, 29, 35, 53–8, 80, 123

Civil Service Department, 56

Clark, Alan, 43, 103, 112, 141, 142

Clarke, Kenneth, 68

Clegg, Hugh, 18

Common Agricultural Policy, 82–4, 87

Common Market, *see* European Economic Community
Commons, House of, 4, 11, 22, 28, 37, 112–13
Commonwealth, 95, 102
Communism, *see* Marxism
Community Charge, *see* Poll Tax
Conservatism, 2–3, 14, 40–1, 44–6
Conservative Party, 1, 2–3, 5, 7, 12, 14–18, 21–2, 24–6, 28, 34–5, 40–52, 58, 63, 76–7, 89, 108–13, 116
consumerism, 30, 117
Cook, Robin, 109
Cosgrave, Patrick, 1, 137
council houses, sale of, 26–7, 34
crime, 21, 75–8
Critchley, Julian, 49
Czechoslovakia, 103

Dayell, Tam, 99
defence policy, 93–5, 104
Defence, Department of, 56, 75
Delors, Jacques, 84–5
dependency culture, 3, 65
devaluation, 9
devolution, 11, 13
Disraeli, Benjamin (Prime Minister, 1874–80), 3, 17, 40, 42, 58
Docherty, Brian, 68
doctors, 66–9
dries, 44–5

economic policy, 2, 4, 6–10, 12–13, 18–21, 29–37, 45, 111–18
economic performance, 8–10, 17, 31–3, 116–18
economic cycles, 6, 32
Economist, The, 41
Eden, Anthony (Prime Minister, 1955–7), 91
Education, Department of, 4–5, 70–1
education, 4–5, 70–4, 77
Education Acts, 1980: 71; 1986: 71; 1988: 71–4
Eisenhower, Dwight. D (President of the USA, 1953–61), 91
Elizabeth II, 1, 13, 95, 102
Empire, British, 3

Employment Acts, 1982: 37; 1988: 37
Employment, Department of, 22
employment policy, 19–20, 37, 117–18
Energy, Department of, 22
Enfield, Harry, 121
England, 17, 25, 27, 46
English Literature, 73
Environment, Department of, 56, 62
European Economic Community, 8, 30, 80–9, 91, 106–7, 108, 110, 113–14
European Monetary System, 85, 110
European Community, *see* European Economic Community
European Union, *see* European Economic Community
Exchange Rate Mechanism, 86, 111–12

Falklands War (1982), 25, 80, 90, 93, 95, 96–100, 102, 104, 108, 114, 120
Financial Times, 60, 97
Finchley (MT's parliamentary constituency when Conservative leader), 43
Foot, Michael, 22, 94
Foreign Policy, 2, 79–107
Foreign Office, 80, 85, 98, 104, 113
Fowler, Norman, 37
France, 8, 32, 81, 83–4, 87, 98
free markets, 4, 6, 18, 50, 65, 71–2, 121–3
Friedman, Milton, 6, 40

Gamble, Andrew, 42
Gaullism, 85–6, 91
General Elections, 1970: 4, 75; 1974 (Feb): 5,7; 1974 (Oct): 5–6, 7; 1979: 11–13, 15–17, 47, 75, 111, 116; 1983: 24–6, 35, 47, 59, 93, 96–7, 108, 111, 116; 1987: 25–8, 94, 109, 111, 116; 1992: 116; 1997: 5, 116
Germany, West, 8, 61, 72, 81, 83, 87, 98, 104–5, 112, 117

Gilmour, Ian, 2, 13, 21, 44–5, 46, 141
Giscard D'Estaing, 82
Gladstone, William (Prime Minister, 1868–74, 1880–85, 1886, 1892–4), 3, 40
Gorbachev, Mikhail, 105–6
Government, Local, *see* Local Government
Gray, John, 69
Greater London Council, abolition of, 61
Grenada, 95
Guardian, the, 97, 114

Haig, Alexander, 98
Hailsham, Quintin Hogg, Lord, 13, 61
Hall, Stuart, 28, 120, 140
Hansard (Official report of parliamentary speeches), 51
Harewood, Earl of, 119
Hatton, Derek, 60
Hayek, F.A., 6
Healey, Dennis, 10–11, 13, 14, 22, 51, 113
health service, 28, 65–9
health service managers, 68–9, 77
Heath, Edward (Prime Minister, 1970–4), 4–7, 8–9, 13, 15, 18, 38, 41–2, 54, 58, 81, 91–2
Hennessy, Peter, 54, 139
Heseltine, Michael, 44, 56, 100, 108–9, 111, 113–14
history, 73
Home Office, 75–8
Hong Kong, 102–3
Hoskyns, John, 55
hospitals and hospital trusts, 67–9
housing, 26–7, 34, 48–9, 59, 62–4, 74, 117–18
Housing Act (1980), 59
Howe, Geoffrey, 18–20, 44, 47, 80, 86, 95, 112–13
Howell, David, 22
Hungary, 103
Hurd, Douglas, 114

ideology, 3, 18, 33–4, 121–4
imports, 33

Income Tax, 3, 19, 31, 116–18
indirect taxation, 19, 31, 116–18
Industry, Department of, 108
inequality, 31, 117–18
inflation, 6, 9, 18, 20–1, 29, 33, 112, 117
Ingham, Bernard, 46, 110–11
Institute of Economic Affairs, 42
Iran, 93
Iraq, 93
Ireland, Northern, 22

Japan, 9, 32, 33, 117
Jaruzelski, General Wojciech, 106
Jenkins, Peter, 17, 27–8, 137
Joseph, Keith, 6–7, 13, 19, 41, 44, 47

Kennedy, John F. (President of the USA, 1961–3), 91
Keynesianism, 6, 8–9, 13, 29, 45, 107, 112
Kinnock, Neil, 25, 39, 94, 109
Kissinger, Henry, 81
Kohl, Helmut, 101, 104–5

Labour Party, 5, 8–11, 13, 15–17, 22, 25–8, 38–9, 46, 48, 54, 58–61, 67, 93, 112, 116–17
Lawson, Nigel, 20, 22, 25, 30–1, 47, 63, 86, 110–12, 117, 140
Liberal Party, 9, 24, 92
Libya, 93
Liverpool, 21, 60
Liverpool, Lord, (Prime Minister 1812–27), 1
living standards, 5, 8
Livingstone, Ken, 61
Lloyd George, David, (Prime Minister 1916–22), 2, 41
Local Government Acts, 1985: 60–1; 1988: 61–2
local government, 29, 40, 58–64, 71, 123
London, 21, 58–61, 69, 112, 114, 121
Lowestoft (Suffolk), 97

MacGregor, Ian, 38
Mackintosh, Cameron, 119

Macmillan, Harold (Prime Minister, 1957–63), 14, 26, 36, 41, 91
Mail, Daily, 97
Major, John (Prime Minister, 1990–7), 58, 114
Malvinas, the *see* Falklands
Manchester, 21
manufacturing industry, 9, 20–1, 32–3
Marks, John, 68
Marquand, David, 122, 139
Marxism, 2–3, 28, 95, 102, 106, 120, 123
mathematics, 73
Maude, Angus, 13
Maudling, Reginald, 13, 79
Medium Term Financial Strategy, 19–20, 30, 33
Meyer, Sir Anthony, 111
Middle East, 93
middle classes, 3–4, 28, 43, 50, 75, 118
Militant Tendency, 60
Miller, Jonathan, 118–19
mine workers, 5, 37–9
Minford, Patrick, 29, 119
Mitterand, Francois, 105
monetarism, 6–7, 18–21, 31, 33, 43, 45, 113
money supply *see* monetarism
Mortgage Tax Relief, 33
Mugabe, Robert, 101–2
Muzorewa, Abel, 101

National Union of Teachers (NUT), 70
National Curriculum (education) 72–4
National Health Service, 65–9, 70, 77–8
Needham, Richard, 34
Neighbourhod Watch, 76
newspapers, 2, 11, 19–20, 26, 46, 51, 82, 86, 97, 106, 110–12
Nicholson, Emma, 24
Norris, Stephen, 50
North Atlantic Treaty Organisation (NATO), 10, 94–5
Northcote-Trevelyan Report (on Civil Service 1853), 58

Nott, John, 21, 99–100
nuclear weapons, 80

Observer, the, 97
oil, 9–10, 19–20, 33, 88
Oxford University, 50, 119

Paris, 114
Party Organisation, 45–7, 51, 112
Party Conference, Conservative, 14, 47–8, 66, 94, 109
patriotism, 3, 25, 41, 79, 98, 120–1
Patten, John, 76
Peel, Robert (Prime Minister, 1834–5, 1841–6), 40
Peru, 100
Plaid Cymru see Welsh National Party
Poland, 106
Police, 18, 75
Policy Unit (Conservative), 55
Poll Tax, 62–4, 112
Ponting, Clive, 99–100, 123
Pope, Alexander, 124
populism, 34, 48, 64, 66, 82, 93, 96, 121
poverty, 117
Powell, J.Enoch, 6, 41, 44
Powell, Charles, 80
Prime Minister, power of, 46
print workers, 39
Prior, James, 2, 13, 19, 22, 43–4, 46, 97, 141
Private Eye, 118
privatization, 34–7
productivity, 32
professions, 3, 28, 65–78, 118, 123
public sector (of the economy), 28, 34–5, 39, 53
public examinations, 74
public schools, 48–9
Pym, Francis, 22, 43, 47

rates, 59–60, 62–4
Rayner, Derek, 55
Reagan, Ronald (President of the United States, 1981–9), 88, 90, 93–5, 106
Reece, Gordon, 15
Rhodesia, Southern, *see* Zimbabwe

Ridley, Nicholas, 62, 112
riots, 21, 63–4, 76, 112
Roberts, Alderman (father of Margaret Thatcher), 21

Salisbury, 3rd Marquess of (Prime Minister, 1886–92, 1895–1902), 3
Scargill, Arthur, 38–9, 60
Schmidt, Helmut, 82
Schools Curriculum and Assessment Authority, 74
Scotland, 11, 13, 25, 27, 59
service industries, 21, 27, 32, 77
Shaw, George Bernard, 65
Sherman, Alfred, 13, 22
Single European Act (1986), 83–4
Situational Crime Prevention, 75–6
'sleaze', 37, 51, 122–3
Smith, Adam, 3
Smith, Ian, 101
Social Democratic Party, 22, 24–5
Social Contract, 10–11
socialism, 35, 60, 65, 85, 107, 116
Spain, 106–7
Spectator, The, 95
standards of living, 30
Star Wars, 94–5
Stevas, Norman, St John (Fawsley, Baron), 21, 45
Stockton, Earl of, *see* Macmillan, Harold
Strategic Defence Initiative *see* Star Wars
strikes, 5, 11, 16, 37–9
Sun, The, 97

Tate, Nicholas, 73
taxation, 3, 6, 9, 18, 19, 21, 31, 116–17
teachers, 28, 70–4
Tebbit, Norman, 21–2, 29, 37, 47, 109–10, 141
Telegraph, Daily, 2, 97
television, 20, 47
Thatcher, Dennis, 50
Thatcher, Margaret (Prime Minister, 1979–90), achievement, 1–2, 115–24; as Leader of the Opposition (1975–9), 8, 10–11, 13–17; attitude to the United States, 10–11, 81, 88, 90–6; Communism, 102–7; conviction politics, 2, 4, 15, 18, 22–3, 33–5, 54; desire for change, 1, 15, 29, 33; early career, 4–8; economic views, 2–4, 6–8, 18–21, 34, 39, 40–1; fall from power, 108–14; foreign policy, 79–106; influence of father, 3; iron lady, 106; morality, 2–3, 6–7, 98, 121–4; nature of support, 6, 17, 62–4, 75; patriotism, 46, 86, 96, 98; political views, 1–4, 18, 86, 140; relations with professional, academic and artistic groups, 33, 65–74, 76–7, 118–21; relations with grassroot supporters, 8, 14, 26, 28, 47–9; relations with Cabinet colleagues, 6, 21–2, 24, 31, 42–7, 109–14; relations with colleagues in the European Community, 80–9, 98, 101; sense of humour, 16, 54; society, 21, 115–16; values and beliefs, 3–4, 32, 35, 51, 58, 65, 75, 121–4
Thatcher, Mark, 93
TINA ('There is no alternative'), 45–6
Trade and Industry, Deptartment of, 103
Trade Unions, 3, 6, 8, 11, 14–17, 27, 29, 35–6, 37–9, 45, 123
Trade Union Act (1984), 37
Transport Act (1985), 61
Transport, Department of, 37
Transport, public, 61
Treasury, 22, 29

Ukraine, 103
unemployment, 9, 13, 16, 20, 29–30, 33, 107
Union of Soviet Socialist Republics (USSR), 90, 94, 97–8, 103–7
United States of America, 8, 10–11, 32, 48, 61, 81, 88, 90–6, 98, 104, 117
United Nations Organisation, 80–1
universities, 119–20
Urban, George, 44

Value Added Tax, 19, 31
Victorianism and Victorian Values,
   3, 31–2, 40, 51, 121–2

Wales, 11, 25, 27
Walker, Peter, 44, 47, 58
Walters, Alan, 22, 57, 110, 119, 140
Wandsworth (south London), 61–62
Webber, Sir Andrew Lloyd, 119
Welfare State, 65
Welfare policy, 6, 8
Welsh National Party (*Plaid
   Cymru*), 97
Westland, 108–9
wets, 2, 34, 41–8

whips, parliamentary, 51
Whitelaw, William, 7–8, 43, 47, 54
Wilson, Harold (Prime Minister,
   1964–70, 1974–6), 5, 9–11, 18,
   54
Winter of Discontent, 11, 14–16
Women in Thatcherite Britain, 24,
   117–18
working classes, 16–17, 26, 43, 74,
   97

Yuppies (Young Upwardly Mobile
   Professionals), 32, 35, 121

Zimbabwe, 101–2

Katy's Pony Challenge

Victoria Eveleigh

Illustrated by Chris Eveleigh

Orion
Children's Books

First published in Great Britain in 2015
by Orion Children's Books
An imprint of the Hachette Children's Book Group
Published by Hodder and Stoughton

Carmelite House
50 Victoria Embankment
London EC4Y 0DZ
An Hachette UK Company

1 3 5 7 9 10 8 6 4 2

A catalogue record for this book is available from the British Library.

ISBN 978 1 4440 1451 8

Typeset by Input Data Services Ltd, Bridgwater, Somerset

Printed in Great Britain by Clays Ltd, St Ives plc

www.orionchildrensbooks.co.uk

Katy's Pony Challenge

For Vanessa Bee. Many thanks for your generosity and for everything you've taught me about horses, especially Exmoor ponies.

"Competitions are not that important to me. I am all about the riding and the horse."

Steph Lloyd, a rider at the Conquest Centre for Disabled Riders.

Exmoor

BRISTOL CHANNEL

COMBE MARTIN
PARRACOMBE
LYNTON
BRENDON
MALMSMEAD
PORLOCK
MINEHEAD
BLACKMOOR GATE
CHALLACOMBE
DUNSTER
SIMONSBATH
WHEDDON CROSS
EXFORD
WINSFORD
WITHYPOOL
HAWKRIDGE
TWITCHEN
DULVERTON

Contents

1   Viking   1

2   A Moorland Ride   8

3   The Jumping Lesson   19

4   A Gentle Hack   27

5   Horse Agility   40

6   The Trouble With Tinkerbell   48

7   James   57

8   A Lost Lamb   67

9   The Courage To Say Something   77

10   Third Time Lucky   87

11   At Liberty   99

12   Everyone's A Winner   114

1

Viking

This place is like a completely different country, Katy thought.

When they'd left Exmoor that morning, streaks of snow had been lingering on the high moors, but here in the Cotswolds it was definitely springtime. The mellow landscape changed constantly: newborn lambs gambolling in meadows, soil the colour of rich chocolate, crops emerging in neat green rows, towering trees, a manor house surrounded by parkland, paddocks grazed by horses and ponies, a pretty village . . . The sandy-coloured limestone of the houses and stone walls blended perfectly with the countryside.

"Great Turville Farm. We've arrived," Melanie said, turning the Stonyford lorry onto a lane flanked by post and rail fencing. Clumps of daffodils created splashes of bright yellow along the neatly trimmed verges.

Horses swathed in rugs trotted up to the fence as the lorry passed by.

Katy turned to her friend, Alice, who was sitting next to her in the lorry cab. "This is so exciting, isn't it?"

"Mm, very," Alice replied. She didn't seem very excited, though, which was odd considering she was about to collect Viking, the fabulous pony her dad had bought for her.

They drove past a large house and into a beautiful stable yard. Several elegant equines watched the visitors with interest from the comfort of their loose boxes.

"Wow!" Katy exclaimed. So this was where people came to buy top-class competition ponies.

"See? I wasn't exaggerating, was I?" Alice said.

Melanie parked the lorry, and they jumped down.

A tall man wearing riding boots, creamy breeches and a fleece jacket walked over to greet them. "Did you have a good trip?" he asked as he shook Melanie's hand.

"Yes, thanks. A slight hold-up on the motorway,

2

but nothing major," Melanie replied. She put her arm around Alice's shoulder. "You remember my daughter, Alice?"

"Of course!"

"And this is her friend, Katy, who often helps out at our riding stables."

"Nice to meet you," he said politely before turning to Alice and grinning. "Excited?"

"Yes," she replied, giving him a dazzling smile that faded too quickly.

"Come on, then. Let's go and tell Viking you're his new owner, shall we?"

Viking was even better in real life than in the photos Alice had shown Katy. Although his body and legs were hidden from view by a royal blue rug and matching travel boots plus tail guard, the quality shone through from his intelligent head to the tip of his tangle-free tail. His recently clipped grey coat shone like silver. Katy couldn't help comparing him with her muddy, hairy ponies back home on Exmoor. She wouldn't have swapped Jacko, Trifle and Tinkerbell for anything, but Viking was proof – if proof were needed – that Alice was racing ahead of her in almost every way.

The two girls had been neighbours and best friends

at primary school, and they'd had a lot of fun riding together. In fact, it was Alice who'd encouraged Katy to start riding in the first place. But now Alice was away at boarding school for most of the year, and in the holidays she often went on exotic trips with her dad or travelled miles to compete in horse shows. She'd be travelling even further now and competing against the best in the country.

The man handed Melanie a large envelope. "Here's all the paperwork," he said. "Passport, five stage vetting, height measurement certificate – fourteen-two exactly, you'll be glad to know – and a few other bits and pieces, including a photo of him jumping at the Horse of the Year Show, which I thought you might like."

"Thanks." Melanie opened the envelope and glanced inside, discreetly checking everything.

"I wish I'd had a father like yours when I was a teenager," the man said to Alice. "Viking is quite some birthday present." He untied the pony's lead rope from a ring on the stable wall. "Well, my lad, we'd better get you loaded before I change my mind about selling you. Time to go and see what Exmoor's like, eh?"

"Rather bleak at the moment, I'm afraid," Melanie said. "It's like the tropics here in comparison. He'll definitely need an extra rug or two with us."

As they walked across the yard, a couple of grooms

called out farewells and good luck messages.

Viking walked up the lorry ramp without a moment's hesitation, like a true professional.

Horses are amazingly trusting, Katy thought. It can't be much fun being trapped in a box on wheels, wondering where you're going to end up. Perhaps he thinks he's off to a competition somewhere. I bet he doesn't realise he's off to a new home.

The return journey took ages. To Katy's amazement, Alice fell asleep almost immediately. She was sure she wouldn't have been able to sleep a wink if it was her new pony in the lorry.

Melanie seemed taken aback by her daughter's lack of enthusiasm as well. She kept making excuses for her, emphasising that Alice was always exhausted when she came back from boarding school.

As they crawled along in a traffic jam, Katy remembered all the times when it had been her ponies in the Stonyford lorry: Trifle's first show at Exford – where she'd bolted out of the Exmoor pony ring and created chaos in the hunter class – travelling to Pony Club competitions and rallies with Jacko and, of course, taking Trifle to Dunster Show . . .

It didn't seem very long ago that Katy had found Trifle on the Common on a freezing cold day at the beginning of April, struggling for survival. Yet the sturdy little mare had a baby of her own now.

Exmoor pony foals were usually born in early spring, but Tinkerbell had done things differently – she'd been born just before Christmas, which had taken everyone by surprise.

Tinks had led a charmed life so far, free from hunger, fear or discomfort of any kind. Her upbringing and outlook on the world were certainly very different from her mother's.

"How are those ponies of yours?" Melanie asked, as if reading her mind.

"Fine, thanks," Katy replied.

"I expect Tinkerbell's grown since I last saw her."

"Yes, Granfer thinks she's going to be taller than Trifle. He says Exmoor foals born on farms are often bigger because they have better food than the ones that grow up on open moorland."

"What your grandfather doesn't know about Exmoor ponies isn't worth knowing, so I'm sure he's right."

"Hm, I hope he's not right about Trifle."

"Oh?"

"He says she's too fat. He says it's always a danger when ponies are taken off the moor because they get too much food and not enough exercise. The trouble is that she seems to get fat on nothing, even though she's feeding a foal."

"Perhaps the moor would be the best place for her, then?"

"No, she hated it when I tried to set her free before."

"Hm, I'd forgotten that."

Katy took a deep breath. Now would be a good time to ask. "Actually, I was wondering whether you'd like to borrow her. Tinks can be weaned in July, so you could have Trifle for the summer holidays when it's really busy at Stonyford."

Melanie's smile was apologetic. "That's a really kind thought, Katy. I love Trifle dearly, but she's too quick-witted to be a riding school pony. She needs a one-to-one relationship with somebody rather than lots of different people coming and going. As you know only too well, we get visitors who haven't a clue about horses, and they can do the silliest things. Riding school ponies need to be phlegmatic."

"Oh, okay, not to worry," Katy said.

But she couldn't help worrying about Trifle for the rest of the journey home.

2

A Moorland Ride

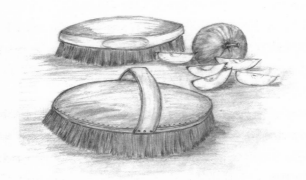

"**Y**ou need to be phlegmatic," Katy told Trifle as she leaned over the stable door and stroked the warm fur on her pony's neck. "No, I didn't know what it meant either, so I looked it up last night. It means thoughtful, reasonable, calm, patient and tolerant. D'you think you can manage to be all those things at once?"

Trifle shook her long forelock away from her eyes and nudged her owner hopefully.

Katy rummaged around in her coat pocket. "One more piece, okay? Even apples can make you fat if you have too many."

A tiny mealy muzzle appeared, whiffling around, straining to get as high as the door.

Katy giggled. "You want some too, do you, Tinks? Cheeky monkey!" She held a thin slice of apple just out of reach. "Hup, then! Hup!"

The little foal reared momentarily onto her hind feet and snatched the treat from Katy's hand.

"What a clever girl!" Katy gave another piece to Trifle so she didn't feel left out. Her phone buzzed in her pocket. She glanced at the screen and smiled. "Hi, Alice!"

"Hi, are you doing anything today?"

"Nope, not really," Katy replied. "I've got some school stuff to do sometime during half term, but it can wait. Actually, I was going to take Jacko out. I haven't ridden him for days. It's so difficult during the winter, isn't it?"

"Yes, I suppose it is," Alice said. She didn't have that problem because there were stables on site at her boarding school and riding lessons were built in to the timetable. "Mum thinks Viking should have the day off to settle in," she continued, "but I could bring Max over so we can go for a ride together, if you like." There was a pause. "Unless you've got anything else planned, of course, in which case I don't mind."

It was the same whenever Alice came back from boarding school. They had to ease back into their old friendship tentatively, like trying on favourite clothes to see if they were still comfortable. A few years ago they would have visited each other's houses without even asking.

"Don't be silly, I'd love you to come for a ride with me!" Katy said. "But we'll have to go steady because Jacko won't be as fit as Max and he hasn't been clipped since November."

"No probs. I feel like having a walkie-talkie ride."

"Great! See you soon – not too soon, though. It'll take me a while to groom my hairy monster."

Jacko took his morning treat politely, his lips barely touching Katy's outstretched hand.

She wrapped her arms around his neck and laid her head against his cheek. His hair, roughened with dried mud, smelled of horse and earth, and the rhythmic sound of his jaws munching travelled as a hollow echo to Katy's ear. Dear, kind Jacko. In the five years they'd been together he'd taught her how to ride, taken her on adventures over the moor and competed successfully at local shows and Pony Club events. In fact, he'd done everything she'd asked with unfailing generosity. They enjoyed the same things: long hacks over the moor, fun rides with friends, inviting-looking jumps lower than a metre, occasional local shows and as little schooling as possible. At fourteen hands high, Jacko was on the small side for a Welsh cob but he was sturdy and well up to weight. Katy hoped she'd never grow out of him.

"I'd better smarten you up a bit," she said, and started rummaging around in the grooming kit bucket that was strategically placed between the two stables. A body brush would be no use at all, and Jacko didn't like the prickly dandy brush, so she chose a rubber currycomb, put a hoof pick in her pocket and entered his stable.

He was, quite literally, plastered from head to hoof. She imagined the smart grooms at Viking's former residence fainting at the sight of him.

Where to begin? She'd start with the places that mattered most, which were where the saddle and bridle would be, and see how far she got . . .

Not as far as she'd hoped. In no time at all, the sound of shod hooves on tarmac announced the arrival of Alice.

Katy kept brushing manically, like a contestant on one of those TV cookery programmes frantically trying to get everything finished in the countdown to stop.

It was hopeless. All she'd succeeded in doing was to convert most of the mud into powder. She could taste the gritty particles in her mouth and feel them up her nostrils. The finer dust hung in the air like fog while the rest settled deeper into Jacko's thick winter coat. He was supposed to be liver chestnut but he looked more like iron grey.

Jacko pushed against the stable door, eager to see who was coming, and then gave a rumbly whinny – the sort he saved for good friends.

11

Glancing up, Katy saw why. "Yes, we're going for a ride with Max. That'll be fun, eh?" she said. The two horses had known each other ever since Jacko had arrived at Stonyford, before Katy's Granfer had bought him as a birthday present for her.

In his prime, Max had been Melanie's top-class show hunter, so he had perfect manners and looked fantastic.

"Katy? Are you okay?" Alice called out, her voice high with alarm.

Katy looked over the stable door. "Yes, fine. Why?"

"There's smoke coming out of Jacko's stable!"

Katy looked behind her at the dense cloud of dust, and started to giggle. "Oh, I see! Don't worry, it's only dust from grooming him."

"Oh, Katy!" Alice exclaimed. "Only you could have a pony that muddy!"

Jacko and Max greeted each other with staccato grunts and a couple of high-pitched squeals. Trifle craned her neck over her door, eager to join in.

Alice moved over to the other stable, but Trifle wasn't at all friendly. She flattened her ears and tried to lunge at Max, teeth bared. Alice made him back away. "Don't be daft, you two! You've met each other loads of times."

"I expect she's trying to protect her foal," Katy said. "I'll bring Jacko out and tie him up to the ring in the wall so you can put Max out of harm's way in here. Then I'll be able to show you Tinks."

Alice did as Katy suggested before entering Trifle's stable. "Oh, Katy! Tinkerbell's gorgeous! How old is she now?"

"Almost exactly two months," Katy said, joining her. "She's really bright. I'm teaching her tricks already. Want to see some?"

"Ooh, yes please!"

"Okay, wait here a sec, I'll just go and get more apples from the kitchen."

Katy dashed back to the farmhouse. She could hear her mum vacuuming upstairs. As it was half term, the farmhouse was fully booked with bed and breakfast guests. Katy scuttled into the kitchen, scooped two apples from the fruit bowl, chopped them into thin slices on the draining board, stuffed them into a plastic bag and scuttled out again.

Back in Trifle's stable, Katy found Alice brushing Tinks, who stood motionless with a blissful look on her face.

"You've found a friend, by the looks of it," Katy said. Why didn't Tinks behave like that with her?

"Mum always says the best way to make friends with a horse is to groom it," Alice said quietly, as if afraid to wake the little foal from her trance. "Seems to be working, doesn't it?"

"Hm, yes." Not to be outdone, Katy said, "She loves having her bottom scratched. It's so sweet, she backs up to me and asks me to do it." She pulled the bag out of her coat pocket. "I got the apples."

Alerted by the familiar rustle, Tinks raised her head, opened her eyes and hurried to the stable door.

Katy had no trouble getting her to perform the rearing-for-apple trick. Then, as Tinks reared up, she took hold of the little foal's hooves and moved around with her for a few steps, as if they were dancing.

"She's like a mini circus pony," Alice said, but she didn't seem to be particularly impressed.

"Wait, there's more." Katy went out of the stable, emptied most of the apple pieces into a bucket but kept a couple in the pocket of her coat, and then went back into the stable again. Holding her hands in the air, she said, "Find it, Tinks!"

The foal homed in on Katy's jacket, snuffling around and then nudging the pocket where the bits of apple were.

"Clever girl!" Katy exclaimed, and gave one piece to her and the other to Trifle.

"Um, do you think it's a good idea to train her with so many titbits?" Alice asked.

Typical Alice – always has to know best, Katy thought. "Apples are okay," she replied. "They're natural and good for her. I never feed her mints or anything – I'm not stupid."

Alice shrugged and said no more.

Anxious to show she knew what she was doing, Katy

demonstrated some other tricks they'd been mastering.

Soon Tinks became rather silly and nippy, like an overexcited child, so the girls decided to go for their ride and leave her to calm down.

They took their favourite route through the fields to the Common above Barton Farm. Once on the open moorland, they were free to go wherever they wanted.

They headed for the hills, riding higher and higher until a vast, glorious landscape spread out before them, with the Bristol Channel and Wales in the distance.

Crystals of crunchy snow lingered among the gnarled, charred heather. A moorland fire had blazed over the Common the previous summer, increasing in intensity as it progressed up the ridge. It was amazing how quickly everything had recovered, though. Within a few weeks, new shoots had pushed up through the wreckage, and the commoners had built a brand-new boundary fence to replace the one taken by the flames. In a year or two it would be hard to tell there'd been a fire at all.

At the top of the ridge they stopped to let Jacko get his breath back. Sweat had turned his dusty winter coat into slick, feathery curls, and he stood steaming in the ice-cool breeze. He'd kept up with Max valiantly, but Max was much larger, hunting fit and clipped out, so he definitely had an unfair advantage.

Alice took a few photos with her phone. "I love this place," she said. "It makes everything else in life seem unimportant, somehow."

"Are you okay?"

Alice looked thoughtful for a moment. "Yes, fine." She flashed Katy an unconvincing smile.

"Sure?"

"Positive."

Katy scanned the moorland below and spotted a cluster of dark dots – the Barton herd of Exmoor ponies. "Oh good, there they are! I was wondering where they'd got to," she said, pointing. "Barton Farm looks perfect from far away, doesn't it? Like a model."

"And there's Stonyford, in the next valley. Our homes seem much closer from up here. You can't see how many gates there are, for a start. Max is so tall that I had to get off for every single one when I rode over to you this morning. I began to wish I was riding Trifle, the best gate-opener in the world."

Katy smiled as she remembered how she'd trained Trifle to stand close to the gate so the latch could be undone, push the gate open with her chest and then turn in a tight circle and stand so the latch could be done up again. Thinking about Trifle made her happy and sad at the same time. They'd grown up together and taught each other so much. It seemed so cruel that Katy had trained her from scratch and, just when they could be having a lot of fun together, she'd grown out of her. "I've been thinking—"

"There's a first time for everything," Alice teased.

Katy made a face. "No, this is serious. I've been thinking about Trifle, and what I should do after Tinks has been weaned. I think I'm going to have to sell her to a good home." Saying it made it real, and Katy had to fight back the tears.

"Oh Katy, I'm sorry. Can't you keep her at the farm and breed more foals from her?"

"Nope. Dad grumbles about me having three ponies. He wouldn't let me collect any more. Anyway, my main problem is that I haven't got enough time to look after three properly and give them the attention they deserve, what with school and everything. Trifle needs plenty of exercise to keep her healthy, and she loves to be out and about, doing things, rather than stuck in a field."

"What about your little cousin, Heather? I started riding when I was her age. I could ride before I could walk, apparently."

"I've already asked Auntie Rachel, but she doesn't want a pony for Heather yet," Katy replied. "She and Mark are expecting another baby."

"Oh dear," Alice said. "I mean, not for them, but for Trifle."

"Hm. I even asked Sharon, because she used to love riding her, but she's got a horse of her own now and she's really busy running the stables at Exford. *And* she's got a new boyfriend; he's a vet somewhere in mid-Devon."

"That's a pity. I mean, not for her—"

"But for Trifle." Katy said, giving Alice a wry smile. "And for me. I really like Sharon."

"Sorry, I haven't been here much either recently – there seems to be so much going on at the moment . . . Never mind, all sorts of things could happen between now and the summer," Alice said. "There's a solution to most problems – the trick is spotting it when it comes along." Max pawed the ground, and she stroked his neck. "I think he's getting cold. Let's move on."

They set off down the hill, letting the horses pick their way on a loose rein over the uneven ground while they chatted away about anything and everything. They even talked about the possibility of doing a long trek over the moors again during the summer holidays – like they had with Melanie a couple of years ago – only this time it would just be the two of them and they'd take a tent so they could camp overnight on Mrs Soames' farm near Withypool.

Katy managed to put Trifle to the back of her mind for a while. It was difficult to worry about the future when they were immersed in the present, relishing every moment as they rode over the astonishingly beautiful moorland.

Alice had been right: it made everything else in life seem unimportant, somehow.

3

The Jumping Lesson

The following morning was taken up with a trip into town for dreary things like the dentist, a haircut and a 'big shop' at the supermarket with Mum. Katy munched a couple of doughnuts and an apple in the car, and as soon as they got home she changed into her outdoor clothes and collected Jacko from the field. It was a raw, windy day, but not actually raining, so she hardened her heart and left Trifle and Tinks pacing around in the field, whinnying for their friend. They'd be better off there than stuck in the stable all afternoon.

Katy gave Jacko a handful of pony nuts in a bucket,

collected the grooming kit and glanced at her watch. Half past two. She'd have to make him as presentable as possible, and it would take at least twenty minutes to ride to Stonyford. There was no time to lose. Melanie was giving Alice a lesson on Viking at three, and Katy had been invited to join in.

Viking arched his neck and walked around the outdoor school with the swagger of a super-fit athlete. Katy followed on Jacko.

"Okay, let's start off with some flat work. Spread yourselves out, and if one of you gets too near the other, circle round so you don't have to break your rhythm," Melanie said, projecting her voice across the outdoor arena. "Sorry about Dean's toys under the tarpaulin at the far end. As soon as he gets the shed cleared out, they're going there. They take up far too much room out here."

Katy wondered what lay under the mound of blue sheeting. *Toys.* If Dean was like Dad and Tom, new toys meant new machinery of some sort . . .

"Ride around the jumps and don't take any notice of them for now," Melanie added.

Jacko settled into a steady walk. Viking bounced along at something between a walk and a trot, barely able to contain himself every time he went near a jump.

"You need to get him listening to you, Alice, so stop him, back up a couple of paces and walk on again."

Alice followed her mum's instructions.

"Now then, let's trot those ponies around and get them loosened up – terrott!"

Jacko recognised the command and shifted up a gear before Katy had given him any aids at all.

What a clever boy, she thought.

"Jacko's had too many lessons from me. He should have waited for you to ask him rather than second-guessing, Katy."

Why did Melanie never miss a thing?

"Right, now that you've both established a rhythm, condense your trot along the ends of the arena and lengthen down the sides. Always be in control before you turn the corner and bend your pony around your inside calf. Alice, you need to keep the balance in your half halts so that Viking's hind legs can step through properly. And Katy, you'll need to ride forward into your corners, otherwise Jacko might use them as an excuse to slow down." Melanie started laying poles down along one side of the arena. "And keep the tempo going over these trotting poles . . ."

Dark brown patches of sweat appeared on Jacko's furry neck. "If it's any consolation, I'm finding this hard work too," Katy whispered to him.

After what seemed like a long time, Melanie said,

"Good, and walk. Let them stretch out on a loose rein while I rearrange a few fences."

Soon a course of four inviting jumps had been built – the sort of thing Katy would have been happy to try with Trifle.

"Can you go and stand outside the arena with Jacko for a moment while Alice and Viking pop round?" Melanie asked.

Pop was the right word. Katy had never seen a pony with so much bounce. Melanie was careful to build up Alice's confidence, first asking her to trot over some poles and a small cross-pole before attempting it in canter. It was odd to see Alice, who'd been fearless over huge obstacles with her old pony, being taught like a beginner. Melanie's cautious approach paid off, though, and before long Alice and Viking were soaring over the cross-pole and a couple of other fences with ease.

"Wow!" Katy said under her breath. Jacko pricked his ears and watched with interest.

"Well done! Much better!" Melanie said.

Alice grinned, stroked her pony's neck and said, "Good boy!" several times.

"Your turn, Katy," Melanie called. "Warm him up with a few transitions and circles, then off you go."

Katy felt a familiar tingle of anticipation as Jacko strode back into the ring, much more lively now he knew he'd be jumping. She loved it when he was like this: keen but always controllable. He bowled around the course like clockwork.

"What a pro," Melanie said. "Go round once more if you like, and then I expect that'll be enough for him."

It was even better the second time. Katy's spirits soared with every fence. They hadn't jumped anything for a month or so; she'd almost forgotten what sheer, undiluted *fun* it was!

"Well done. You make a good team," Melanie said. "If you don't over-face him he'll never let you down."

Katy dismounted, gave him a hug and led him outside the arena to cool off while Alice had another turn.

"Canter him in a circle again to get a good rhythm going while I raise these jumps," Melanie said.

Here comes the serious jumping lesson, Katy thought as she watched the obstacles grow. Definitely outside our comfort zone, Jacko.

"Okay, Alice, now try the whole course: cross-pole, vertical, parallel and then the oxer to finish. Sit tall, land straight and look up to the next fence. Be positive off the corners and don't faff with him too much. Let him jump the jump, and as soon as you land let him travel."

Viking flew over the cross-pole and the vertical jump as if they were twice the size.

"Good. Now shorten him up to go round the corner. Keep looking at the parallel, and count your strides in."

Viking started to fight for his head, eager to tackle the next jump. Alice seemed to give up the unequal struggle and let him go, or perhaps she was trying to let him jump the jump. Whatever the reason, he took off a stride too early, launching himself upwards and outwards with astounding force. By the time he landed, Alice was sitting in front of the saddle, clinging on to his neck. Somehow she managed to heave herself into the right position again, but it didn't look pretty. She'd lost her stirrups and her reins were like skipping ropes. Viking was already locked on to the big oxer, powering towards it, no doubt delighted to see what he considered to be a proper jump.

"Circle! Turn him away!" Melanie shouted.

Too late. Viking kept going and leapt over the oxer as if his life depended on it. Alice didn't have a hope. She was catapulted out of the saddle and landed on the ground like a rag doll, narrowly missing a wing of the jump.

Melanie rushed over to help her while Katy led Jacko back into the arena and attempted to catch Viking. For a while he galloped around, startled and wide-eyed. He even went over the cross-poles again, with no rider and his broken reins dangling. Gradually his gallop slowed to a canter, then a hesitant trot. At last he walked up to

Jacko. Katy grasped the limp reins and stood between the two ponies, saying comforting things in a soothing voice.

Alice struggled to her feet with Melanie's help. "I'm fine. Just winded, that's all," she croaked.

Katy remembered being winded at Pony Club camp when she'd fallen off Trifle. She'd been unable to breathe. It had been horribly scary.

"Wait there. I'll get another pair of reins from the tack room," Melanie said.

Katy looked at her in disbelief as she walked away. "You're not going to get on again today, are you?" she asked her friend.

"Yes, I must. Need to get his trust back. It wasn't his fault. He did everything right. It was me who fluffed it. He took me by surprise. Honestly, it was like riding a rocket!" Alice said, breathing heavily between each short sentence.

The broken reins were taken off Viking's bit and new ones secured somehow while he fidgeted and tossed his head. Still shaky, Alice was given a leg-up onto his back. Although she gave her mum a watery smile, she looked anxious.

Katy's heart went out to her as she stood with familiar, dependable Jacko by her side.

"Okay, Alice, just walk him in circles before doing a few transitions, to get him relaxed and listening to you again." Melanie's voice was reassuring. "Well done. That's really nice. Now, when you're ready, go forward into working trot, establish a good rhythm and then trot over the poles . . . Super . . . Okay, this time around I want you to trot over the poles, circle in trot at the far end of the arena and then trot over those cross-poles I've put up. Don't break that rhythm . . ."

Alice stiffened visibly as she approached the cross-poles, and Viking put in an extra stride before cat-leaping over, as if unsure what to do with such a tiny jump, but Alice managed to stay with him and let the reins slip through her fingers so she didn't jab him in the mouth.

"Well sat!" Melanie said. "Can you do it once more? Try to relax, keep looking up and visualise a perfect jump in your head. I'll count the strides with you . . . That's nice! Keep that rhythm . . . One, two, three . . . *Much* better! Excellent! Let's end on a good note and leave it there." She beamed at Alice. "Good girl. I'm really proud of you."

As Katy rode home over the moor, she thought about the importance of Alice jumping Viking again, and the courage it had taken to do it. She felt full of admiration, and grateful that she hadn't needed to be brave like that with either of her ponies.

4

A Gentle Hack

Perhaps it was the cold wind swirling around the buildings, the fact Jacko was still in his stable, whinnying for his friends, or a sense that her owner was in a hurry, but for the first time ever Tinks ran off, bucking and sprinting in different directions when Katy led Trifle out to the field the following morning. Trifle became anxious and unusually bargy, so Katy let her go in the field and turned her attention to Tinks.

Images from the *First Foal* book Rachel had lent her played in her head, especially the one of two people guiding a thoroughbred foal to a field with a folded towel looped round its chest and their hands linked around its bottom while a third person led its calm mother in front. As far as she could remember, the caption was something like: *Competent assistants are essential when handling the young foal. A folded stable rubber or tea towel can be used to guide it out to the field if the weather is good.*

The weather isn't good and I haven't got any assistants, competent or otherwise, Katy thought as she tried to corner her rebellious young foal. But you'll have to go in that field whether you like it or not because you can't stay inside all day.

Eventually Tinks ran back into her stable. Katy took Jacko's head collar and put it on the foal as Granfer had shown her, with the noseband around the base of her neck and the long strap around her tummy so it fitted like a body harness. There seemed to be lots of conflicting advice about handling foals, but one thing everyone said was that if they pulled back while wearing a head restraint when young they could damage their necks forever. Katy wasn't sure when a foal stopped being young, but she didn't want to risk putting a foal slip on Tinks just yet.

Trifle was going ballistic out in the field and Jacko wasn't helping by answering her urgent whinnies every time, but at least Katy could now control Tinks – sort of. She bounced out to the field, apparently infuriated by the unfamiliar power over her. Once in the field, it was all Katy could do to hold her for long enough to release the buckles, and as soon as she was free she dashed off.

Katy didn't have time to watch and worry. She brushed away the remains of Jacko's dried sweat, picked out his hooves, tacked him up and went. Perhaps she'd work out a good plan for handling Tinks as she rode to Stonyford. She often had her best ideas while riding.

As it turned out, the main thing she thought about as she battled to open gates with the wind against her was that she should have taken the longer, more sheltered route via the road. By the time she reached Stonyford she was wet, muddy and no further forward with a plan of action.

Melanie was in the yard with Viking, who was tacked up and impatient to get going. "Do you mind riding out again, Katy?" she asked.

"No, of course not."

"I'd go myself, but I've got a ten-thirty lesson booked and Dean's taking out a two-hour ride. It really would be a great help – just to settle Viking and stretch his legs before the journey. We're dropping him off at Alice's school on the way, you see. She'll be going straight there from her father's, as he lives so near." She looked towards the house. "What on earth is Alice *doing?* Rupert! Can you go and find your sister? Katy's waiting for her."

Rupert sauntered over to the house.

"Run!" Melanie called after him. "What is the matter with everyone this morning?" She stroked Viking's nose. "You seem to be the only one with any get-up-and-go today, don't you?"

Alice emerged from the house, walking stiffly from her fall the previous day.

"It'll be good for you to loosen up with a gentle hack," Melanie said brightly as Alice reached them. "Take a safe, sheltered route, like around the lanes to Wellsworthy and back."

Even the mention of Wellsworthy made Katy feel tingly.

Alice did look rough. Her normally pretty face had a puffy bruise on one cheek and a swollen lower lip – she must have bitten it as she fell.

"Nice day for a ride," Katy said jokily.

"Here, I'll give you a leg-up," Melanie said as she pulled Viking's stirrups ready for Alice to get on. "One, two, three . . ."

Riding instructors must spend their lives counting to three, Katy thought.

As soon as Alice landed in the saddle, Viking was off, dancing out of the yard. Alice found her stirrups quickly and managed to control him. Even though she was obviously sore, she sat beautifully.

"Let Jacko go first. Just walk!" Melanie called after them.

"Okay!" Katy replied over her shoulder, but Melanie had already turned away to greet some visitors.

Viking didn't like following Jacko. He cantered on the spot with his neck arched and ears back, occasionally giving a frustrated buck.

Katy kept glancing behind, hoping he'd settle down. "Would you prefer to be in front?" she asked.

"I don't dare; not at the moment, anyway," Alice said breathlessly.

She really is an excellent rider, Katy thought. But I wouldn't want to swap ponies for anything.

They drew near to some cattle behind a gate, bellyaching for food.

"Hello, hasn't Tom fed you yet?" Katy asked as she rode by.

There was a rumble in the distance. As it came closer, Katy recognised the noise of the engine. "Just our luck!" she muttered, and with that the Barton Farm tractor appeared, carrying a big round silage bale. Ribbons of plastic had peeled off the bale and were flapping erratically in the wind.

Jacko stood still, unconcerned but awaiting instructions.

Katy knew that if Tom had seen them he'd have

stopped and turned the engine off. Her big brother wasn't at all horsey, but he wasn't stupid – not when it mattered, anyway.

The tractor kept coming . . .

"Quick! Follow me," she said to Alice, turning Jacko around and trotting back to an open gate she'd noticed as they'd gone by. Granfer had taught her to make a mental map of things like possible escape routes when out riding, and it was amazing how often it came in useful.

Tom ground to a halt by the entrance to the field and opened the door of the tractor cab. "Hi, girls! How are you getting on?" he shouted above the sound of the wind whipping streamers of silage wrap into a frenzy.

Viking snorted and ran backwards, threatening to rear, but Alice sat still and managed to stop him.

"Go on, Tom!" Katy yelled.

"What?" Tom climbed out of the cab and came across to them.

Viking shied away, pirouetting on his haunches. He looked as if he'd explode with pent-up energy at any minute. The field was huge. If he decided to bolt there'd be no stopping him.

"I like your horse, Alice. He looks proper," Tom said, and winked. "Not like Katy's boring old donkey."

Katy refused to rise to the bait. "The tractor's upsetting the ponies," she said.

Tom looked surprised. "Okay, bossy boots. Sorry for being sociable. Bye, Alice. Good to see you – *briefly*." He walked away, climbed back into the tractor and drove off.

They walked on and, after a while, managed to ride side by side so they could talk. But just as Viking had really begun to relax, some mountain bikers in day-glo clothing appeared around a bend, their wheels making a whooshing noise on the wet tarmac.

Viking stopped dead, snorted and tried to turn for home. When Alice checked him, he reared up, his hind shoes slipping precariously as he nearly overbalanced. She clung on, leaning forward and letting the reins go slack to give him the best chance of recovery.

Katy jumped off Jacko and held on to Viking while Alice dismounted.

"Sorry!" the first cyclist said. "We didn't realise. Would it help if we walked?"

"Worth a try," Katy said.

Obligingly, the cyclists got off their bikes and pushed them, one by one, past the ponies, nearly falling in a ditch in their efforts to keep as far away as possible.

"Thank you so much! My friend's pony is very young. We're just breaking him in," Katy said.

"Since when was ten very young?" Alice asked after the bikes had disappeared from view.

"I had to say *something*." Katy studied her friend. "Are you okay?"

"Bit wobbly."

"We can go back, if you like."

"Hm, we might meet the tractor. Let's lead the ponies as far as Wellsworthy and wait in the yard for Tom to go by."

"Good idea."

They set off again, with Alice and Viking following Katy and Jacko for safety. After a while they turned left into the lane to Wellsworthy and Barton Farm.

Alice brought Viking alongside. He made a face at Jacko and tried to forge ahead, but Alice checked him. "I wish we could still be at primary school, doing Pony Club and local shows together," she said suddenly. "We had so many laughs, didn't we?"

Katy smiled. "Yes, good times."

Alice attempted a smile in return, but she looked close to tears.

Katy longed to say something like, "It's no fun having a pony you're afraid of riding. Perhaps it isn't too late to send Viking back." She didn't know how to word it tactfully, though.

A collie dog rushed down the lane to greet them, tail wagging. For a brief heart-stopping moment Katy thought he was Greg's sheepdog, Jed, but almost immediately she realised he belonged to a builder whose van was parked outside Wellsworthy.

"Dean's giving the place a makeover before the new people move in," Alice explained.

"Wow, he hasn't wasted much time! Who are they?"

"The family of an old friend of Dean's. The husband's a helicopter pilot, so it'll be his wife and child living here mainly. Anyway, they can't wait to move from London, so everything fitted in really well with Greg leaving." She noticed Katy's expression. "Sorry, that came out all wrong – *stupid* me."

Alice knew better than anyone how much Katy adored Greg, even though he was ten years older and obviously thought of her in the same way as a little sister.

When Greg had moved into Wellsworthy just before Christmas, it had been like a dream come true for Katy. For a while each day had brought with it the happy possibility of seeing him by chance, especially as she had to pass by Wellsworthy to get to the main road where she caught the school bus. He'd intended to set up a business at the old farm, but planning permission had been refused and shortly afterwards he'd been offered a well-paid job on an estate in Wiltshire. It was an opportunity everyone had said he'd be a fool to miss – everyone except Katy. Life had definitely lost some of its sparkle without Greg around.

"It's odd to think that two years ago Dean was

living here – and he hadn't even met Mum then. Now they're married and it seems as if he's been with us forever," Alice said as they stood in the yard waiting for Tom's tractor to go by. Their ponies homed in on the grass around the edge of the yard, and ate it hungrily.

Katy smiled. "I remember the first time I met Dean. It was just up the lane there. I was riding Trifle, and she hadn't been broken in for long. She was horrified when she saw the removal van, and even more horrified when Dean came up to say hello in his super-cool sunglasses and leather jacket. First he insulted her by calling her a *Shetland*."

Alice giggled.

"And then he gave her a walloping great pat so she nearly jumped out of her skin!"

Alice looked amazed. "But he's always the one who tells the visitors to stroke the horses rather than pat them. Ha! I'll have to tease him about that. Mum says he's got 'the zeal of a convert' where horses are concerned. Even she's worn out by his enthusiasm sometimes. He's into all the modern ideas – natural horsemanship and stuff. Mum calls it hippy horsemanship, which makes him cross. He says she should be more open-minded. Horse agility's the latest thing. That's what all the equipment in our arena's about."

"Oh, you mean the toys under the tarpaulin!" Katy exclaimed.

"Yes, that's another thing: Dean says if hoops and seesaws are toys then show jumps are too."

Tom rattled by in the tractor.

"Hoops and seesaws really *do* sound like playground equipment, though," Katy said. "What on earth is horse agility, anyway?"

"Well, you've heard of dog agility?"

"Yes, the dog whizzes around an obstacle course while its owner runs along giving instructions. I love watching it on TV at Christmas time when they have highlights from the horse show at Olympia."

"Brilliant, isn't it? Well, horse agility's like that, but with horses."

Katy looked at her, amazed. "But you'd have to use a head collar and lead rope, wouldn't you? I mean, you couldn't get a horse to follow you and do obstacles running free, like a dog?"

"That's the goal, yes," Alice said. "You start off doing groundwork exercises, then you lead the horse round the obstacles and then, after a lot of practice, you do it without anything on at all."

"Ooh, really?" Katy said in mock surprise, and started laughing.

Alice realised what she'd said, and soon both girls were in fits of giggles. "Not the *handler* – the horse, you numpty!" she said eventually. "Apparently it's becoming really popular all over the world – like a whole new sport. And there's no need to travel to competitions because they're judged by video. Dean's got a book that explains it all. I'm sure he'd lend it to you."

"Thanks," Katy replied, not really intending to do anything about it. She had enough going on at the moment without trying to learn anything new, especially if it took a lot of practice. "D'you think we ought to get going, if you're leaving after lunch?"

Alice nodded. She drew the reins over Viking's head and guided him away from the grass, ready to mount.

"I don't mind walking and leading, if you'd prefer," Katy said.

"Thanks, but I'd better ride." Alice winced. "Standing still and getting cold aren't great for bruised muscles, are they?"

"Here, I'll give you a leg-up." Katy got Alice onto Viking, and mounted Jacko. Then they set off back down the lane towards Stonyford.

Viking seemed much more settled now, which made Alice more relaxed and talkative.

"That was quick! Look, we're nearly there," Katy said as they passed the field with the open gate where they'd taken refuge from the tractor.

"All's well that ends well," said Alice.

But she spoke too soon. It began to rain: spots, then large drops and then an ice-cold deluge, blown head-on by the wind.

Jacko walked on with dogged determination, while Viking tucked his chin into his chest and skittered about, trying to wheel round and protect his head from the onslaught.

"So much for a quiet hack!" Alice said, cantering sideways past Jacko. "Thank goodness for sticky bum jods!"

Katy couldn't help laughing, although her heart was in her mouth at the thought that a vehicle could appear around the corner at any moment.

Luckily, they only encountered a lady wearing an inadequate waterproof coat, walking a dog that appeared to be too miserable to take much notice of anything.

The squall stopped as quickly as it had started, but Viking was shaking.

Alice stroked his bare, slippery neck. "Poor chap. Exmoor must be a terrible shock for him."

"And he hasn't even seen the wild part yet," Katy said.

5

Horse Agility

Melanie, Alice and the twins left Stonyford after lunch. Viking was in the back of the lorry, cocooned in his padded rug, travel boots and tail guard. Katy felt happy for him. He'd be going to a place he understood – a carefully controlled environment where he'd be pampered and expected to jump things.

Alice waved through the rain-spattered window.

"Good luck!" Katy called, waving back. "Keep in touch!"

The lorry drove away, and soon all she could hear

were the sounds of horses munching and rainwater trickling.

Dean looked at a text message on his phone. "The people booked in for a moorland ride this afternoon have cancelled. Can't say I blame them, even though the weather's improving."

"I'll still muck out a few stables before I ride home, if you like," Katy said. That had been the original plan.

"It's really kind of you, but I don't see why you should," he replied.

"I don't mind, honest."

"Well, if you're sure . . . It'll mean I'll have time to do some horse agility with Max. I promised Mel I'd move the equipment to the old hay shed today."

"Fine. I'll just check Jacko's okay and then I'll get to work," Katy said.

Jacko didn't even look up as Katy walked into his stable. He was too busy eating the top-quality haylage that Melanie bought in for her horses. At Barton Farm he had to make do with homemade hay. Katy put her hand underneath his cooler rug. He felt dry and warm.

He turned his head to nuzzle her briefly, then carried on chomping, making the most of every second.

By the time Katy had gathered together a wheelbarrow, dung fork and yard brush, Dean was already pulling equipment out from under the tarpaulin while Max wandered around the outdoor school without any tack on – not even a head collar.

She glanced in the direction of the arena every time she went to the muck heap, fascinated by what she saw. Some of the stuff was quite ordinary – traffic cones, poles, a small tarpaulin and a couple of plastic hoops arranged on the ground – but there was also a giant inflatable ball, a circular jump made from what looked like drainage pipe, and an archway supporting a curtain of ribbons that fluttered in the wind. Katy put down the wheelbarrow and watched in amazement as Max followed Dean through the curtain without a moment's hesitation. Trifle would never, ever go through something like that! Her two least favourite things were narrow spaces and anything flapping.

By the time Katy had finished the row of stables, some flags, a large wooden seesaw and an A-frame with a wide, non-slip surface had been added to the assortment of obstacles that littered the arena. She could see why Melanie called them toys; they looked much too fun to be serious equipment.

Katy looked at her watch. If they set off soon she'd have plenty of time to muck out her own stables and get the ponies settled before dark.

She tacked up Jacko and led him out. Dean was heading for the seesaw, with Max walking freely at his shoulder as if connected by an invisible thread . . . She had to see this!

Max hardly missed a beat. He put his head down to take a good look at the seesaw, stepped onto it, calmly kept going as it reached the point of balance and walked off the end when it had tipped the other way.

Katy looped her arm through Jacko's rein and tried to clap, but with riding gloves on it didn't make much sound. "Brilliant!" she called out.

Dean beckoned her over. "Want to have a go with Jacko?"

"Can I? Really? Without tack or anything, like Max?"

"Er, you could try, but I expect you'll need a head collar and lead rope to begin with. Max had to learn to work at liberty – it didn't happen overnight." Dean collected Max's head collar from the gatepost. "I'll put him back in his stable and grab a head collar for Jacko, okay?"

Katy led Jacko into the arena, took off his tack and put it on the gate. He was usually pretty good, and it would be so lovely to impress Dean . . .

She walked a few steps, hoping Jacko would follow, but he just stood still and stared as if to say, "Are you mad? I thought we were going home."

"Come on, there's a good boy!" Katy said in what she hoped was an encouraging voice. She held out her hand and then tapped her thigh. "Come here, good boy!"

Jacko put his head down and pawed the sandy surface of the arena.

How can I get him to understand? Katy wondered. I know! Trying her best to sound like Melanie, she called, *"Terrott! Good boy, come on, Terrott!"* and ran away from Jacko with exaggerated high steps. Glancing behind to see if he was following, she saw him crumpling onto the ground. She stopped and glared in disbelief as he rolled vigorously, got up and snorted with pleasure. Then he walked over to Dean, who was now standing by the gate with a head collar and long lead rope in his hand.

You infuriating pony! Katy thought. So much for showing Dean what a strong bond we've got. He must think I'm an idiot, trotting off by myself like that!

Dean buckled the head collar. "Okay, let's start with a few basics. Horse agility's all about good two-way communication between horse and handler."

"I was trying to show him what to do, but he just wasn't listening," Katy said defensively. "I think he knows me too well, because he always obeys Melanie when she tells him to trot."

"Jacko adores you," Dean replied. "Anyone can see that. But you've still got a long way to go before you know each other well enough to do horse agility at liberty. He wasn't being uncooperative just then; he simply had no idea what you wanted him to do." He smiled. "Think about it from his point of view. When you lead him into an open place, remove his saddle and bridle and set him free, what does that usually mean?"

"Well, it's usually in a field, and at home, and it means he's off duty, I suppose." Katy realised what Dean was getting at. "Oh, and the first thing he does is roll – always."

Dean nodded. "And what do you do when you want to catch him?"

"I just go to the field with his head collar. I never have to go in and catch him, though. He always comes as soon as he sees me." Katy paused. "I think I see what you mean," she said slowly. "You came to the gate with a head collar, so he came to you. He wasn't trying to snub me by going to you rather than me; he was doing what he usually does." She stroked Jacko's neck. "Oh, it's so *frustrating*. It's like the more time I spend with horses, the more I realise I don't know anything!"

"Only ignorant people think they know it all," Dean commented. "If you're willing to keep learning you'll find each new discovery leads to another and another. Don't let it frustrate you – it's what makes life so fascinating and fun." He handed Katy the lead rope. "Loop it to and fro, so you can let it out easily without getting your hand caught. You'll need to give Jacko room to work at a safe distance."

The rope was about twice as long as the ones Katy

was used to. She liked the heavy, pliable feel of it.

"You'll find it easier to communicate clearly but softly with this," Dean told her. "Remember, you've got to be able to understand each other really well before you can do things at liberty together. Try to learn as much as possible about Jacko so you can read his body language easily. Be clear in your body language, too. And if you use words, make sure they always mean the same thing."

Surely that's obvious, Katy thought.

"For instance, if you praise him when he does something right by saying, 'Good boy', try to avoid saying it as encouragement when you want him to be a good boy."

Katy remembered what she'd done a few moments earlier, and felt herself blushing. "Oops, sorry."

"Don't worry, it's surprisingly common. I've noticed the vet says it when she's about to give one of our horses an injection. It's lucky she doesn't come here often, because they'd soon associate the word 'good' with being jabbed!"

Katy smiled. Somehow Dean managed to point out mistakes without making her feel bad. She wished some of the teachers at school were more like him.

The next thirty minutes or so were spent finding out about things Katy had never rated as particularly important: the best way to lead Jacko – on a loose rope with his head in line with her shoulder – and all sorts of groundwork exercises she'd never encountered before, like getting him to lower his head or bend it round, and asking him to move without using the rope at all.

By the time they called it a day, Katy realised that horse agility was much more than just games, even though it was great fun. She'd been shown a whole new way of thinking about horses, and there was so much more to discover.

As she rode home in the fading light, buzzing with enthusiasm, she could hardly wait until she'd be able to have another lesson with Dean. The only trouble was that by tomorrow morning all the horse agility equipment would be stored away in the shed at Stonyford. What a waste.

6

The Trouble With Tinkerbell

With half term nearly over and lots of homework to do, plus meeting her school friends in town on Saturday, Katy's intentions to practise her new skills with Jacko every day didn't come to much.

There was even less time to do things with the ponies once school started again. Two hours every day were spent on the bus, and the teachers seemed to be piling on the work all of a sudden. The word *exams* cropped up far too often for Katy's liking.

Alice kept in touch regularly. She always seemed to be worrying about something, whether it was a show jumping competition, the school play, exams or the incomprehensible twists and turns of her friendships. Katy felt grateful she had a bunch of school friends she could rely on. They were the quiet ones in her class: the unremarkable, uncomplicated lot who attracted little attention and did their own thing. Katy's school life was more tedious than stressful. For Alice it seemed to be the other way around.

Anyone looking at recent posts on Alice's Facebook page would have thought she led a charmed life. There were photos of Viking jumping, lots of glamorous school friends and a weekend in London with her dad and the twins. Scrolling down, Katy featured too, looking rather less glamorous on an unclipped, sweaty Jacko as they paused for breath on the Common, with Max's elegant ears and neatly pulled mane in the foreground and a stunning view of Exmoor in the background. Alice had written the comment *A fab ride with Katy*. Hardly any of Alice's friends had liked it. They'd probably wondered who Katy was.

Most of Katy's photos were of Tinkerbell looking adorable. They always got masses of likes and comments, especially from Alice. She asked after Tinks regularly, and Katy told her she was "thriving" or "fine".

Well, it was sort of true; health-wise she was fine. It

was her behaviour that wasn't at all fine. In fact, as she grew larger it was getting downright dangerous.

Katy had only ever shown Tinks kindness and love, yet she was becoming the worst-behaved pony she'd ever met! Nothing seemed to work – not even her newly acquired groundwork skills for horse agility. Tinks didn't respond to subtle, soft cues. Actually, she didn't respond to anything much, unless it involved something to eat. She bit, reared up whenever she felt like it, kicked and barged like a playground bully. In desperation, Katy tried pretty well everything she could think of, including slapping the foal's nose if she nipped. Tinks reacted by nipping quickly and then pulling away, as if it were a game.

Trifle had never been a problem like this, although she hadn't been handled by anyone until she was weaned. She'd been scared of people for ages, and she was still wary of people she didn't know, but she'd always been well-mannered. In fact, looking back on it, she'd been pretty easy to train.

Katy was too embarrassed to tell anyone about the problems she was having – least of all Alice, who'd probably been right about those titbits.

Instead, she began to search the Internet for advice. Everyone seemed to be in agreement that you should be patient, persistent, kind, gentle and consistent. Easier said than done, Katy thought. She trawled through endless success stories, hoping to discover useful nuggets of advice. There were plenty of accounts of how people had turned fearful, abused rescue horses around, transforming them into prize-winning mounts or dependable family friends. But Tinks had never been abused – unless you counted a few taps on the nose to warn her against nipping – and she didn't appear to be afraid of anything.

Katy, on the other hand, was becoming afraid of Tinks. It was impossible to ignore a nagging feeling that she was out of her depth where foal training was concerned. She needed help from someone she trusted – someone with lots of experience, who knew how to handle foals . . .

It was almost the Easter holidays before she finally asked Granfer, and even then it took a bit of encouragement on his part.

Rachel and Mark had brought Heather over for Sunday lunch, as it was her first birthday, but they'd had to leave immediately afterwards because they were already lambing on their farm. Dad and Tom had gone outside as well. Lambing at Barton Farm was due to start soon, so there was lots of work to do. Katy and Granfer were washing up while Mum and Gran chatted in the sitting room.

"I forgot to say, we passed a removals lorry in the lane. Looks like the new people at Wellsworthy are moving in," Granfer said.

"Oh, right."

"Come from London. A woman and her child, by all accounts."

"Yes, Alice told me." Katy didn't really care who was going to be living there if it wasn't Greg.

They worked on in silence for a while. Katy stacked the dishwasher while Granfer cleaned the pots and pans.

With the final saucepan put away, Granfer asked, "How's your youngster getting on?" He hardly ever called horses by their names. It fitted with the slightly detached, down-to-earth way in which he treated them.

"She's lovely. Cheeky, but lovely."

Granfer's wise eyes met Katy's. "Hm, cheeky as in badly behaved?"

She laughed nervously. "Yes, sometimes. I was going to ask you what to do about it."

"No time like the present. Let's go and take a look at her."

The ponies were at the far end of the field, grazing on the first shoots of spring grass.

Katy called to them. Tinks gave a shrill whinny

and cantered over to the gate, where she put her head on one side and pushed her muzzle between the bars, nibbling Katy's hand when she tried to stroke her.

"Hello, gorgeous," Katy said, pleased that she'd come so readily. Granfer was bound to be impressed.

"Feed her a lot of titbits, do you?" he asked.

"Only sometimes."

Tinks pulled back, kicked her heels and sped over to her mum, who was ambling over with Jacko.

"What have you just taught her?" Granfer asked.

"To come when she's called," Katy said proudly.

"After that."

Katy felt put out. "Um?"

"It looks to me like you've taught her to take you or leave you, on her terms."

"But I can't do much to stop that, can I? Unless I put a head collar on her in the field, and you always say I should never leave head collars on because they can get caught up in things and cause terrible injuries:" Katy heard her voice rising with indignation.

"There's no need to catch her. Just be the first one to walk away, while she's still interested," Granfer said. "You're in charge; you must be the one who walks away first. You've got to train her, not the other way round. Things she learns now will last a lifetime. It's much easier to start as you mean to go on than break a habit later. Kinder, too."

Granfer was right, Katy realised. She thought about Tinks, and how she was now rearing up and expecting a titbit rather than waiting for Katy's cue. Tinks was training *her*, slowly but surely, and she hadn't realised it. Did she really want a grown mare who mugged people for titbits or kicked out if they didn't scratch her bottom when she backed up to them?

All the ponies were by the gate now, side by side.

"Hey! That's no way to treat your mum!" Katy exclaimed as Tinks nipped Trifle's neck. "Don't let her get away with it, Trifle, bite her back!"

Trifle nudged her foal affectionately.

Granfer propped his stick up and leaned on the gate. "It doesn't help that she's the spoilt first-born. That mare won't be so tolerant after she's had a few foals."

"Jacko never tells her off, either," Katy said. "It's so sweet – he's like an adoring uncle. They play together, but he always gives in to her. He's a true gentleman."

"Hm, a herd's the best place for a foal," Granfer said. "Siblings to play with and plenty of adults to teach right from wrong. It's hard for youngsters to get above themselves in a herd."

Like in a big family, Katy thought. There's always someone to put you in your place, or help you if you need it.

"In many ways a tame foal is more tricky to train than a newly weaned sucker from the moor," Granfer added. "It misses out on all that education from its own kind. And foals that are handled a lot from the start have no inbuilt fear of people. In fact, sometimes they end up wondering whether they're horse or human, I fancy."

Tinks tried to nip his hand as it rested on the gate. He waved his arms. "Back up! Back up!" he growled, staring her in the eye.

She stepped backwards, amazed, and then came towards him again, as if sure there'd been some mistake.

"Back up!" he said again firmly, waving her away.

She stood a few paces away from the gate, licking her lips.

"That's better. She learns quick, I'll give her that," he said.

"But I want her to love me – I don't want to scare her away," Katy protested.

"You weren't looking, were you? Not properly," Granfer said. "As soon as she did as I asked, I stopped asking. That's the opposite of being scary – that's creating rules, and rules make us feel secure. Love isn't enough. You need to set boundaries as well. She'll be much happier for it."

Katy began to see what he was getting at. "Hm, I suppose so."

Granfer put his hand on her shoulder. "Look at it this way: if your mum and dad had let you do whatever you wanted, you'd have been in a fair mess by now, wouldn't you? They've taught you right from wrong and the good manners that make you a nice person to be with."

Katy smiled and gave a little bow.

"Your foal hasn't got a herd to teach her how to behave, but she's got you. You're the leader of this little herd, and like any good leader you must stick by the rules you make. The first lesson this filly must learn is to respect your space and move when you ask her to. Everything else will follow. If you're firm and fair, she'll love you for it; if you're not, she'll walk all over you."

7

James

S oon it was the first day of April and Katy's birthday. Trifle's too, of course.

"I can't believe it was six years ago that I found you on the Common, all wet and new," Katy said as she watched Trifle tuck into a horsey birthday treat of apples, carrots and a few pony nuts.

Chomp, chomp, chomp!

"You were so tiny and cold that nobody thought you'd survive. But you proved us wrong, didn't you? I wasn't really interested in ponies until that moment, you know. You've got a lot to answer for, my beautiful Trifle."

At the mention of her name, Trifle lifted her head from the feed bucket and studied Katy with her large amber eyes.

Tinks had been nursing from her mum, but now that she'd drunk her fill she came up to say hello. Katy stroked her before walking away to make a fuss of Jacko. He'd already scoffed his share of the birthday meal. Tinks stayed by the stable door, eager for more attention, so Katy picked up her birthday present from Granfer – a brand new head collar with red webbing, brass buckles and a matching lead rope – and went into the stable.

"Look what Granfer's given you!" she said. "We needn't use Jacko's head collar as a baby harness any more."

Tinks sniffed the shiny new gadget, explored it with her lips and stood quietly while Katy adjusted the buckles so it fitted snugly. She tilted her head and tried to nip Katy's hand, but Katy managed to carry on regardless, as Granfer had told her to.

"You do look grown up," she said, thinking that Tinks wasn't much smaller than Trifle had been at six months old. Trifle, however, had taken ages to realise that a head collar wasn't a terrifying instrument of torture. Yes, there were definite advantages to handling foals from birth.

Trifle's faded, worn head collar and mud-coloured

lead rope looked particularly shabby alongside her daughter's as Katy led them out to the field, one in each hand. She set them free – Tinks first, then Trifle, went back to get Jacko, put him in the field as well and then went inside for an extra-special birthday breakfast.

"Has Alice come home for the holidays yet?" Mum asked as she handed Katy a warm plate of bacon and eggs.

Katy shook her head. "Nope. She's doing work experience with her godmother, who's a vet in Newmarket."

"Goodness, that sounds very grand."

"It is. She specialises in racehorses."

"Alice wants to be an equine vet, then?" Dad said.

"Yes, I think so."

"I imagine she'd do well at that," Mum said. "She's good with people as well as animals, and that's so important."

Dad poured himself another cup of tea. "You need first-class exam results, though. Apparently even if you get straight A grades there's no guarantee of a place to train nowadays."

"Which is why she's trying to get as much experience as possible, even though it means she'll hardly have any time at home," Katy said. "Afterwards she's going to stay with her dad and then she's off to some sort of show jumping clinic."

"How's she getting on with that pony of hers?" Dad asked.

"Much better now, I think, although they were eliminated at an inter-schools competition the other day. Viking's such a perfectionist that if anything goes wrong he loses his confidence and starts refusing."

"I thought he was supposed to be the best of the best."

"He is. He's like a show jumping genius when everything goes right, but he's so highly strung that he tends to have hissy fits when things go wrong. That's why Alice is going to have the extra lessons with a top show jumper, to prepare for POYS."

"Poys sounds like a disease – the sort of thing a sheep might get," Tom said.

Katy laughed. "It stands for Pony Of the Year Show. It's a big show jumping event over the Easter weekend. She said she's dreading it because her mum *and* her dad are going to be there. Poor Alice, there's always something stressing her out."

"Huh, she should try being a farmer, with nearly six hundred ewes to lamb down," Tom replied.

And the conversation inevitably turned to lambing.

After breakfast, Katy mixed some powdered milk with warm water and poured it into bottles with screw-on teats. Year by year, she was being given more jobs on the farm. The orphan lambs were now her responsibility, and she took great care over them, sometimes spending hours teaching a frail one to suck. As she frequently had to explain to their guests, most of the lambs weren't actually orphans but the weakest member of a twin or triplet, so they were often small and vulnerable. They had to be fed at least every four hours when they were little – it was almost a full-time occupation.

"You going up to the lambing shed, Tom?" she asked hopefully, looking into the kitchen.

He groaned, got up and stretched. "Suppose so. A few days in, and I'm knackered already. I'll give you a lift up on the quad bike, if you like."

On the way, Tom stopped to let the two sheepdogs out of their kennel. Sky immediately jumped onto the back of the vehicle, where she stood poised and ready for action. Moss, her mother, clambered onto Katy's lap.

Katy hugged her close as they sped up the track, a milk bottle clasped in each hand.

When they reached the shed, Moss stayed with Katy.

There were only a couple of lambs to feed but they

were both hungry, which was a good sign. If they went off their feed it usually meant they were poorly, and an ill lamb without immunity from its mother's milk was difficult to cure.

"There! All gone," she said with satisfaction as both bottles were sucked dry and the lambs tottered off to curl up under the warm glow of the infrared light in the corner.

The wind had got up and a fine, misty rain was falling when Katy left the shed. *Typical! It could have stayed dry for a little while longer.* She looked at her watch – just over an hour to wash, get changed, walk to the bus stop and catch the bus into town to meet her friends. Not much time to spare.

Moss followed her back towards the farmhouse, but as they drew near she peeled away and ran off.

"Moss! Here!" Katy called several times, but it made no difference.

There was the sound of barking. Something wasn't right. She put the bottles down in the lee of a wall, so they wouldn't blow away, and ran to see what was the matter.

She found Moss standing between a boy and the ponies' field, blocking his way. He was small and thin

– about eight years old, at a guess – and he was holding his hands over his ears while rocking to and fro.

"That'll do, Moss! Here!" Katy said sternly.

The collie came reluctantly.

"Good girl. Stay!"

Moss lay with her belly pressed to the ground, eyeing the boy as if he were a stray sheep.

"Don't worry about the dog, she won't hurt you," Katy said as she approached him.

He carried on rocking and staring at the ground.

"I'm Katy. What's your name?"

He didn't even look up.

She put her hand on his shoulder, and he flinched away as if she'd given him an electric shock. For some reason it reminded her of how Exmoor ponies from the moor reacted to being touched. She was wondering what to do next when she heard voices. Looking up, she saw Mum hurrying towards her with a small, dark-haired woman by her side.

The woman knelt down in front of the boy, and hugged him. "Oh, James! You can't go wandering off like this. We've been looking for you everywhere!"

"Olivia and James popped in to say hello just after you left to feed the lambs. They've moved into Wellsworthy," Mum explained to Katy in a half-whisper. "James has autism."

Katy wasn't too sure what that meant. She wondered

how much he understood and whether he ever said anything.

The ponies had come over to take a look at the people gathered by their field.

Olivia glanced up at them, then smiled at Katy. "James is like a moth attracted to a light bulb where horses and ponies are concerned."

"Does he ride?"

"Not any more. He used to – at our local Riding for The Disabled centre – and he got on really well, but we made the mistake of letting him go pony trekking when we were on holiday. They all went too fast, and James tumbled off and hurt himself. He's refused to ride ever since. Melanie very kindly said he could go and spend time with a pony they've got at Stonyford, Misty—"

"Dear old Misty! I learned to ride on him," Katy said.

"The idea was to get his confidence back, but sadly it had the opposite effect," Olivia continued. "There was too much going on there – lots of people, horses and noise. I think the thing that triggered his panic attack, though, was Misty being grey."

What colour do you expect a pony called Misty to be? Katy thought.

"You see, James was riding a grey pony exactly like him when he had his accident."

"Rachel, my aunt, told me horses seem to focus on details like that," Katy said. "When she was in Australia she worked with a horse who'd been treated badly by a man wearing a leather bush hat. Apparently it was fine with everybody except people wearing leather bush hats. She says a horse's behaviour can seem illogical if you don't know what's happened to it in the past, but there's always a reason."

"How fascinate—" Olivia's reply was cut short as James broke away and ran towards the ponies. "James! No, wait!" she shouted.

Katy ran too, but before she could stop him he'd scrambled through the fence into the field. She grabbed the head collars from beside the gate. Three inquisitive ponies were already milling around James. "It's okay, they won't hurt you!" she called, hoping he wouldn't do anything silly. "Just stand still, and I'll come and catch—"

They moved so fast that for a moment it was difficult to work out what had happened, but Katy realised with astonishment that it was Trifle who was the troublemaker . . . No, that was unfair; she'd actually driven Tinks away from James, and was now protecting him by warning Tinks and Jacko not to get too close. Tinks looked as surprised as Katy felt.

Trifle went right up to James, and he wrapped his arms around her neck.

Katy felt sure the mare would send him flying at any moment – she hated being held like that, especially by someone she didn't know – but a dreamy look came over her face. She lowered her neck and stood as still as a statue while James leaned against her shoulder.

Olivia looked worried. "He will be okay, won't he? I mean, they're perfectly tame?"

I hope so, Katy thought. "Yes, he'll be fine," she said. Trifle was certainly giving a good impression of being perfectly tame. Perhaps she's phlegmatic after all, Katy thought. But she knew there was more to it than that. James and her pony had found an instant connection unlike anything she'd witnessed before, and she couldn't stop a twinge of – yes, she had to admit it – jealousy.

8

A Lost Lamb

Katy was running so late after the incident with James that Mum drove her to the bus stop. She arrived just in time, and spent the rest of her birthday in town with her school friends, looking around the shops, eating pizza and watching a film. In some ways she envied the freedom her friends seemed to have. For most of them Easter meant having fun, shopping for summer clothes and eating chocolate eggs rather than lambing, calving and lots of hard work. However, deep down, Katy knew she'd hate to live anywhere but Barton Farm and she wouldn't know what to do without her ponies.

One thing she thought she would be able to do without was James, but it was too late to do anything about that now. She'd told Olivia she didn't mind him coming to 'help' with the ponies, although what help he'd be was hard to imagine.

Sometimes it doesn't pay to be nice and have good manners, Katy thought, brushing Jacko while she waited for James and Olivia to arrive the next morning. She looked at her watch: they were twenty minutes late already.

"Hi there! Sorry!" Olivia said breathlessly. "James isn't having a good day, I'm afraid."

Oh help, what on earth have I let myself in for? Katy thought. "Don't worry. The ponies needed a good brush," she said, although it had been a pretty pointless exercise. They were only going out to the field to get muddy again.

Trifle gave a maternal, loving whinny. For a moment Katy thought she was directing it at Tinks, but it was definitely for James, who was resting his forehead against hers. She seemed to be trying to get as close to him as possible. Extraordinary.

"Ah, Trifle's your special friend, isn't she, James?" Olivia said. "She's been waiting for you!"

She's not the only one, Katy thought crossly.

"Can he brush her?" Olivia asked.

Katy hesitated. The lambs were due a feed, and

she had a suspicion that Tom hadn't spent much time making sure the weakest one had drunk its fair share yesterday. "Okay," she said. "But he should be careful to do as I say. The foal is quite cheeky sometimes, and Trifle can be protective of her with people she doesn't know. Wait while I put their head collars on."

With the two ponies tied to separate rings in the wall of the stable, she let James in. "Don't get too near the foal," she warned, but James went straight to Trifle anyway. She found his silence disconcerting.

"Um, shall I explain to you about grooming, or—?" she asked awkwardly, looking first at James and then at Olivia.

"Showing him what to do works best, but he understands words, too, especially clear instructions," Olivia replied.

"Do you want to use your right hand or your left hand?" Katy asked him, holding up her hands in turn.

He put up his right hand, but his eyes didn't leave Trifle.

She chose a body brush from the grooming bucket. It wouldn't do much good, but at least it was so soft that James wouldn't hurt Trifle if he used the wrong amount of pressure. "Okay, you slip your hand through the strap, like this, and brush her gently in the same direction as her hair." Katy demonstrated what she meant. The amount of scurf scattered over the mare's broad back was embarrassing. It was easy to by-pass grooming when she wasn't being ridden, and she was moulting in earnest now.

Katy handed the body brush to James. "Here, you have a go. Don't tickle her, but don't be too rough either."

He brushed Trifle with great care, a look of deep concentration on his face.

The pony's head lowered, her bottom lip went wobbly and her eyelids drooped.

Katy took another brush, and groomed Tinks.

Granfer's retraining programme – firm, consistent handling and fewer treats – was already working. Tinks relaxed as Katy smoothed her dense, downy coat.

"There's a good girl," she whispered.

"There's a good girl," James said.

Katy glanced at him, then carried on brushing in an attempt to hide her surprise.

"There's a good girl," he repeated, more confidently this time. "There's a good girl."

Because Trifle seemed to be so happy with James, Katy allowed him to lead her out to the field while she led Tinks. It certainly made things easier, especially as Olivia went ahead and opened the gate for them.

Tinks trotted off when Katy let her go, but Trifle

stayed put for a while. Usually she only did that when the weather was awful or there wasn't much to eat, but it was a beautiful spring day and the field was bright green with tender new shoots of grass.

James jumped up and down joyfully as Trifle eventually wandered away, circled, crumpled to the ground, rolled, hauled herself upright and shook vigorously with ecstatic grunting noises. Tinks rushed over to join in the fun, and the two ponies tore across the field together, leaping and bucking. Trifle farted loudly several times in the process.

Katy giggled. "Typical Trifle! Alice says she's gas-powered."

"Pumbaa!" James said, loud and clear.

"Yes, just like Pumbaa," Olivia turned to Katy. "James loves *The Lion King*."

Katy made the connection. "Of course! Pumbaa's the warthog who farts a lot, isn't he? That film was one of my favourites. I haven't seen it for ages, though."

"Well, if you ever feel like watching it again, James plays it at least once a day."

"Really?" Katy said, amazed. "He must know it off by heart!"

"Believe me, he does," Olivia said. "Anyway, what can we help you with now? If you show us how to do it, I'm sure we could clean the stables – 'muck out' or whatever you call it."

Katy knew that teaching them how to sort out the dirty straw, take it to the muck heap and pile the clean bedding against the walls to air the stables would take ages, and those lambs had waited long enough. "Would you like to feed the tame lambs?" she asked.

Olivia's face lit up. "We'd love to!"

To begin with, James couldn't get used to the fact you had to tip the bottle up so that milk, rather than air, went into the teat, but once he got the hang of it he was meticulous about doing it correctly.

With three people to hold three milk bottles, lamb feeding was completed in no time.

"What else have you got lined up for us?" Olivia asked.

Katy's next job was best done quietly, with Moss the sheepdog for company. "Er, if you'd like a cup of coffee at the house, I'm sure Mum would love to see you. I'm just going to look around the fields quickly."

"What are you looking for?"

"Oh, just the ewes and lambs. It's my job to make sure they haven't become separated during the night."

"Does that happen a lot?"

"Often enough to make it worth checking twice a day. Lambs are good at wriggling through gates or fences and then not being able to find their way back, or falling asleep, or following the wrong ewe."

Olivia was amazed. "But why don't their mothers look after them? I thought animals were good at that sort of thing."

"Some ewes are wonderful mothers, and others aren't so good," Katy said. "To be fair, though, there are so many sheep in each field that it's easy for the lambs to become mixed up, especially the twins and triplets."

"It sounds fascinating. Do you mind if we come with you?" Olivia asked.

"Er, okay, but it involves a lot of walking, and being very quiet, and remembering where things are, or were – rather like that game where you have to match the pairs, only instead of cards there are ewes and lambs with numbers on, and they're constantly moving."

"James is brilliant at that sort of thing." Olivia looked round at where James had been, but he'd wandered off to the other end of the shed. "If nothing else, I can tell your ewes I understand their problems!" she said, and went to get him back.

The lambs in the first field were the oldest. They were past the frail newborn stage and were beginning to jump about and run races together.

"Oh, aren't they *sweet*?" Olivia whispered. "Why have some of them got a dot and then a number?"

"They're singles," Katy explained. "Doubles just have a number. Then if one twin dies we can put a dot in front of the number on the living one."

Olivia looked rather shocked. "You're very down-to-earth about such things, aren't you?"

Katy thought about it. "I suppose farmers have to be. It doesn't mean we don't care, but livestock farming's all about life and death, isn't it?" Trying to include James in the conversation, she said, "It's the circle of life, as in *The Lion King*."

"The circle of life," he repeated, and for a moment their eyes made contact before he looked away.

After a while Katy found the lamb she'd been watching out for, limping behind its mother.

"Poor thing! What's happened to it?" Olivia said.

"It's got joint ill," Katy said.

"Shall I go back and tell someone?"

"No, it's okay, I've got everything I need in my pocket," Katy said. With help from Moss, she managed to catch the lamb with her crook without disturbing the other sheep, inject it and return it to its mother. Then she wrote what she'd done in her notebook so Mum could update the farm records.

"You're amazing, you know," Olivia said.

"Not really. Just doing what I've been taught to do,"

Katy replied. It was lovely to be called amazing, all the same.

She knew there'd be a problem in the next field because there were frantic bleating noises coming from several sheep. When they reached the gate they found a ewe wandering aimlessly, claiming random lambs, walking away with them, deciding they weren't hers after all, bleating loudly and repeating the process all over again. The lambs in this field were younger and not as good at finding their mothers, so there were a lot of upset sheep.

"What shall we do?" Olivia asked.

Katy was tempted to go and get Dad or Tom, but it was difficult to admit she was out of her depth. "Er, it would help if we could find the missing lamb," she said, reading the blue number sprayed onto the ewe's fleece, "dot sixty-seven."

Before she'd finished speaking, James was running back to the gate.

"James, wait! Where are you going?" Olivia called, but he didn't seem to hear her. He climbed over the gate and disappeared from view behind the high hedge separating the two fields.

Katy and Olivia hurried after him.

They found him crouched down, looking at something.

As Katy got closer she could see it was a lamb, curled

up and sleeping soundly. She knew what number it would be before she read it out loud: "Dot sixty-seven! How did you know it was here?"

"It was here," James said.

"He memorises what he sees in remarkable detail," Olivia explained, "rather like a pictorial map."

The lamb woke up, stared at them in horror and made a desperate attempt to flee. Katy just managed to grab it with her crook, and held it close. She could feel its little heart hammering underneath its ribs. "Poor thing, we've scared you witless, haven't we?" she murmured. "Let's find your mum."

They got as close as they could, and let the lamb go. It stood there, lost and alone in a huge, scary world, and gave a desperate bleat. The distraught ewe stopped in her tracks and blared a reply. The lamb took a few steps towards the noise, and bleated again. With that, the ewe came running, and soon the lamb was suckling, its tail wriggling blissfully.

With James' help, it didn't take long to sort out the others.

"Do you mind if we come every morning?" Olivia asked as they walked back to the farmhouse.

"Not at all," Katy said. "There's so much to do at this time of year. It's great to have willing helpers."

And this time she wasn't just being polite.

9

The Courage To Say Something

At last lambing was nearly over, the weather improved after a solid week of rain and Alice returned to Stonyford for a couple of days before the beginning of the summer term.

The girls wasted no time in seeing each other. Alice rode Max over to Barton Farm because she wanted to say hello to Tinks before she did anything else.

"My, you've grown! You're nearly as tall as your mum," she said, standing between Tinks and Trifle in their stable. "And you're both getting beautiful, glossy summer coats already! How did that happen?"

Katy grinned. "Constant brushing by James. At least, he brushes Trifle so I have to brush Tinks to keep an eye on things. She's getting much better, but she can still be quite bolshie sometimes."

"Well, shows she's clever and testing the boundaries," Alice said, smoothing the babyish mane, which had reached the stage of nearly flopping over.

"Oh, she's much too clever for her own good. She learned all those silly tricks I taught her far too well – especially the rearing-up one – and she soon worked out how to get food from me. You were right about not giving her too many titbits."

"It's sometimes easier to see things when you're looking in from the outside," Alice said. "You've done a great job with her, honestly."

They looked at each other and began to giggle. "This is making me nervous. We're being much too nice to each other!" Katy said.

"Scary, isn't it?" Alice replied.

Katy gave her the small red head collar. "Come on, you can lead the little monster out to the field and I'll have Trifle for a change. James always leads her everywhere now."

"Where is he? I'd love to meet him properly."

"Olivia's taken him to the dentist today. I do hope he'll be okay. He gets really scared about that sort of thing." Katy felt her chest tighten at the thought of what he'd be going through.

"You really care about him, don't you?" Alice said.

"Hm, he's sort of grown on me, I suppose. To begin with I found it quite difficult finding things for him to do. But he's actually been very helpful." Katy led Trifle out of the stable, and Alice followed with Tinks. For once Jacko didn't whinny, as he had Max for company. "James has made me think about so many things I used to take for granted. I mean, for me talking's easy—"

"Impossible to shut you up," Alice agreed.

Katy made a face. "Seriously, though, have you ever thought what it would be like to be terrified of speaking, in case you got the words wrong, or they sounded peculiar or came out too loud? The funny thing is, he talks much more when he's with the ponies, and he never does his stressy things like rocking to and fro. Olivia says Trifle's the best therapy James has ever had, and she should be available on prescription."

Alice smiled. "A Trifle a day keeps the doctor away."

"Absolutely," Katy gave her pony a rub on the withers as they walked along. "The more I get to know James the more I like him. He's kind, and very clever, and completely honest. It's difficult for him to hide his feelings like we can, and it doesn't enter his head to be untruthful about anything." Katy undid the latch of the gate into the field. "I'll wait for you to undo Tinks' head collar before I undo Trifle's, so she's less likely to go charging off. Ideally, you want to release her so she doesn't even realise it's happening, and then be the first to walk away." It was odd telling Alice what to do, when she'd always been the one who knew more about horses and . . . well, everything, really.

When the two girls went back to the gate, the ponies followed them and seemed reluctant to be free.

"That's unusual. Normally Tinks can't wait to let off steam," Katy said. "She must love you very much."

Tinks rested her head in the crook of Alice's arm while she gently scratched underneath her jaw. "Feeling's mutual," Alice said. "Ah well, I suppose we'd better go on that ride we've been promising ourselves."

The girls rode in short-sleeved shirts, eager to tan their pale arms in the warm sunshine. Jacko felt like a different pony from the one Katy had ridden during February half term – sleek and fit instead of hairy and tubby. He walked with a spring in his step, and kept up with Max easily.

A few Exmoor ponies emerged from some gorse bushes, curious to see the horses. "Oh good, I was hoping they'd be here," Katy said. There was one mare in particular she wanted to show Alice.

Jacko, always a little confused by the fact that the moorland ponies looked like his best friend, pricked his ears, arched his neck and blew a soft greeting to them through his nose. They responded by coming closer and soon he was exchanging squeals with a couple of mares. She laughed. "You big wuss! Let's go before that stallion comes over to see us off."

Around the next gorse bush, Katy saw them: Tormentil and her one-week-old colt foal. "Aha! I *knew* they'd be here somewhere," she said.

"Oh!" Alice exclaimed. "Nothing has the right to be that cute!"

The foal studied them intently, half hidden behind the mare.

"Isn't that Trifle's mum?" Alice asked.

"Yes, she's usually one of the first to foal."

"So that's her half-brother, then. What a cracker! Are you going to keep him?"

"I'd love to, but he wouldn't be able to become herd stallion. He's too closely related to most of the others in this herd."

"Still, you could train him and sell him to somebody else for showing, or breeding, or both. I'd help you!"

Katy didn't like to point out that Alice was hardly ever at home. "Hm, I'll see," she said. "I really can't have four ponies back at the farm."

"Any further forward with finding a home for Trifle?" Alice asked.

"Nope, not yet. I've been too busy lambing, and James has been having such a good time with her.

Anyway, I don't want to spoil today by thinking about it. Tell me all about POYS. Was it amazing?"

"Yes, I must admit it was, and it was nice that Viking went so well when Mum and Dad were both watching. There were lots of big names there, too."

"What? Were they jumping?"

"No, helping with the competition, seeing the people they coach, and also talent spotting. A lot of that goes on. Oh, and there was this place that sold the most *delicious* hot chocolate. You could have it with sprinkles and marshmallows – all sorts of yummy stuff!"

Katy laughed. "You're impossible!"

They'd reached one of their favourite cantering places: a gently sloping incline of close-cropped heather with hardly any gorse, bracken or boggy areas – far too good to walk over. The two girls looked at each other, knowing they were both thinking the same thing, and their mounts began to dance on the spot, sensing what was afoot.

"Race you!" Alice shouted.

The horses surged up the hill, their hooves eating up the ground. Max pounded along in front, kicking up an occasional clod of peaty earth, his chestnut tail streaming out behind him.

They pulled up at the brow of the hill, and took a while to calm the horses down. Their blood was up and they kept breaking into a jog trot, eager to be off again.

"I feel bad that I haven't managed to get over to

Stonyford this holidays, what with lambing and everything," Katy said finally.

"Your absence has been noted and commented upon," Alice remarked. "Actually, it's true. Last night Dean said he'd missed his gate-opener-in-chief, especially when Mum was away with me at POYS."

Katy grinned. "Nice to be appreciated. Is he still into horse agility?"

Alice rolled her eyes. "Is there sand in the Sahara? He went on a course just before the Easter holidays, and now he wants to set up a club on Exmoor and do training days at Stonyford."

"Great! That's brilliant news!"

"Ah, it *would* be brilliant news if Mum were keen, but she says there's too much going on already and there's nowhere to put all the equipment." Alice paused. "I think she's secretly fascinated by horse agility, but in a way she feels threatened."

Katy frowned. "Why?"

"I don't know exactly. Perhaps it challenges her beliefs about how horses think and what they're capable of. Anyway, Mum says Dean can have a dedicated area when the indoor school has been finished in the autumn, but until then his horse agility stuff has got to stay in its shed."

"Hang on a minute, I've got a brilliant idea!" Katy exclaimed.

"Oh-oh."

"No, it isn't oh-oh at all, it's pure genius! Our sheep shed's empty now lambing's finished, and it won't be used again until the autumn, so we could keep it in there. And in return, perhaps we could use some of it. You see, I've been thinking about what James can do with Trifle that's safe and doesn't involve riding her. We've been on short walks around the fields, with him leading her and me leading Tinks, but we get in muddles because she often gets excited or wants to eat grass. I can't help him much when I've got Tinks. But in the sheep shed we could put Tinks in one of the pens so she can see us, which would free me up to show James how to handle Trifle. I could do some of the exercises with Tinks as well. Perhaps Dean could even come over and give us a few lessons."

"No harm in asking," Alice said, gathering up her reins. "Time for another canter?" And she was away before Katy had time to answer. They were heading for home now, and this time they stretched out into a flat-out gallop. Jacko's hooves skimmed the ground, ironing out bumps and dips as they powered along. It was difficult to stop, but the girls didn't try too hard. First Max slowed down so Jacko overtook, encouraging Max to speed up again, and then Max overtook Jacko, and so it went on all the way to the gate, where they ground to a halt, breathless and giggling.

"I've just remembered why I love riding so much," Alice said.

Katy grinned. "Me too."

The gate was a tricky one, half off its hinges, so Katy had to dismount to open it.

"Anyhow, you've told me about POYS, but what about your time with your godmother?" she asked when she was back in the saddle.

"Oh, it was *amazing*," Alice said. "Really interesting. Racehorses are so beautiful. Mindboggling how much some of them are worth, though, and awful that one little problem can end a promising career. It's a high-pressure job, with a huge amount of responsibility, but I'm now certain I want to be an equine vet."

Katy smiled at her friend. "I expect you're getting used to pressure, what with school work and being in the jumping team and everything."

"I must admit it was lovely not having to ride for a while."

"Sorry, I shouldn't have suggested a ride today. We could have stayed at home or gone into town."

Alice stroked Max. "Not this sort of riding. I meant schooling, and jumping, and endless competitions."

"But when we were doing Pony Club together you told everyone you wanted to become a top show jumper."

"Mm, I know, but I had no idea what hard work it would be and how much courage it would take, over and over again." She looked miserable all of a sudden. "Oh, I hate myself for being so ungrateful!"

"How can you be ungrateful when you never asked for Viking in the first place?" Katy asked.

"Because I did, sort of, didn't I? I mean, Dad knew I'd wanted to be a champion show jumper ever since I was a little girl, so he must have thought he was making all my wishes come true when he bought Viking for me. I wish I'd said something then, but I didn't have the heart. And now it's too late."

"But I thought you were both getting on really well now, what with two clear rounds at POYS and everything."

"Yes, I know it sounds silly, but that's the trouble: it's impossible to admit I don't want to do show jumping any more now that Viking and I are finally doing well. I mean, it's understandable to give up when you're hopeless at something, isn't it? But crazy to want to stop when you've given it everything and are beginning to get results. I'll never have the courage to say something now – not with all the outdoor competitions coming up plus the big one at Hickstead. It's never-ending."

"Granfer always says it's best to quit when you're ahead," Katy said. "Showing everyone what you're made of and going out on a high is much more honourable than admitting defeat when you're doing badly. And if you hate it, what's the point?" She smiled. "Follow James' good example: be totally honest."

10

Third Time Lucky

It was half term by the time the sheep sheds were completely cleared out and Tom collected Dean's horse agility equipment with the tractor and trailer. There was even more of it than Katy remembered, including a sturdy bridge, a tunnel and a podium made from a huge tractor tyre.

"Wonderful having it all indoors like this," Dean said, admiring the new setup.

Tom grinned. "I can see what Melanie means about toys. Playgroup for gee-gees, eh?"

"Careful, or I'll withdraw my offer of a pint or two

in the pub this evening," Dean said. He turned to Katy and James, who'd been helping with the lighter things. "I want to get as much practice as possible, so any time you'd like a lesson, just say the word."

"What word?" James asked.

"Er, good point. What word would you like to say?"

"Mafusa!"

Dean looked baffled.

"He's Simba's father in *The Lion King*," Katy explained. She didn't add that it was what James called his father. As she'd got to know him better, she was beginning to realise how much he missed not having his father around. James seemed to find it difficult to grasp the fact he was such a long way away, flying helicopters for the army. In his *Lion King* world, his dad was King Mafusa and he was Simba, trying to get back to the Prideland.

"Mafusa it is, then," Dean said.

"I'm way out of my depth here," Tom said. "See you this evening, Dean."

"Mafusa," James said again, and jumped up and down with excitement.

"Yes, can we start as soon as possible?" Katy said. "It's half term this week, so there's plenty of time, and Alice is coming home tomorrow for a couple of days, so she can join in too. I'm sure it would do Viking good to try something completely different."

"I'm afraid he'll be staying at school," Dean said. "It's not worth bringing him back for such a short time."

"Well, there's always Tinks," Katy said. "Alice gets on really well with her."

"We'll be busy at Stonyford during the day, but there'll be time in the evenings. I'm sure we can work it in somehow," Dean replied.

"I'll come and open gates when you take rides out, for free!" Katy said.

Dean looked amused. "Deal."

The following evening, Katy, James and Alice arrived in the lambing shed with Jacko, Trifle and Tinks for a 'playgroup session', as Tom insisted on calling it.

"Okay, let's think about horse agility obstacles for a moment," Dean said. "Toys are actually a good name for them because good toys are fun and useful. Playing with them teaches us all sorts of skills we need in real life: communication, cooperation, problem-solving, cause and effect and lots more besides. Each of these obstacles will prepare your pony for the real world in a different way."

Tinks nibbled at Alice's clothes, played with the rope and refused to stand still.

"Let's give Tinkerbell something to do. You go first, Alice," Dean said.

Tinks jogged into the arena with the look of a child let loose in a toyshop.

"Just walk her around and try not to take any notice of the equipment for the moment," Dean said. "Try to be firm but soft, if that makes sense. Set your boundaries and stick to them. Keep your shoulder in line with her head. Be soft but precise with your body as well as your hands, and give release as soon as she does the right thing."

Soon Tinks was walking calmly alongside Alice. Katy had to stifle a momentary feeling of jealousy. It was hard to let go.

"Okay, see what she thinks of some of the obstacles," Dean said. "Perhaps you could start by showing her the tarpaulin. Remember, she's young. Let her explore it."

The foal's dark nostrils flared and she snorted suspiciously at the tarpaulin. She pawed experimentally at the unusual surface, but nothing would induce her to step onto it with all four feet.

Katy could see that Alice was beginning to get cross, although she was trying to hide it. A part of her was glad that Tinks wasn't being totally obedient.

"Relax, have a looser rope and give her time to investigate," Dean said, straightening out the tarpaulin again. "You've got to be a strong, calm leader. If you get uptight she'll think there's something to worry about. Have you heard of the candle trick?"

"Er, no," Alice said.

Katy wondered what on earth Dean was going to suggest. Using a candle to get a pony to move didn't sound much like 'natural horsemanship' to her.

"Okay, close your eyes," Dean said. "I want you to imagine you've got a candle deep inside you, and you're in control of the flame. If you want to be very calm, take the flame right down low, and if you want to give yourself more energy, make the flame larger. It's a great way of learning to control your emotions. If you're in charge of yourself, your pony will sense you're a good leader."

"Wow, that's powerful," Katy said, opening her eyes and seeing Alice doing the same. James still had his eyes shut, and so did Trifle.

Dean walked over to the tarpaulin and folded it several times so that it was a long, thin strip. The feed barrier was on one side and he stood on the other. "Right, then, Alice. You are a positive, reliable leader. Take Tinks for a walk and go over this while you're about it. No big deal."

Tinks baulked the first time, and then did a cat-leap over, as if it were a deep ravine.

"That's one of the reasons for a long rope," Dean commented. "Bring her round again."

The next time her jump was smaller, and when she went round again she walked over it as if it were a pole.

"Good," said Dean, unfolding the tarpaulin so it was slightly larger.

Tinks trod on it for a stride, but hardly seemed to notice. Soon she was walking over the fully extended tarpaulin without the slightest hesitation.

"Excellent. You've achieved a tremendous amount in that simple exercise. Building trust is what it's all about." Dean said. "I think that's enough for her, as she's so young, and James has been watching patiently for a long time."

"Yes I have," James agreed.

Dean gave James some tips about leading, and then they weaved in between a line of cones, walked over the tarpaulin and navigated their way between some parallel poles on the ground.

To finish off, Dean rolled a huge green ball into the arena.

"A ball!" James said happily, and hurried towards it. To his dismay, Trifle wasn't so keen. She pulled back, eyes bulging, and refused to go near it.

What a pity, Katy thought. She's been so good until now.

"It's okay, she's scared of it, James," Dean said.

"I know!" he cried, and tried to pull her closer.

"Stop," Dean said. "If you pull her you'll make her

even more scared. It's far better to show her it isn't scary, like this." He took Trifle's lead rope from James. "I'm going to bring the ball as close as I can, but as soon as she looks worried I'll roll it away again. See?" Dean did it a few times, getting closer and closer. Each time, as the ball rolled away from her, Trifle began to look more interested and less scared. Eventually it came so close that she reached out and touched it with her nose. "Good girl!" he said. "Okay, James. Will you walk just in front of us, pushing the ball along, and we'll follow?"

James did as he was asked, and Trifle followed the ball willingly. "If a horse is scared of something, following it often makes them braver," Dean explained.

Trifle was occasionally touching the ball with her nose, almost helping to push it along.

"I've just thought of something!" Katy said. "I used to say *push* when I wanted her to push a gate open. I wonder if she'll remember."

In answer, Trifle pushed the ball with her nose.

James jumped up and down with delight. "Push!" he said.

Trifle nudged the ball with her nose.

"Push!"

Dean had some difficulty persuading James to stop while Trifle was still enjoying the game.

"Why don't riding lessons include things like you're teaching us?" Alice asked.

"Beats me," Dean said.

James looked confused.

"Beats me means I don't know," Katy explained. It wasn't until she'd met James that she realised how ridiculous some sayings sounded when taken literally, and he couldn't help taking things literally. If something was cool it was cold, or if it was all the rage it was very angry.

"Is it true you're starting an Exmoor horse agility group?" Katy asked.

"Yep, I'd like to, if I can get enough people interested," Dean said.

"Well, I've been thinking."

"Not again! That's twice in one year!" Alice joked.

Katy made a rude noise, and James laughed.

"This really *is* becoming a playgroup," Dean said, but he was laughing too. "Okay, please tell us more."

"Well, how about having a horse agility event here during the summer holidays? Anyone who's interested could come along and see what it's about."

"You know what? That's the most brilliant idea!" Dean said. "We'll have to ask your mum and dad, though."

"I'm sure they won't mind. It needn't be a competition or anything – just a sort of fun day."

"A fun day. Yes, I like the sound of that." Dean looked pleased. "It'll give us something to work towards. Now, where were we? Ah yes, it's your turn! Again, do some leading exercises between the obstacles first. Keep the rope slack and your mind focused."

Katy tried to remember everything she'd been taught about leading during February half term. It seemed such a long time ago – before she'd met James, even.

"Very good. Once he's doing everything you ask without any input from the rope, you'll be at the stage when you can see if he'll follow you freely," Dean remarked.

Katy had watched lots of videos of horse agility on the Internet, and it was incredible what some people managed to do with their horses at liberty. The thought of becoming that good seemed an impossible dream.

"Right then, I'd like you to try the hula hoop. Ask him to stand with his front legs inside it."

Katy felt disappointed. It would have been nice to impress Alice with something more exciting than standing in a circle of plastic on the ground. She walked up to the hoop with Jacko beside her, but when they got there he skirted round the edge and flatly refused to put his feet inside. No matter what she did, he avoided it.

This is ridiculous! You're Mr Dependable, for goodness sake! Katy thought. Why do you always show me up in front of Dean? She knew she shouldn't get cross, but she couldn't help it.

"Think of that candle," Dean said calmly. "If

something isn't working, don't keep doing the same thing or you'll teach him the opposite of what you're aiming for.

After a while he added, "I had a feeling this would be his weakest link. If it's any consolation, a lot of horses – even highly successful ones – are frightened to put their feet inside a closed ring like this. It seems they feel they'll be trapped if they do. Let's build the solution up gradually, like we did with the others."

Dean made a circle of clean straw so Jacko could get used to standing in that first, followed by a broken hoop to get him used to an open circle. Finally, he enclosed it.

"That didn't take long, did it? What a good boy," Dean said, rubbing Jacko's forehead affectionately. "Now the idea is to get him to stand still while you go to that other hoop a couple of metres away."

"Stand." Katy said, but as soon as she walked away to the other hoop, Jacko followed. "It won't work; he's too used to following me now," she said.

"You've got to give the right signals," Dean said. "Have a signal to stand that's completely different from your signal to walk on."

Katy asked Jacko to back up again by tapping the lead rope. "Good boy. Stand."

This time she made it to her hoop before he stepped sideways out of his.

"He *nearly* did it," she said, eager to get on.

"Not good enough, I'm afraid," Dean replied. "You've both got to stand still in your hoops for the count of six. Walk away slowly and smoothly, looking out for any slight shift in his body so you can stop him before he takes a step."

She sighed. Dean was right, of course. This simple exercise had exposed a weak link in Jacko's training. He'd never been good about standing still when she mounted him, but she'd become used to getting on quickly and adjusting the girth and stirrups as they walked along. It had never entered her head to retrain him to make life easier and safer. She walked back to Jacko, and did as Dean said. As she reached her hoop, Jacko shifted his weight, preparing to move. "Stand," she said firmly.

"One, two, three, four, five, six," Dean counted. "Excellent. Third time lucky."

"Why?" James asked.

"Why is the third time lucky?"

"Yes."

"That's a very good question," Dean said. "Three is considered a lucky number by some, but also people who work with horses say you often have to show a horse how to do something three times before they understand what they're supposed to be doing."

Three seems to be a very horsey number, Katy

thought, and suddenly realised that she hadn't moved out of her hoop and Jacko hadn't moved out of his. In fact, he seemed to be dozing. "Look!" she said.

Dean laughed. "He's not only parked, he's turned his engine off! Get his attention by saying his name and creating a connection with the rope, and ask him to walk towards you. Nice. Now have a go at the other obstacles – whatever order you like."

Jacko walked over the tarpaulin as if it wasn't there; kicked the ball rather than nudging it, which made James laugh; hesitated about stepping onto the seesaw but eventually walked over it twice without faltering and followed Katy through the curtain of brightly coloured plastic ribbons.

Dean told James and Alice they could go and have a play after that.

Katy grinned. "Phew! It's amazing how much concentration you need, isn't it?"

"That's because you're learning something new. Before long it'll become second nature. As you all get better at it, horse agility will open up a whole new world of possibilities."

"I think it already has," Katy said, looking at Trifle. The little mare was pushing the large green horse ball across the shed with her nose, accompanied by James, who was laughing and jumping up and down with excitement.

11

At Liberty

The beginning of the summer holidays was Katy's favourite time of year – even better than Christmas – and Alice staying for the weekend was making it better still. It really did feel like old times as they sat in their pyjamas on Katy's bed, snuggled under her duvet.

The video they were watching ended with a burst of applause as Alice cantered out of the International Arena at Hickstead with a huge grin on her face.

"I still can't believe you did it," Katy said, staring at her friend with a mixture of awe and horror. "You jumped a double clear on Viking at Hickstead and *then* you told everyone you didn't want to do competitive show jumping any more?"

Alice grinned sheepishly. "Well, you were the one who told me to quit while I was ahead, and you can't get much more ahead than that."

"But it must have been the most brilliant feeling, jumping in that massive arena where all the top riders compete! Are you absolutely sure you won't regret this?"

Alice became thoughtful. "I'm really glad I did it, but I wouldn't have been able to take the pressure much longer, juggling all that training with schoolwork. Good exam results are the priority if I'm going to become a vet, which I want more than anything." She sighed. "I'll miss Viking, of course, but I would have grown out of him soon, and he's going to a really nice girl who's a good rider."

"Didn't your mum and dad go ballistic when you told them?"

"No, that was the really peculiar thing: they almost seemed relieved. I think Dad was trying to please me and show he cared, Mum was trying to please me and show Dad she cared as much as he did, and I was trying to please both of them and make us a family again. That was the crazy part, because Mum and Dad were never particularly happy together. And Dean's great.

I wouldn't want Mum to split up with him, not for anything."

"No, I really like Dean as well, and he's a brilliant teacher. I've learned so much since he's been doing horse agility with us."

"Yes, I've got some catching up to do. There's only a week to go before the fun day."

"Ah, now that's what I wanted to talk to you about. You see, I've been thinking—"

"Not again! This isn't like you – should you go and see the doctor?" Alice said with mock concern.

Katy tried to thump her through the duvet, but it didn't work very well.

"Ow – not!"

Katy ignored her. "I've been thinking about each of us doing a mini demonstration, to show people what we've achieved, as a surprise thank you to Dean."

"Hey, that's a really good idea!"

Katy bopped Alice over the head with her pillow. "Don't sound so surprised! I'm full of good ideas."

"Including the solution to your problem about what to do with Trifle?" Alice asked.

Suddenly the evening wasn't such fun after all. "No, I can't bear to think about it – not now that James loves her so much."

Alice grinned. "You really can be a numpty sometimes."

Katy scowled at her.

"The answer couldn't be any more obvious if it jumped up and went *Boo!*" Alice said, doing both those things. She flopped down again on the bed, giggling. "Do I have to spell it out?"

Katy was rapidly losing her sense of humour. She hated it when Alice made fun of her. "Go on, then. As long as it's short. Spelling's never been my strong point."

"J-A-M-E-S."

"James. What about him?"

Alice clapped her hands against her forehead in despair. "Can't you *see*? He's the ideal solution! If you don't want to actually sell Trifle to him, perhaps you could have some sort of loan agreement. That way, Trifle could stay here, his parents could pay something for her keep, and he and Olivia could help with mucking out and things. Even if James doesn't want to ride, he loves doing horse agility and taking her for walks, doesn't he?"

Katy felt an uncontrollable grin spread across her face. "Alice Gardner," she said slowly, "I hate to admit it, but you really are rather brilliant."

Olivia was delighted when Katy suggested it to her the following day. "Isn't that wonderful, James?" she said to him. "You'll be able to come here and see Trifle whenever you like, and look after her and take her for walks, you lucky boy!"

James looked unimpressed. "I do that already."

"But from now on it'll be like owning her," Katy said. "I mean, I'll still own her but you'll act as if you do."

"Like an actor in a film?"

"Um, no, not really . . ." Katy looked to Alice and Olivia for help.

"And your parents will be paying for all the things she needs, like hay," Alice said brightly.

James looked mystified. "Is that good?"

"Er . . ." Katy and Alice said together, trying their best not to laugh.

"Is Trifle happy?" James asked.

Katy smiled. "Yes, she's very happy that you're going to have her on loan."

"Good," he said.

And that was that.

They all worked hard on their horse agility skills in the run-up to the fun day. Dean came over and helped for the first two evenings, but on the third he had to go to a committee meeting. It gave Katy, Alice and James a chance to plan what they were going to do for their surprise demonstration.

"It would be brilliant if we all did something at liberty, wouldn't it?" Katy said.

"Will that be safe if there are crowds of people there?" Alice asked.

"I don't see why not. We'll be inside the arena and they'll be outside, and we can let each pony off in turn."

To increase their chances of success, they chose the things they were best at.

For James and Trifle, that meant the ball. Trifle was drawn to the ball like a magnet. She pushed it whenever James shouted, "Push!" – and sometimes when he didn't, as well.

Tinks made a bee-line for the podium, climbed up the ramp onto it and then flatly refused to come down again.

Eventually Alice put the head collar on to lead her down. "I know you've got a no-treats policy with her now, but what if I just had a few pony nuts in my pocket to encourage her to come to me?" she said.

"Oh, okay, just a handful," Katy agreed. She fetched some, and Alice tried again. It worked!

Tinks soon realised what she was supposed to do. At the third attempt she trotted up the ramp, turned round, waited for Alice to walk away and call her, then raced down the ramp for her reward.

Katy clapped her hands. "Whoohoo! Perfect!"

James joined in too.

Startled by the sudden noise, Tinks dashed around the arena, leaping and bucking.

"Oh dear, I hadn't thought about that," Katy said. "She's never heard clapping before, has she? We'd better get her used to it."

So they spent the next quarter of an hour clapping and shouting things like, "Hurray!" and "Whoohooo!" when Tinks dashed about, but falling silent when she stood still. James thought it was a great game and, after a while, so did Tinks.

"It's amazing how quickly horses learn not to be afraid if they feel in control of the situation," Alice said.

"I suppose we're all like that, aren't we?" Katy said.

James nodded in agreement.

Alice pointed at the agility curtain. "Oh, look at her!"

Tinks had walked part of the way through so that her head was sticking out, looking at them, and the multi-coloured strips of plastic were draped over her like a fancy dress costume.

"I don't like the curtain." James said exactly the same thing several times during every horse agility session. "Trifle doesn't like the curtain."

"It's okay," Katy reassured him. "Nobody's asking you and Trifle to go through the curtain. You won't have to do anything you don't want to do."

"Good," he replied. "I don't like the curtain."

"Your turn, Katy," Alice said.

Katy took Jacko's head collar off and signalled with her body that she was walking forward. He moved forward with her and walked through the curtain as well as he would have being led. She hadn't had to give him any signals using the rope for a long time, anyway. It had only really been there for security.

"Hang on a sec, and I'll lower the jumping hoop," Alice said.

Katy thought of the imaginary candle inside her and made the flame larger, as Dean had taught her, to increase her energy. She began to run, and Jacko trotted by her side, matching her stride step for step. As she drew near to the jump, she indicated he should go through while she ran on. He jumped it enthusiastically, and even slowed to a walk when she did afterwards. "Good boy!" she said, stroking his neck. "Good boy!"

"Go round again, to prove it wasn't a fluke!" Alice called.

"Oi, cheeky!" Katy replied, but she couldn't wait to try it again.

Alice rushed into the arena. "I'll raise it for you."

The jump looked trickier now. It was higher off the ground and the space to jump through had been reduced. Oh well, it was only made from lightweight drainage piping, so even if they crashed right through it no harm would be done.

She needn't have worried; Jacko soared through.

"Again?" Alice asked.

"I think I'll quit while I'm ahead," Katy said breathlessly.

The following morning, three days before the fun day, Dean decided that as the weather forecast was good for a while he'd move all the horse agility equipment into the paddock next to the lambing shed. "There'll be more room for everyone out here," he said, "and it's so much nicer being outside in weather like this."

"What are we going to do about our liberty demonstration?" Katy said to Alice when they were out of earshot. "It'll be really difficult to prevent the ponies from eating the grass. I bet Dean knows how to stop them, but it'll give the game away if we ask him."

When Katy and James met up with Alice the following afternoon for an outdoor training session, she said, "I managed to ask Dean about preventing the ponies from grazing." She put on a jokey secret agent pose. "And he didn't suspect a thing!"

"What's the answer?" Katy asked.

"No magic wand, unfortunately, just more of the same: be firm, clear and consistent," Alice said. "Oh, and it could take a bit of time if the pony in question is used to diving for grass whenever she feels like it." She looked at Trifle, munching happily while James daydreamed.

Following the instructions Dean had given Alice, they alternated walking around with standing still, and whenever any of the ponies looked as if they were about to put their heads down to eat, they gave a quick, decisive jerk on the lead rope and said, "No!"

Jacko soon got the message, and completed most of the obstacles at liberty without any problems. He even jumped higher than he had in the shed.

Trifle was okay on the lead rope, but they couldn't get her to stop eating when she was at liberty, especially when James was supposed to be in charge.

"I think you'll have to do your show leading her," Alice said.

"Good," said James.

"And, sadly, I think I'd better lead Tinks as well. There are too many things that could go wrong out here," Alice added. "But everyone's going to be blown away by your demo, Katy! We'll save you and Jacko 'til last, before the break."

As she lay in bed that evening, reliving every moment of her horse agility demonstration, Katy became so fizzy with excitement that it was impossible to get to sleep. Who'd have thought Jacko would turn out to be such a star? They'd learned so much in just a few months; what would they be able to achieve in the future? Tomorrow they'd do a final run-through, and then it would be the big day – the day they'd been planning for ages . . .

One of Granfer's many sayings was, "You can plan for everything but the unexpected."

Katy was reminded of that the following morning. Even from a distance, she could see that Jacko wasn't walking freely when she went to get him from the field, and as he came closer she realised he was lame.

The vet was called, and found an abscess in Jacko's hoof. She removed his shoe, released the pus and applied a poultice. "There. Nothing too serious," she said. "He should be fine in a week or so, as long you keep it clean."

Katy felt numb. *Nothing too serious? It's a catastrophe!*

The vet gave her poultices, bandages, a hoof boot and detailed instructions, and left with a cheery wave.

Alice and Katy returned to Jacko's stable in silence, and stared in disbelief at his poulticed foot.

"Let's think positive," Alice said at last. "Jacko will recover in time for our ride across Exmoor, and the fun day can still go ahead more or less as planned. We'll just have to share Trifle and Tinks. There'll be other fun days, and there are agility competitions that you can enter, so all your hard work with him won't go to waste."

Katy knew all that was true, but she still couldn't help being bitterly disappointed.

"In fact, I've had a brilliant idea!"

Katy wasn't in the mood for Alice's brilliant ideas.

She carried on regardless. "You could teach Trifle to go through the agility curtain! She's never been through it, has she?"

"No, I don't suppose she has," Katy said, unable to ignore the spark of enthusiasm igniting inside her.

"Come on, then. Let's give it a go now, before James gets here."

So Katy and Alice took Trifle and Tinks to the outdoor arena.

Even though it was a calm day, the curtain rustled with the slightest breeze. Trifle eyed it suspiciously and tried to keep as far away as possible.

The girls decided to tie all the strands up out of the way to begin with and release them gradually, to build Trifle's confidence. She was still hesitant, so Katy suggested Alice should lead the way with Tinks.

Trifle followed her daughter with an anxious whicker. Strand by strand, they let the curtain down. To begin with Trifle rushed through, but after a while she became used to the feel of the curtain brushing against her body and walked through calmly.

Katy gave her lots of praise. It was lovely to be

working with Trifle again, and to put her new-found knowledge to good use. It was especially satisfying that they'd managed to get Trifle over her fears without asking for help from Dean or anyone else.

By the time James arrived she was walking through the curtain as if it didn't exist.

"Trifle doesn't like the curtain!" he said indignantly.

"She *didn't* like the curtain, but she's okay about it now," Katy said. "Look, no worries." She led Trifle through again. "Would you like me to show you how we did it?"

"Can we sing the no worries song?" James asked. If he was scared, singing the *Hakuna Matata* song from *The Lion King* often helped.

"Of course we can."

So, with Katy leading Trifle on one side, James on the other and Alice walking in front with Tinks, they repeated the process, singing all the way.

"I'm getting a little hoarse," Alice said.

"But you've got one already," James said. "Why are you laughing?"

"Because you make us happy," Katy said truthfully.

"Oh. Good."

That evening, Katy and Alice decided to have a final practice with Tinks and Trifle.

"I'd love to do something at liberty with her for

the demo," Katy said. "I wonder if she'll weave in and out of the cones with me."

"Worth a try," Alice said.

Katy tried, and tried some more, but half way through, at the same point every time, Trifle wandered off course and put her head down to eat.

"Try Dean's Plan B: say 'no' and whack the ground just in front of her nose when she goes to eat," Alice suggested.

"Sounds horribly violent. I don't want to hurt her."

"You're not going to whack her, just the ground – and preferably while she's putting her head down, before she's even eaten anything."

Katy tried it. The second time round Trifle was more hesitant about putting her head down, the third time she obviously thought about it but decided against it and the fourth time she followed Katy without faltering. Katy praised her and scratched her withers as they walked along.

"Well done!" Alice said.

Katy was going to stop there, but something made her keep going, over the tarpaulin and towards the curtain, fluttering in the breeze.

"Hang on! I'll tie it up for you," Alice called out, but Katy had a good feeling about Trifle, steadfastly by her side. There was an invisible, unbreakable thread between them. She could feel it . . . A few more steps, and they were through with a rustle of streamers.

"Wow! Will she do that again?" Alice asked.

"Only one way to find out," Katy said. She turned and walked back through the curtain with Trifle by her side, and repeated the process once more.

"You've cracked it!" Alice cried. "That's our jaw-dropping surprise for Dean sorted!"

Katy felt as if she might burst with pride and love. "Good girl!" she said to Trifle. "What a good pony!"

Everyone's A Winner

"FUN is a really odd word when you look at it a lot," Katy said.

She and Alice had got up early, and had been walking around the lanes with signs saying FUN DAY to put at the road junctions.

"DAY is too," Alice said, studying the few remaining signs, "and CAR PARK. How about *TOILET?*"

"Words are weird, full stop. Come on, let's get these done and have some breakfast." Now that Sunday had arrived, clear and calm, Katy felt on edge. Everything was ready. They simply had to wait for people to arrive, but nobody had yet. She began to worry that nobody would. After all, it was perfect beach weather . . .

Luckily, her fears were unfounded. Things started to happen soon after breakfast – slowly to begin with, then gaining momentum like an unstoppable wave.

First Dean, Melanie and the twins turned up, followed by Olivia, James, Rachel, Mark, Heather, Granfer, Gran and Mrs Soames in quick succession.

"I'd say there's enough for a party already," Granfer said as they all crowded into the kitchen. He loved a good get-together.

James looked overwhelmed.

"Shall we go and see the ponies?" Katy asked.

He nodded.

"Are you alright, James? Do you want me to come too?" Olivia said anxiously as he headed for the door with Katy and Alice.

"No thanks," James said without a backwards glance.

Granfer guffawed. "That told you!"

"Yes, it did rather, didn't it?" Olivia said. "I couldn't be more delighted, though. A couple of months ago he wouldn't have been nearly so confident. In fact, he probably wouldn't have answered at all."

Trifle's coat shone like a polished conker and her hooves glistened with hoof oil.

"Well done, James. She looks fab!" Katy said.

"Yes, she's the best thing since sliced bread," he said solemnly. "Sliced bread is my favourite. Trifle's my favourite too."

"Completely logical," Alice agreed.

"Brilliant," Katy added. "I'll just put some fly repellent on the ponies, as we're going to be outside. The horse flies are awful at the moment."

In the background the two sheepdogs barked incessantly as people arrived with their horses. Jacko, Trifle and Tinks raised their heads and swivelled their ears to and fro, trying to make sense of all the commotion.

Alice looked around the corner. "Wow! I don't think you needed to worry about nobody turning up!" she exclaimed.

Katy and James joined her.

"Blimey!" Katy said. "Looks as if someone's even come by taxi!"

"I'll stay here," James said, and went back to be with Trifle.

Katy knew how he felt. Now that everything was actually happening she wanted to hide away until someone told her it had been a huge success and she could relax. "I'll join you," she said, only half joking.

"Oh no you don't!" Alice said. "Don't be such wimps. What is there to be afraid of? It isn't as if this is a competition or anything. Everyone who's here today is coming because they're interested to find out more. They'll all be on your side. It's a *fun day*, remember?"

Katy thought of the courage Alice must have found to take part in all those show jumping competitions – and in front of competitors who wanted to see her fail, too, so they would do better or at least be able to criticise her. She was right. There wouldn't be any winners or losers today, unless failing to turn up when Dean was relying on them counted as being a loser. "Why don't we sing the *Hakuna Matata* song?" she said. "It'll make us brave and fearless."

"Good idea. It worked going through the curtain, didn't it?"

"Ready? One, two, three," Katy said, and they all started singing together, drowning out all the other noise.

Two other, much deeper, voices joined in all of a sudden. Katy thought she was imagining it to begin with, but the singing became louder and nearer. She looked round the corner. Dean was walking towards them with another man, and they were both singing.

James appeared by Katy's side, and she heard his voice falter as his hand reached out for hers. "Mafusa!" he shouted.

For a moment she thought he was saying the word for the horse agility session, but then she realised.

James ran to his father, wrapping his arms around him just like he'd done with Trifle when he'd first seen her.

Melanie appeared round the corner. "Everybody ready?"

"As ready as we'll ever be," Katy said.

"Great. Lots of people have turned up – many more than we thought. Your mum's terrified she'll run out of pasties."

"She should face her fears, like Simba," James said.

The two girls grinned at each other.

Katy led Trifle and Alice led Tinks while James followed along behind, clutching his dad's hand.

Tom had been busy that morning as well, putting rows of small straw bales around the arena for everyone to sit on. Earlier it had looked as if there'd be far too many bales, but now there were hardly enough. Barton Farm had never had so many visitors!

Dean tapped the microphone attached to his shirt. "Testing, testing, one, two, three... Can everyone hear me?"

The members of the audience nodded silently or said, "Yes."

"Well, it's great to see so many of you here. I hope you'll get a lot out today and will go back home fired up with enthusiasm to play with your horse and explore what's possible. That's one of the fantastic things about horse agility: the more you learn, the more you'll realise how much you've been underestimating the ability of your horse and yourself.

"Horse agility is a relatively new, exciting horse sport that can help everyone improve their horsemanship skills. It builds trust between horse and handler, and can be enjoyed as a sport in its own right or to create a firm foundation for riding or driving. It's also wonderfully inclusive. All shapes and sizes of horses, and people, can take part. For instance, I know of a lady who achieves amazing things with her Shetland pony from the confines of her electric wheelchair," Dean said. "Okay, that's enough of me waffling on. The best way to tell you what it's all about is to show you with the help of Katy, James and Alice, together with two very wonderful Exmoor ponies: Trifle and Tinkerbell, her eight-month-old foal."

The audience clapped. Tinks pulled back in alarm and skittered around Alice, but she stood firm and the filly calmed down again.

"Well, there's our first demonstration of horsemanship," Dean said. "If you can remain calm inside and stand still even if your horse is making all sorts of fancy moves, it's amazing how quickly it'll calm down. Alice here just showed Tinks there was nothing to worry about, and she picked up on that pretty quick. Let's have Tinks in the arena first, please."

With Alice leading her around some of the obstacles, he explained how horse agility could be very helpful in a foal's education, but it was important to keep lessons short and fun.

"Right then, there's a young man here I'd love you to meet," Dean said. "Trifle needs no introduction for most of you; she seems to make an impression wherever she goes, from local shows to national television. But I doubt many of you have met James before, as he's a relative newcomer to Exmoor, having moved to Wellsworthy a few months ago. Now, James is a remarkable young man who seems to have forged a special friendship with Trifle. In fact, I think it's fair to say they're inseparable."

Katy felt a lump growing in her throat.

"Talking is immensely hard for James, so it's a mark of this boy's courage that he's asked me if he can borrow my microphone. Perhaps he's just fed up with me blathering on."

The audience laughed.

James looked startled, but stood his ground with Trifle, steady as a rock, beside him. Dean unhooked the microphone and transferred it onto James' shirt.

"Hello," James said. There was a long pause. "I am James." Another long pause. "This is Trifle."

The audience started shifting uncomfortably on the straw bales.

Katy's heart went out to him. She willed Dean to take the microphone away and carry on with the demonstration, but he just rolled the ball towards James.

"The best toy is the ball," James said with a little more confidence.

Trifle instantly started to push the ball along with her nose.

An "Ahhhh!" sound came from the audience.

"The worst is the curtain. We don't like things we don't know touching us. We don't like doors."

He's right, Katy thought. Trifle used to hate being touched as a foal. Also, it took me ages to get her confident about going through the door into her stable.

"But together we are brave, like Simba and Pumbaa. Mafusa is watching us," James said, walking towards the curtain with a look of grim determination on his face. A slight breeze made the curtain flutter, and for a moment it looked as if Trifle was going to shy away, but she kept going.

There was an audible sigh of relief all round.

James told Trifle she was a good girl and led her to

the podium, but instead of asking her to walk up the plank onto it, he asked her to stand alongside, climbed onto it himself and hauled himself onto her back.

Katy and Alice looked at each other in utter amazement.

"Has he ever done that before?" Alice asked in a half-whisper.

"No, never," Katy replied.

"Trifle knows how I feel. She knows what it's like to be afraid and not be able to tell anyone," James said, then he leaned forwards and hugged her neck.

Everyone started clapping. A few people stood up, then more and more, and the clapping became louder and louder.

When, eventually, it died down, Dean said, "Thank you very much, James. That was truly magnificent. And now it's Katy's turn. It's a great shame that her lovely Welsh cob, Jacko, is lame at the moment, but I gather she's been practising some things with Trifle in the past couple of days, and I, for one, would love to see them."

Katy looked at the spectators. So many people she'd love to impress were there: Granfer, Gran, Mrs Soames, Dad, Melanie, Rachel, and even – oh, how lovely – Sharon! She knew she couldn't go through the curtain at liberty now, not after James had been courageous enough to go through it himself. "What

James has done with Trifle is fantastic. I can't possibly follow it," she said.

Dean smiled at her. "Well then, why don't we break for twenty minutes so anyone who's brought a horse can fetch it, and then we'll all have fun trying things out."

James went to the farmhouse with his mum and dad, saying he was as hungry as a lion, so Katy stood holding Trifle and chatting to people while Alice held Tinks nearby.

Dean brought her a cup of tea. "Well done," he said.

"I haven't done anything yet," she replied.

"Oh yes you have. It was a noble thing you did just then." He grinned. "I know what you were planning. I saw you practising with Alice yesterday, and I was so impressed. That pony of yours would follow you to the ends of the earth. You know that, don't you?"

Katy felt herself blushing. "I wasn't sure, until yesterday. In fact, I often felt she preferred James to me. She's so sort of *motherly* towards him."

"We all need to be looked after. Trifle decided she had to look after James, just as you decided you had to look after her all those years ago when you found her on the moor. You've made her confident enough to look after others now, but that doesn't mean to say she'll ever stop needing you," Dean said. "Come on, we've got a busy afternoon ahead, teaching all these keen people and their horses."

Katy had never been to a horsey event like it. The atmosphere was serious yet fun, and everyone was eager to learn from each other.

Eventually Dean turned his microphone on again. "Before you all go home, I'd like to say a big thank you to everybody for coming, to the Squires family for hosting this event and to my helpers, Katy, Alice and James."

Everyone clapped.

"Horse agility can be done for fun, or if you enjoy competitions you can take part in local and online competitions. If you'd like more details, please come and see me afterwards. One of the unique things about the scoring for horse agility is you're scored not only on how the horse completes an obstacle but also on horsemanship. So if the horse is, say, scared of the tarpaulin and takes a long time to cross it but the handler responds to the situation well, the pair could still get a relatively high score."

Dean reached into the bag by his feet. "This wasn't a competition, but I reckon everyone's a winner today, so you all deserve a rosette. Katy, can you do the honours, please?"

Katy felt rather like Father Christmas as she

distributed rosettes among the delighted participants.

Finally, she came to James. He was sitting on Trifle again, with his parents standing close by on each side. She clipped a rosette onto Trifle's head collar.

James frowned. "Why?"

"Because you and Trifle did really well today."

"I know."

"So this is like a prize, to say well done."

"Is it important?"

Katy had never considered whether rosettes were important before. "Um, no, not really."

"Good," James said. Reaching forward, he unclipped the rosette and handed it back to her. "I love Trifle. That's important."

Katy grinned. "James," she said, "you're by far the cleverest person I've ever met!"

Author's Note

This is the fourth book about Katy and her Exmoor pony, Trifle. Many people and ponies have helped me along the way.

Of the ponies, I'd like to mention Jacko, Tinkerbell, Trifle and Viking. Jacko was my first pony – a liver chestnut Welsh cob – and he was just as wonderful as the Jacko in this book. Tinkerbell was our daughter Sarah's Exmoor pony when she was a young girl. She taught Sarah the importance of bravery and a non-slip saddle pad, among other things, and they both gave me lots of ideas for my stories. Our herd of free-living

Exmoor ponies, which we keep on the moorland above our farm, has also provided me with a great deal of inspiration, especially a mare called Trifle. When our children were growing up they had riding lessons at Dean Riding Centre, which is owned by Tracey and Ashley Eames. There was a fantastic jumping pony there called Viking, who'd won many prizes with their daughter Shelley. Sarah was having a jumping lesson on him one day when he locked on to a huge jump that wasn't part of the plan. Unfortunately Sarah parted company with him in mid-air, rather like Alice in this story!

Many thanks to Tracey and Shelley Eames for their help with the show jumping theme in this book, and also to Rosie Andre for giving me some idea of what it's like to take part in big show-jumping competitions like POYS. Rosie and her pony, Frankie, have done incredibly well together, having started from scratch as two inexperienced youngsters. She has a huge following on Facebook and YouTube, where her videos can be found under littlecreamconnemara. Rosie has managed to combine competitive riding with having fun and building a unique bond with her pony.

Vanessa Bee has been a friend and invaluable source of information about horses for many years. She is an incredibly busy lady, but she still found time to answer my questions and read through my manuscript.

Several years ago, when Vanessa and her husband Philip were teaching Exmoor pony foal handling at our farm, Vanessa said she'd had an idea for a new equestrian sport. "You know dog agility?" she said. "Well, how about doing the same thing with horses?"

We all laughed and told her it would never work, especially as her ultimate aim was to work her horses free, without a head collar and lead rope.

Luckily she took no notice. Horse agility is now an international equestrian sport, and Vanessa and Philip travel all over the world teaching it.

Vanessa is always keen to stress that the main purpose of horse agility is to build a better relationship between horse and handler through playing together and having fun. The Horse Agility Club runs online competitions because some people enjoy them and find them useful, but at its heart the sport is non-competitive and all about the relationship between human and horse. Vanessa's *Horse Agility Handbook* is dedicated to *all the horses – and their people – who just want to have fun!* That, to me, says it all.

The main reason I included James in this story is that once he entered my head he refused to leave. My ideas for his personality came from talking to people with autism and reading books by Temple Grandin, Rupert Isaacson and Charlie Avent. I especially like this quote from Charlie:

"I had to learn humour, imagination and sarcasm as well as learning different expressions and sayings. Yes, I know the books all say we can't, but I did. So there!"
Following the Hoofprints: From Unteachable Child to Student Horse Whisperer by Charlie Avent

The staff at the Calvert Trust, Exmoor, kindly allowed me to spend a very interesting afternoon at their riding centre. The Calvert Trust provides activity holidays for disabled people, their families and carers.

Especial thanks to the staff at the Conquest Centre, particularly Chantal Bannister and Jess Dixon, for their help, introducing me to some autistic riders and their parents and inviting me to attend a fascinating training session with Rupert Isaacson.

Steph Lloyd was very generous with her time, answering many questions about what life's like for her as an autistic person, and how riding at the Conquest Centre has helped her in so many ways.

Fiona Kennedy, Fliss Johnston and the team at Orion Children's Books have, as always, given me encouragement and invaluable advice every step of the way.

Most of all, love and thanks to my husband, Chris, for his patient support and wonderful illustrations.

If you'd like to find out more about some of the things I've mentioned, here are some useful websites:

Exmoor Pony Society:
http://www.exmoorponysociety.org.uk

Exmoor Pony Centre:
http://www.moorlandmousietrust.org.uk

Exmoor National Park:
http://www.exmoor-nationalpark.gov.uk

Dean Riding Stables:
http://www.deanridingstables.co.uk

The Horse Agility Club:
http://www.thehorseagilityclub.com/your-club/great-britain/

The Calvert Trust Exmoor:
http://www.calvert-trust.org.uk/activities/horses

The Conquest Centre:
http://www.conquestcentre.org.uk

Charlie Avent:
http://www.autismmeetsnaturalhorsemanship.com

Horse Boy (Horses Helping Children With Autism):
http://www.horseboyworld.com

Victoria Eveleigh
North Devon
March 2015

Exmoor Ponies

Exmoor ponies are a common sight on the moorlands of Exmoor National Park in south-west England. Their distinctive appearance is one of the things that makes them so special: their bodies are various shades of brown with black points, and they have predominantly dark manes and tails and a 'mealy' buff colour on their muzzles, round their eyes and inside their flanks. There are no white markings on an Exmoor pony. For a few months during the summer they look sleek and glossy, but as winter approaches they grow thick double-layered protective coats to keep them warm and dry.

At a preferred height range from 11.3 hands (119cm) to 12.3 hands (130cm), the Exmoor is classified as a small British native pony breed. Its origins have become the subject of debate following recent research, but there's no doubt it's founded on the ponies that grazed the rough pastures in and around Exmoor for centuries – probably as far back as the Bronze Age.

The Exmoor Pony Society was founded in 1921 to establish and promote the breed, and to ensure the ponies were kept true to type. This was partly in response to a fashion for 'improving' ponies by using thoroughbred or Arab stallions.

During the Second World War, many ponies were stolen for food and fewer were bred. In the end, only about forty-six mares and four stallions were left on Exmoor. A remarkable lady called Mary Etherington encouraged some local farmers to re-establish their herds so that the breed was saved. Today numbers have increased to about 4,000 mares, geldings and stallions worldwide, but only about 500 of these are breeding mares that have had a foal in the past five years. The Exmoor pony is classified as a native breed at risk, and it's likely to stay that way due to its small gene pool.

Even though Exmoor ponies can now be found all over the world, Exmoor is still where most of the free-living herds can be seen. These herds fend for themselves for most of the year, but in the autumn they are gathered in by their owners so that the foals can be weaned and registered, the health of each pony can be assessed and the stallion can be swapped if necessary. The surplus foals that aren't needed as future breeding stock are usually sold to new homes at this time.

Taming a completely unhandled pony requires skill and patience, but it can be very rewarding.

If you'd like to find out more about Exmoor ponies, the Exmoor Pony Society has a very good website packed with information: www.exmoorponysociety. org.uk.

A visit to Exmoor isn't complete without a trip to the Exmoor Pony Centre, near Dulverton. This is the headquarters of the Moorland Mousie Trust, a charity dedicated to the welfare and promotion of Exmoor ponies. For further details see the website: www.exmoorponycentre.org.uk.

The Trust runs a pony adoption scheme – the next-best thing to owning an Exmoor pony!